D0505221

THE REAL BLUE WATCH

EXTRAORDINARY TRUE STORIES FROM BRITAIN'S FIREFIGHTERS

Geoff Tibballs

First published in Great Britain in 1996 by
Virgin Books
an imprint of Virgin Publishing Ltd
332 Ladbroke Grove
London W10 5AH

A catalogue record for this book is available from the British Library.

ISBN 0 7535 0082 5

Typeset by TW Typesetting, Plymouth, Devon

Printed and bound by Cox & Wyman Ltd, Reading, Berks

Contents

Introduction and Acknowledgements

For years, the Fire Brigade were the nation's unsung heroes. Most of us took them for granted. Whenever there was a fire to put out or someone or something to be rescued, they would instantly appear, anywhere, day or night. And then when the job was done, rather like the Lone Ranger, they would ride off into the sunset. Despite the bright red engines and two-tones, the Fire Brigade never had the high profile of the other emergency services. There was no *Z Cars* or *The Sweeney, Emergency – Ward Ten* or *Dr Kildare* to dramatise their work. Indeed, for many years the most famous firefighters were Pugh, Pugh, Barney McGrew, Cuthbert, Dibble and Grubb.

Then in the mid 1980s, that all changed. *London's Burning* gave us an insight into the world of the modern firefighter – the camaraderie, the practical jokes, the professionalism and, above all, the bravery. No longer were firefighters faceless people in helmets, they were real human beings. As we marvelled at the exploits of *Blue Watch*, so our awareness of what the Fire Brigade was all about increased.

When the bells go down, the nation's firefighters spring into action. Every 'shout' represents a step into the unknown, for they never know exactly what they will encounter. Even the most routine fire can turn to tragedy in a split second.

Apart from the flames themselves which can maim or kill, many fires produce clouds of thick, deadly black smoke. Once that smoke gets into your lungs, life expectancy can be measured in seconds. That firefighters make light of such ever-present danger and repeatedly risk their own lives to rescue others is why the public hold them in such high esteem.

Humour is the firefighter's defence mechanism but some incidents to which they are called are so horrific that even the most battle-hardened individuals are deeply affected. Nobody who fought the

King's Cross Underground fire of 1987 or who helped free bodies from the Kegworth air crash two years later will ever forget the experience.

In this book, I have covered some of the most dramatic events of recent years, together with those curious rescues of hapless animals and embarrassed humans which are part of a firefighter's everyday life. It would have been impossible to compile this book without the help of many people within the Fire Service. My grateful thanks go to the following Brigades for generously supplying information and reminiscences: Avon, Buckinghamshire, Cambridgeshire, Cheshire, Cornwall, Hampshire, Kent, London, Merseyside, Norfolk, Northamptonshire, North Yorkshire, Nottinghamshire, Staffordshire, West Midlands and Wiltshire. I would also like to thank Nottinghamshire Library Services, the *Lancashire Evening Telegraph* and the British Newspaper Library for background material and Rod Green and Lorna Russell at Virgin Publishing for their enthusiasm and support.

1 Commercial Fires

The Valley of Death

It should have been an afternoon of great celebration. Bradford City Football Club had won the Third Division Championship, their first title for 56 years, and a bumper crowd of over 11,000 had gathered at their Valley Parade ground for the presentation of the trophy followed by the team's final game of the season, against Lincoln City. They came from all over West Yorkshire on that Saturday afternoon of 11 May 1985 – young and old, singly and in families, committed fans side by side with those who had never even been to a football match before.

Into the latter category came Jayne Sampson. A few days before her nineteenth birthday, Jayne travelled to the game from her home in Leeds with friends who had got her tickets for seats in the main stand. She was excited about going to a football match – her mother, Jean, recalled her happy, smiling face as she set off. Tragically, it was to be Jayne's first and last game. For along with 55 others, she was killed in the raging inferno which engulfed Valley Parade and turned a carnival atmosphere into a full-scale disaster in a matter of minutes.

For some 40 minutes, the occasion was one of typical end-of-season good humour. Events on the pitch took second place to the celebrations off it. City fans weren't used to success – now they were determined to make the most of it. Among the VIP guests in the exclusive suite section of the stand was a group of civic dignitaries from Bradford's twin town of Hamm, West Germany. Yorkshire Television cameras were also present to witness the promotion party. That old wooden main stand, one of a number of similar structures in the Football League, was packed with over 3000 supporters, many of them pensioners who preferred to sit in relative comfort and peace rather than run the gauntlet of the unruly hooligan element which plagued the terraces of Valley Parade much as it did at other grounds throughout the country. One hundred police officers were on duty that afternoon to ensure law and order.

There were just a few minutes to go until half-time and PC Adrian Lyles, who was patrolling the corridor at the back of the stand, was looking forward to the possibility of a quick cup of tea. Suddenly he was alerted by a fan in G Block, in the north corner of the stand, at the Kop end, who said that he had spotted smoke seeping up from beneath the floorboards. PC Lyles immediately made his way to the wooden tip-up seat three rows from the back of G Block and investigated. It seemed nothing more than a minor fire. PC Lyles sent a colleague to find a fire extinguisher and asked the people in the vicinity of the smoke to move away. There was little response.

Almost at once, PC Lyles realised that the fire was getting worse. The flames were beginning to lick through the floorboards and starting to burn his legs. A fellow officer tried unsuccessfully to rip up the boards to get at the fire. In an attempt to command attention, PC Lyles stood on a seat and asked people to go down on to the pitch for their own safety. Again he didn't get much reaction so he shouted at the top of his voice. Finally, people got the message. Seeing the officer and then the spreading smoke and fire, they began to move forward as requested.

Still nobody had any idea of the gravity of the situation. PC Lyles' colleague had been unable to locate a fire extinguisher because they had been moved to the clubhouse at the far end of the stand, ironically as a safety measure. In previous matches, hooligans had let off the extinguishers or, worse still, used them as missiles. PC Lyles remained in the top half of G Block, quickly but calmly helping adults and children over a partition.

'I thought the fire would localise itself,' he said later, 'but then the smoke started to accumulate. We tried to get everybody out. I went into the back passage and there was just a wall of smoke. I could hear people banging at doors, shouting, panicking. I went in to try and help but I wasn't able to get to them. The smoke was thick and black and there was no chance of taking a breath. Choking on the smoke, I escaped over the four foot wall in front of the stand and on to the pitch. Then I turned back to face the stand and the heat was unbearable. I'd got out just in time.'

As the referee brought the match to a halt, fans in other parts of the ground, blissfully unaware of the tragedy that was unfolding before their eyes, continued their chants of 'We love you, City'.

The speed with which the fire had spread through the wooden structure took everyone by surprise. Yorkshire Television cameras picked out the first flames licking beneath the seats in G Block at 3.43 p.m. Just 87 seconds later, it had ripped across the timber, tarpaulin and asphalt roof and engulfed the whole stand, moving faster than the fleeing spectators could run. The roof created a grill-like effect, radiating intense heat downward. As people ran for their lives, they were showered with lumps of molten asphalt falling from the blazing roof.

One fan said: 'It was just a bit of smoke at first. Then suddenly a sheet of flames sprang up. It caught on the tarpaulin of the stand roof and spread right across. As it burned, parts of it were falling on to people below. People started scrambling and screaming but they didn't stand a chance. As the asphalt fell, it was clinging to their clothes. I saw a fellow lying on the ground and burning. There was hardly much left of him.'

All the while, clouds of thick, choking smoke billowed out in relentless waves from under the stand roof, blinding those trying to escape. As panic spread through the stand almost as quickly as the flames, the occupants had to make a split-second life or death decision. Should they head down to the front of the stand and attempt to reach the safety of the pitch via the 4 foot wall, or should they make for the exits situated at the back of the stand?

For many, particularly the elderly and those sitting in the rear section of the stand, the easier option seemed to be to try for the exits which would eventually lead on to the street outside. Not only were the doors considerably nearer than the pitch but also there were no daunting walls to climb. Many of those who chose to find the exit doors would not live to regret the decision, for all but one of the doors were locked and a series of one-way turnstiles were chained to prevent latecomers getting in without paying. A policeman tried to battle through the smoke to unbolt one of the doors but he collapsed and had to be pulled clear by a colleague. The man who had the keys to open the doors didn't have a prayer of getting to them in time. Instead, the rear of the stand, where the fire was at its hottest, became an instant graveyard as people were trapped with nowhere to go. Many burned to death, some died of smoke inhalation, and others were trampled underfoot in the crush as people turned and desperately sought an alternative way out. Eventually, spectators were able to use brute force to smash down some of the gates but the delay claimed many lives.

More fortunate were those supporters who elected, or were physically able, to make for the pitch. Youngsters in particular could clamber across the rows of seats and escape to the safety of the pitch by vaulting over the wall at the front of the stand. Those who couldn't scale the wall without assistance were dragged over by fellow fans and rescue workers. Not everyone made it. Several bodies were later found at the foot of the wall on the stand side.

Saturday 11 May should have been part of PC David Britton's weekend off but he was on duty at Valley Parade that afternoon to earn some overtime. He wasn't remotely interested in the football and would quite happily have settled for being placed somewhere without a view of the match. Instead he was located at the edge of the pitch with a special responsibility for looking after the referee and linesmen. When he noticed the first serious signs of smoke from the stand, he decided that since he was responsible for the safety of the match officials, he ought to step on to the pitch and suggest that the referee stop the game for a few minutes until the problem was resolved. As he consulted with the referee, he looked back towards the stand.

PC Britton later recalled: 'Suddenly smoke had covered the whole stand. Then a ball of fire ripped across the roof. The heat was so intense I could feel it from the middle of the pitch where I was standing. I started to run towards it but felt this terrific blast of heat, like the force of an oven door being opened but much, much worse. I saw a man having difficulty getting over the wall at the front of the stand. The clothes on his back were on fire. I kept running. My helmet dropped off and I could feel my forehead getting very hot. I had developed a form of tunnel vision. I was oblivious to everyone else. All I was thinking was, I've got to get to that man. When I reached him, his clothes were all in flames around him but I just reached over and got my hands under his armpits and, what with me pulling and his own efforts, he managed to get on to the top of the wall. A colleague joined me and we rolled the man over on the ground and put out the flames. Instinctively, I ran my hand through my hair. My hand immediately came up in big blisters. What I hadn't realised was that as I had been running towards the man, my hair had burst into flames.'

PC Britton was to spend nineteen days in hospital. Tragically, the man he had fought so bravely to rescue died nine weeks later of his injuries.

The Fire Brigade received an emergency call at 3.43 p.m. and the first appliances were on the scene within four minutes. Two off-duty firefighters were among the spectators that day and when the fire broke out they immediately ran to the hose, only to find that the nearest hydrant was in the road running along the back of the stand. And there was only one way to reach the road – through the wall of smoke and flames. With no breathing apparatus, it was clearly an impossible mission and the pair had to settle for helping with the rescue.

When the appliances arrived, the firefighters were confronted with the dual task of rescuing people and trying to fight the blaze. Fearlessly they set about plucking spectators, many with their clothes and hair ablaze, to safety. A human chain was formed to bring people out over the wall and on to the pitch. An elderly woman was on fire, stranded on the wall. The first attempt to rescue her was driven back by the heat but the crews persisted. When they finally reached her, they realised that her clothing was melting and sticking to their hands in the ferocity of the flames.

Rescue workers ploughed into the stand, pulling their coats over their heads as protection against the falling asphalt. They spoke of a 'physical wall of unbearable pain' as they approached the burning stand. Hardened policemen were reduced to tears. An inspector managed to get a woman half out but simply couldn't hold on to her and away she went. Witnesses spoke of incredible acts of bravery. A 72-year-old man risked life and limb to pull two children to safety. He was left with burns to his face and hands. Mr Patsy Hollinger, chairman of Bradford City Supporters Club, was left nursing an injured right eye and a burnt face after his heroics. 'It was sheer hell,' he said. 'There just seemed to be this ball of fire everywhere. We were in the paddock when we saw what was happening and three or four of us went into the stand to try and get people out. We just picked up children and threw them on to the pitch to get them away from the flames.'

Twenty-five-year-old Antony Burrows described how he saved an old man's life. 'At first only a few people panicked. They were trying to get on to the pitch because there was nowhere for them to go. There was an old man with his hair on fire. I peeled off my jumper and put it over his head to smother the flames. It was just an instinctive reaction.'

Another fan said: 'We could see the flames creeping along the bottom of the seats, then it seemed as if someone had opened a door at the back. There was a northerly breeze which created a tunnel of wind and it was like a furnace. People panicked and were rushing on to the pitch. I later spoke to a groundsman who said he saw one old man trapped between some seats, burning. I went across to help people into ambulances and there were men with their hair burnt off and their faces burnt. There were children walking around with burns on their hands.'

Some had miraculous escapes from the back of the stand. One who received burns to his face, feet, body and legs recounted how he and his wife had been swept along by the panicking crowd towards the back of the stand even though he knew that the doors would be locked. 'There was no opportunity to do anything else. We were just swept past the shop in the stand and were suddenly hit by a great ball of black smoke. It seemed to come racing past us and then the lights went out with a bang and it all went black. I thought, My God, we've had it now. I took a couple of breaths and clung to my wife. We were lucky because there then appeared to our left some light through a door. I think it was flames but it gave us some help in trying to go forward. It was an inferno. I couldn't believe it because we had only been out of our seats for two minutes.'

He and his wife scrambled over the wall on to the pitch and it was only then that he realised that his clothes were on fire. Spectators and rescue workers quickly seized him and rolled him over on the ground to extinguish the flames.

Fifty-eight-year-old Joan Williamson also related how everyone rushed to the back of the stand in the initial panic. 'When they found that the doors were locked, everybody seemed to be trampling on everybody else. My God, I trampled on old women and old men but I was just being dragged along. I saw that my friend's hair and back was on fire and then a stranger grabbed me and dragged me out of the stand.'

Out on the pitch, the 22 players anxiously scanned the burning stand, praying that friends and relatives who had been sitting there had managed to flee the inferno. City player/manager Trevor Cherry had decided to drop himself from the game in order to give one of the club's promising youngsters a chance to show his prowess. So instead of being out on the pitch, Cherry sat with his wife and small daughter in the directors' box in the stand. His two sons were sitting with friends a few rows away. 'When the fire broke out, my first thought was for my family,' said Cherry. 'A few minutes earlier, my wife had taken our daughter out at the back to the toilet. I found them in the corridor and it was like a dark tunnel in there – you could scarcely see anyone but those nearest to you. The boys and their friends came to us and we left as quickly as we could.'

While Bradford City chairman Stafford Heginbotham helped to supervise the evacuation of the players' bar, the police rescued two prisoners who had been arrested earlier in the afternoon following crowd trouble. The detention room in which they were being held was directly in the path of the onrushing flames. With bodies piling up against the locked doors, people searched frantically for another way out but the thick smoke rendered navigation virtually impossible, even for those with an intimate knowledge of the ground. One man entered a darkened room thinking he had discovered an escape route, only to find himself trapped by the fire. Fortunately, firefighters managed to pull him out in time.

As extra manpower was brought in from across the region, the firefighters' priority remained the rescue of as many people as possible and only when they were driven back by the heat did they turn on the hoses. In truth, the fire was probably beyond recall by the time the first appliances had arrived. It had taken too much of a hold and there was nothing that could be done to save the stand or, sadly, many of the people in it.

'We did what we could,' said one of the firefighters on duty that day, 'but somehow we knew we were fighting a losing battle. The fire was burning too fiercely. It was absolute hell in there. The heat was unbelievable. People were being taken out with the most horrific burns – and they were the ones who were still alive. I never thought I'd see scenes like it and I never want to again.'

At 4 p.m., Jayne Sampson's brother heard on the radio that there had been a fire at Valley Parade but the report said that no one had been hurt. The family breathed a sigh of relief, unaware that casualties were piling up at the city's hospitals.

Fleets of ambulances took some 250 injured to three hospitals. With panic-stricken fans pouring into the narrow side streets around the ground, access to Valley Parade was no easy matter. The scene was chaotic. Paramedics were overwhelmed by the sheer volume of casualties. Whenever they tried to load one batch of injured for removal to hospital, another case needed their urgent attention. One ambulance carrying ten burnt policemen was flagged down by a distressed motorist who handed a child suffering from burns out of the car window and into the ambulance.

From 4 p.m. onward, Bradford Royal Infirmary resembled something out of a battle zone. The majority had burns to their hands, and scalps, wounds sustained as they had used their hands to shield their heads from the lumps of hot asphalt. Children arrived, not knowing whether or not their parents were alive. Old men, their heads swathed in bandages, tottered about in a state of shock. Thirty off-duty nurses came in to help treat the wounded. So severe were the injuries that the hospital had to send to Leeds for extra dressings. Plastic surgeons were drafted in to deal with the worst cases – many of the survivors would require skin grafts.

When the fire had finally burnt itself out, totally gutting the old stand, the grimmest task of all began – that of sifting through the debris for bodies. People who had been happily watching a football match a couple of hours earlier had been reduced to shrivelled, charred corpses. Some were so unrecognisable as having once been a human life form that a pathologist positively identified one pile of remains as a body, only to discover later that it was a piece of plastic. The falling molten asphalt had exacerbated the situation. It had covered some of the bodies and then re-set, forcing the rescue services to use crowbars and axes to prise the corpses from their hideous black shells. Some bodies had been welded together in the heat.

Forty-three of the 56 who died perished at the rear of the stand, hopelessly trapped as they came up against the locked doors and turnstiles. This was where the fire was at its most fierce. At its height, the blaze generated a temperature of over 1000 degrees Centigrade. Sixteen bodies were found piled up by the turnstiles next to G Block where the fire had started. Another heap nearby, near a short passage leading to some double doors, yielded a further dozen bodies. Five more were discovered in the narrow walkway at the back of the stand and three in the men's toilets. Some fans had tried to evade the approaching flames by crawling through the tiny gap beneath the chained turnstiles. They were doomed to die on the spot. Four bodies were found jammed against the turnstiles at the centre rear of the stand. Perhaps through shock, others simply hadn't been able to make a run for it and were burnt alive in their seats.

City fan Andrew Goldsborough usually stood on the terraces, but for such a big game he had decided to purchase a stand ticket for the first time. 'At first, all I saw was some wisps of smoke. I thought it was a few hooligans and didn't pay much attention because I was more interested in the game. I thought the fire, or whatever it was, would all be over in a few minutes. But then the smoke suddenly seemed to thicken up. Lots of people began screaming. I looked towards the back of the stand and there was a man standing there with all of his clothes on fire. He was swaying from side to side and then he fell down and disappeared. And there was an elderly couple sitting side by side. They didn't try to move or anything. They just went on sitting and a big piece of burning tarpaulin from the roof fell down right on top of them. At the back, there was a big crush of people trying to get out so I ran to the front and more or less threw myself over the wall on to the pitch. That saved my life.'

Jean Sampson, Jayne's mother, tuned in to the radio herself at 5 p.m. and heard the awful news that 50 people were believed to have died in the Valley Parade fire. She waited anxiously for Jayne's return, her worst fears multiplying by the minute, until finally she could wait no longer. Her husband contacted the Bradford police. They had lists of those who had been taken to the various hospitals. Jayne's name was not among them.

Throughout the evening, switchboards were jammed as people begged for news of friends and relatives at the match. The hospital corridors were packed with relatives seeking information as to whether their loved ones were still alive. Some were calm, others verging on hysteria. A nursing sister sat them down in a room and produced a list of those admitted with injuries, patiently checking off the names as she went along. She admitted: 'It got very upsetting when people were left there because it slowly became obvious that they were going to be bereaved.'

Identification of the bodies was a painstakingly difficult business. The victims had been so badly burnt that by 10 a.m. on the Sunday morning not one had been positively named. In total, it took 114 police officers three days to identify all of the victims. Since visual identification was impossible, certainly for any of the bodies recovered from the stand, officers had to check dental records and comb the area for any items that had not been destroyed in the fire. Twenty-eight were eventually identified by their dental records – others by jewellery, bags, spectacles, wallets, bus passes, a wages slip and a snooker chalk. A traffic warden from Bradford was named among the dead by his uniform. Jayne Sampson was eventually identified by a small piece of her watch.

The Bradford City fire claimed the lives of eleven children, aged between eleven and sixteen, and nineteen pensioners, the oldest 86. Many had been inadvertently trampled to death by more able-bodied fans desperate to get out. A deputy headmaster died with his two sons, and one family suffered the anguish of losing members of three generations – an eleven-year-old boy, his father, grandfather and uncle. Over the following days, posies of flowers in soft drinks bottles were balanced on the turnstiles through which so many had tried to escape. Other floral tributes were lined against a smoke-blackened wall at the rear of the main stand.

Those who were fortunate enough to have survived continued to relive their ordeals. Seventy-six-year-old retired firefighter Kenneth Perryman was a season ticket holder in the main stand but, fortuitously as it turned out, for this game he had preferred to stand near the directors' box. 'The flames came along the roof so fast that they hit the office buildings and bounced back as a fireball. I thought I was in hell. I prayed. I used my fire service training and dropped to my knees below the smoke to escape. It was horrific – I've never experienced anything like it in all my thirty years in the service. The first night I was in hospital I didn't dare go to sleep because every time I shut my eyes, I saw the area of flames again.'

Geoffrey Mitchell owed his life to three strong men. He said: 'There was just a little bit of smoke in one corner of the stand, then it came up under our feet. It spread in a flash. The smoke was absolutely choking. My son was only a couple of yards behind me. I made my way down a passageway to an exit but the gate was padlocked. Three burly men put their weight against it and smashed the gates open. When I got out, I was so relieved to meet up with my son who had escaped through a different exit.'

In the wake of the fire, there was naturally intense speculation as to the cause. Everyone wanted to know how English football's worst-ever disaster could have happened. Some witnesses suggested a smoke bomb thrown by a supporter, but that theory was later discounted. The inquest concluded that the most likely cause was a discarded cigarette dropped through a hole in the wooden floor of the stand in G Block in the vicinity of seat I 142 or J 142. In a void beneath the floorboards, the cigarette had set fire to debris which had been piling up there for over seventeen years. These piles of litter ranged in depth from 3 inches to 18 inches. A search of the void revealed, among other things, a 1968 newspaper, an empty peanut packet bearing a price of six old pence and an empty ten-pack of Park

Drive cigarettes. The rubbish, allowed to accumulate over the years beneath a wooden building, made for an accident waiting to happen.

The death toll might have been reduced had spectators been aware of the urgent need to evacuate the stand at the outbreak of the fire, but as one member of the emergency services observed, 'It wasn't until the situation was clearly visible to a lot of people that they decided to make their escape and the fire at that stage was chasing them out of the stand.' For their part, the police were handicapped by the absence of loud-hailers and the background noise of the fire also caused communication problems with their radios.

Bradford City came in for criticism although they denied that they had been officially warned about the danger beneath the stand. But there were no trained stewards on duty to guide people out and no indication to spectators about emergency exits. In their defence, the club pointed out that the 25 of those who died from seats in G Block were only feet away from a door which was bolted but not locked and had therefore offered a chance of escape.

Ironically, as a result of promotion, Bradford City had been about to start work on improvements to the main stand, including the replacement of the old wood and felt roof. They were waiting until the season had finished before carrying out the renovation. Work had been due to start on the Monday following the fire.

The Valley Parade disaster served to highlight the hazards which existed at some sporting venues and helped shake the game of football out of its complacency. Wooden stands would become a thing of the past. Its messages were all too quickly forgotten by some supporters however, for just eighteen days later, 38 fans were killed and over 350 injured at the Heysel Stadium in Brussels when Liverpool fans rioted before their team's European Cup Final with Italian club Juventus.

Killed in the Line of Duty

Whenever firefighters tackle a blaze, they are putting their own lives on the line. Fire kills, and so does the smoke which invariably accompanies it. Fire is also unpredictable. The smallest of fires can suddenly flare up in a matter of seconds which means that even the most accomplished of firefighters can find themselves trapped with no way out. Sometimes the consequences are fatal.

The date of one such tragedy was 10 July 1991. Green Watch at Silvertown Fire Station in East London were a typically close-knit group. They enjoyed each other's company in and out of work and liked to bring their families along for social gatherings. In April, they and their families had all been on a three-day trip to Paris and they had already booked a holiday together in Norwich for the coming Christmas. Sadly, the Christmas toast would be to absent friends.

That night in July, Green Watch were called out to deal with a blaze at a five-storey warehouse at Bromley-by-Bow. The fire had started on the second floor of the building which housed business equipment. It spread at an alarming rate, producing thick acrid smoke which greatly restricted visibility. It was also an exceptionally humid evening, making the job more uncomfortable than usual for the crews.

As appliances arrived from other stations, a team was sent in to search the premises in case anyone was trapped. The rest of the firefighters concentrated on trying to bring the blaze under control, playing their hoses on the fiercely burning building.

The team of searchers went in wearing breathing apparatus which would normally supply each of them with around 30 minutes of oxygen. They could scarcely see through the smoke. To make matters worse, the warehouse was a maze of corridors, rendering navigation difficult at the best of times. In these conditions, it was virtually impossible. The corridors were lined with shelves where piles of documents were stored, so there was plenty of material to feed the fire.

Through the corridors they crawled, each passage looking the same as the last. The team split up in pairs to scour different areas, constantly aware of the danger of the heavy shelving collapsing on them. Then one pair, Terry Hunt, a 34-year-old married man with two children, and David Stokoe, 25 and single, became totally lost in the web of smoke-filled walkways. Their oxygen was running out fast. Their colleagues desperately tried to find them to get them out in time but to no avail. When they were finally found, their air supplies had run out. The two men had suffocated to death.

The feeling among the rest of Green Watch was one of stunned disbelief. Outside in the warm night air, the crews wiped the sweat from their brows as word of the tragedy was passed around. Heads were shaken, tears were shed. But everyone knew that there was a job to be finished. In the end, it took 100 firefighters almost six hours to control the blaze, but they did it.

To heighten the feeling of injustice, it transpired that the fire had been started deliberately.

The rest of Green Watch rallied together in these, the most difficult of circumstances. They were all back on duty the day after the fatal fire. Even those on leave cancelled their holiday to join the watch.

The people of the East End raised £100,000 for the victims' families. Tributes to the dead men poured in and the following year two commemorative plaques were unveiled and two trees planted in their memory. Their station officer said: 'Although David hadn't been with us long, he was fitting in well and learning fast. Terry had been here for years and was a very popular man. They were both good firemen and we will miss them both very much.'

*   *   *

A group of revellers dressed as sheep suffered burns when their fancy dress costumes caught fire at a New Year's Eve party in a pub at Cirencester, Gloucestershire. The flock of nine had chosen to see in 1995 dressed in black leotards covered in puffs of cotton wool, but their plans all went up in smoke when one brushed past a lighted cigarette.

The thick glue on the sheep outfits was highly flammable, causing the flames to spread rapidly. As the victims rolled on the ground, a man in a blue Little Bo Peep dress tried to stamp out the fire.

The publican who staged the private party for 70 people, all in their twenties, said, 'By the time seven of them had caught fire, they were walking infernos. One touched a cigarette, the others rushed to his help, and within a matter of seconds they were all alight. I thought at first the decorations were on fire but then I saw someone in a sheep outfit rush past the bar with his costume burning, so I quickly grabbed the fire extinguisher. It was lucky the bar was not as packed as it was last year or we could have had a real tragedy.'

The glue caused burns to the backs and faces of five men and two women, who needed hospital treatment before being discharged the next day. A Gloucestershire Fire Service spokesman said: 'We had a call to say some sheep were on fire. It was the most unusual emergency of the whole year.'

*   *   *

The Real Blue Watch

A Journey into Hell

The Underground complex at King's Cross station is the busiest in London. Not only does it serve two important main line railway stations – King's Cross and St Pancras – but it is also the place where no fewer than five London Underground lines converge. So throughout the day and evening it is seething with passengers rushing to or from trains for the North and the Midlands, as well as commuters making their way across the city. On an average weekday, over 250,000 people use the station with around 100,000 passing through in each peak period.

The early evening of Wednesday 18 November 1987 was no exception. Although the main rush hour was coming to an end, the network of gloomy, dank subterranean passages was still packed with office workers who had stayed on late before embarking on their journey home and people setting off for an evening out on the town.

Neville Eve, a personnel officer for Thames Water and a loving family man, decided to stay on at work that evening so that he could fill in a request for promotion. At 6 p.m., he telephoned his wife Sylvia at their home in Slough to say that he would be late for dinner and asked her to tell their two young daughters, four-year-old Samantha and seven-month-old Suzanna. He eventually left work at 7.24 and travelled to King's Cross by tube where he proposed to change to the Metropolitan Line for Paddington, the British Rail station which serves Slough. Mr Eve was one of 31 passengers whose journey ended at King's Cross that night.

Another innocent to the slaughter was Marco Liberati, a 24-year-old philosophy student from Bologna. Friends in Italy had clubbed together to pay for him to come over to England to join his girlfriend Mariella Santello. It was Mariella's 21st birthday the following day and Marco had bought her a surprise present. That evening, as the pair travelled from Wood Green, where she had been staying with friends, to her new lodgings in the East End, she playfully teased him about the mystery gift. But no matter how hard she tried, he would not reveal what he had bought her. She would have to wait until the next day. Alas, by then Marco would not be alive to hand over the token of his love.

It was pure misfortune that he came to be at King's Cross at all. Mariella hadn't decided which was the best way to get from Wood

Green to the East End and, since she envisaged making the journey on a fairly regular basis, she was planning to try out a number of different bus and tube routes. She opted for the Piccadilly Line from Wood Green to the centre of London and they would busk it from there, perhaps changing at Holborn. But as the train pulled into King's Cross, she spotted on the map inside the carriage that she could get a connection there to the East End. So on the spur of the moment she pulled Marco out on to the platform, just as the doors were closing. A split second longer and they would have been forced to carry on to Holborn. Without a care in the world, the young lovers joined the throng of passengers heading up the escalator towards the booking hall concourse.

The first hint of anything untoward at King's Cross that evening occurred at 7.29 when a commuter travelling on the up escalator of the Piccadilly Line noticed a minor fire beneath a step at the right-hand side of the upper part of the escalator. He duly reported it at the ticket office to a booking clerk who in turn telephoned the relief station inspector. Unfortunately, the clerk gave the location of the smoke as the up escalator on the Northern Line. Two minutes later, Judith Dingley, a BBC radio producer, also saw smoke rising out of the 50-year-old wooden Piccadilly Line escalator and rushed back down to the bottom, warning people not to go up. They simply ignored her.

Another passenger informed the booking clerk that there was a fire beneath the Piccadilly Line escalator. He peered out of his office. 'There didn't seem to be any more smoke than when I previously looked out,' the clerk later told the official inquiry. 'I didn't think it was very serious, so I didn't leave the booking office.'

At 7.32, as more passengers reported seeing smoke, PC Terry Bebbington telephoned the British Transport Police headquarters to raise the alarm. The London Fire Brigade's Wembley HQ was notified. Crews at the nearest fire station to the incident, Euston, were already out on what turned out to be a false alarm at University College Hospital, so four pumps and a turntable ladder were sent instead from Soho, Clerkenwell and Manchester Square fire stations. The Soho Red Watch crew was led by 45-year-old Station Officer Colin Townsley, a married man with two daughters and the firefighter who heroically gave his life that night trying to save others.

While the pumps sped as fast as they could through the busy city traffic towards King's Cross, at 7.38 p.m. the relief station inspector entered the machine room beneath escalator no. 5 and saw smoke and flames beneath the adjoining no. 4 escalator. He tried to douse the flames with a fire extinguisher but couldn't get near enough.

The Soho pump ladder arrived at 7.42, followed a minute later by the Clerkenwell pump ladder under Temporary Sub Officer Roger Bell and the Manchester Square pump under Station Officer Peter Osborne. The three officers went into the labyrinth of subways to investigate. Colin Townsley and Roger Bell walked down the Picca-dilly Line escalator next to the one which was on fire. S.O. Townsley immediately decided that the fire was sufficiently serious to warrant the order: 'Make pumps four – persons reported.' Returning to the booking hall area at the top of the escalator, he ordered S.O. Osborne to arrange for two breathing apparatus wearers and a water jet. Meanwhile Roger Bell carried on down to the bottom of the escala-tor, past the fire, to turn back passengers who were still going up. He was to tell the inquest: 'There wasn't much heat at that stage. The flames merely looked like a cardboard box on fire. It was what I would call complete combustion. It was getting plenty of air – there was little smoke.'

Roger Bell set about stopping people ascending the escalators and began to clear them away from the concourse at the bottom. With a train at the platform, he urged passengers to get back on it.

Down on the platforms, passengers leaving trains could smell the smoke. But a tannoy announcement reassured them: 'Don't panic, it's just a small litter fire.'

Some weren't convinced. Twenty-one-year-old Mark Silver tried to get back on the train but he couldn't battle his way back through the crowds in time. The boarding passengers had filled the carriages to capacity and the doors had closed. The train vanished into the dark tunnel.

By now, the decision had been made to evacuate the station. The police also ordered that no more trains should stop at King's Cross.

Mark Silver and some of his fellow passengers waited on the platform to catch the next train out. They didn't fancy facing any Underground fire, no matter how minor. For their part, the police around the platform did not seem overly concerned and all remained calm until a further announcement said, 'Stand back from the train. The train will not be stopping.' The announcement sent a chill through the passengers. Maybe the fire was more serious than everyone thought. The feeling turned to one of panic. As trains went through without stopping, those on the platform banged furiously on the windows, pleading to be let in. A woman, gripped with terror, jumped on to the line and ran after one of the trains. The police had to go down and rescue her.

Mark Silver went up the Piccadilly Line escalator. 'Everyone was pushing, screaming and shouting,' he said. 'We crushed on to the escalator. People began to climb up using the handrail; others tried to scramble up the steep slope between the escalators. Halfway up, the heat began to increase. I could feel it on my legs, even through the thickness of my jeans. Flames were coming, just little flames around the side of the escalator steps. As we were going up, about seven people, mainly businessmen, were going down. They looked at us as if we were mad – they just wanted to catch their trains. The smoke got blacker, the air got hotter. It was a smell like rubber and litter burning. At the top of the escalator, in the booking hall, the fire was really going. The walls were sizzling. It looked as if smoke was coming out of the ceiling. I saw a guy with his hair on fire. I got through the ticket barrier and went up the stairs to the main line station as fast as I could.'

The apparently innocuous fire had taken a dramatic, deadly turn for the worse. At 7.45, just three minutes after the Brigade had arrived, it suddenly erupted into a lethal flashover, sending a sheet of flame shooting across the ceiling of the booking hall area, swallowing up anyone in its path.

One of those caught in the line of fire was British Transport Police Constable Stephen Hanson, a married man with three children including an eight-week-old baby. 'One minute the fire seemed under control and then whoosh! It was like a shock wave of fire and bellowing smoke. It was like a jet of flame that shot up and then collected into a kind of ball. It completely knocked me off my feet. The fireball just hit me in the face and hands. My hands caught fire – they just melted in front of my eyes. I could see the balls of fire above my head, crawling along the ceiling, so I got down on my hands and knees to get below it. I could smell my own flesh barbecuing but I had to try and rescue some of the others. And all the while there was a sheet of fire hanging in the air about four feet above me with flames swirling down. To avoid the heat, I then flattened myself against a wall, shouted at others to do the same and edged towards the exit. I came across a passenger on the floor. I tried to help but the heat was too intense and I couldn't grip with my hands because they were so badly burnt. On my way out, I collided with the glass in the heel bar shop and cut my hand. I finally managed to get out at the Euston Road south-side exit. I went to a nearby hotel and plunged my hands and arms into a bucket of cold water.'

Leading Fireman David Flanagan had been sent back from the seat of the fire by S.O. Townsley. Ten seconds later and a few yards away in the booking hall area, he met the rest of his crew . . . at the precise moment that the flashover occurred.

'The whole area was plunged into complete darkness,' he recalled later. 'All that could be heard was people screaming. There was no time to start up our breathing apparatus sets. In order that we wouldn't become trapped, I shouted to the crew to get out and we then ran for our lives back along the subway by which we had entered. The only assistance we could offer people was to guide them out. We could feel them holding on to our clothing as breathing became difficult.'

Firefighter Joseph Boland was stunned by the speed of the flash-over. 'All of a sudden, without any warning at all, the whole place was engulfed with heat. Because it happened so quickly, we had no chance even to start our breathing apparatus. People were screaming. Visibility was zero through the thick black smoke. I kept to a left-hand wall thinking it would lead me somewhere. There was a woman clinging to the wall. She seemed to be running into it – she had lost all sense of direction. I got hold of her and shouted to her to keep low. You couldn't breathe, it was so hot. All you could do was hold your breath.'

Unaware of the terrible scenario 70 feet above them at the top of the escalator, British Transport Police and London Underground staff were trying to shepherd passengers away from the Piccadilly Line escalator and up the parallel-running Victoria Line escalator instead. All they were doing was sending them into the very heart of the fire. Not all passengers obeyed the instructions anyway. A woman with a small child ignored directions and went up the Piccadilly Line escalator. There was no way out at the top and she never did come back.

Marco Liberati and Mariella Santello were still joking as they stepped off their train at King's Cross. She remembered: 'I smelled smoke as soon as we got on to the platform. But it was mid-November, just after fireworks night when kids were still playing with fireworks, so I didn't think much of it. Even the policeman directing people didn't show any alarm. I was facing Marco on the escalator with my back to the ticket hall. We were teasing each other about my birthday surprise. Then as I turned round near the top of the escalator, a huge flame spread right across the ticket hall. It just filled the whole space. I don't remember anyone screaming. Panic sometimes makes you shut off. I don't know why we simply didn't run back down the escalator. The way out seemed to be up and into the air – I didn't think of smoke being the killer. I could see a gap beneath the flames and I dived for it. As I went underneath, I shook myself and my hair and threw away my black plastic jacket and bag.

'I turned round to see if Marco had followed me but I couldn't open my eyes. I tried to shout his name but couldn't even open my mouth. I found out later that everyone behind me had died.

'The heat was enormous and was melting my skin. I must have put my right arm over my head because that was burnt more than my left one. I thought, I am going to die here and there is nothing that I can do about it. What came to my mind was my mother, my friends; how far away they all were as I was about to die in those flames. I can't remember feeling pain or fear, just sadness. Then I thought, I can't die – I am too young. There are so many things I want to do.

'Somehow I managed to make my way out to the steps leading to St Pancras. One of the last things I remember was someone putting an oxygen mask over my face and pouring buckets of cool water over my legs.'

Mariella then slipped into a coma for 24 days. She recovered but Marco perished at the top of the escalator.

Student Kwasi Arari Minta was travelling up the Victoria Line escalator as directed when he too was suddenly confronted by the fearsome flashover. 'As I reached the top, I saw a tremendous flash of flame. I saw the flames hit the man who was directing us out – he turned and ran towards the exit with his hands over his face. The flames by this time had spread completely across the booking hall and seemed to be just over my head. At the same time, all the lights went out. I dived head first under the flames and rolled towards the exit barrier. I crashed into what I think was the collector's box. The whole area was in flames. I realised I couldn't use that exit so I turned and ran down the stairs to the Circle Line platforms. There I met two women. One of them shouted, "My God, you're on fire!" She started to tear my clothes off which probably saved me from even more horrific injuries.'

Passengers who could see what was happening tried to flee back down the escalator in the hope of catching a train to safety. But with no trains stopping, they were left with nowhere to go. Others were terrified at the thought of being trapped underground by a fire and reasoned that the only escape was into the outside air. That meant running the gauntlet of the booking hall concourse and many died in the attempt.

One who did get through was classical guitarist Ron Lipsius. He said: 'I knew the station and made for the tunnel which comes up outside St Pancras. I must have looked like a blackened alien because the tramps who sit there said, "Jesus Christ, where has that come from?" '

The skin was hanging from his hands in ribbons and his injuries were so appalling that he had to have a number of skin grafts. His guitar-playing days were over but he was just thankful to have got out alive, particularly as the friend's mother who travelled with him up the escalator died at King's Cross that night.

Another survivor described the horrific injuries on the escalator. 'A thing, I suppose a person, came stumbling down the stairs. His hair was all burnt off, his head was smoking and his skin blistering. He held his hands in front of him and there was smoke coming off them.'

Guardian journalist Richard Bates had been waiting on the north-bound platform of the Victoria Line when he was instructed to leave and directed up the Victoria Line escalator. When he reached the top, he saw orange flames coming from the right-hand side of the Piccadilly Line escalator. He didn't think they posed an immediate threat and so he pressed on into the ticket hall. He had only gone a couple of paces further when he heard a 'whoosh' and flames shot across the top of the Piccadilly Line escalators to where he was standing. They hit the wall where a temporary station operations room was situated. The flames were followed immediately by thick black smoke. He crouched down, put his hands to his face and struggled back towards the escalator.

Station Officer Osborne was in the ticket hall at the top of the Victoria Line escalator. He saw a very severe flame shooting from the direction of the Piccadilly Line escalators, which looked like a flame-thrower. Luckily it missed him as it burst up into the ticket hall. He shouted to passengers on the Victoria Line escalator to go back down. Near the top, he saw the badly burnt Richard Bates emerging from the smoke. S.O. Osborne took Mr Bates to the bottom of the escalator, swearing at him throughout the descent to keep him conscious, and then doused him with a water extinguisher.

Richard Bates believes that he probably owes his life to a platform poster. He had stopped to look at the poster when police officers shouted that everyone should get out as quickly as possible and, as a result, he was near the back of the queue heading up the escalator.

He said afterwards: 'I had only got two strides into the ticket hall and then ... At first there was a noise like a blast furnace, then flames ripped across the ceiling as if they had been shot from a flame-thrower. Then there was the choking smoke, so black and thick it seemed you could grab it by the handful. People who had walked past me further into the hall staggered around unable to see and unable to escape. Their bodies bumped into me. I got out – the only one to stagger down the escalator out of that cauldron.'

The flashover effectively divided the station into two worlds, each believing it had lost touch with the other. Those on the surface believed that those beneath were trapped or probably dead; those beneath had no idea what was happening above. Roger Bell had returned from trying to evacuate passengers to be confronted with a totally different form of fire. The seemingly innocuous blaze had been transformed into one where flames were darting out from the steps and sides of no. 4 escalator, up round the ceiling and back down on to the escalators. The fire was curling up the escalator shaft right through to the crest. He immediately tried to find a branch and hose with which to fight the fire, unaware of the disastrous flashover. Similarly, he did not know that his colleagues on the surface believed he was dead.

Joined by PC Bebbington, Roger Bell climbed the escalator and directed the jet into the flames. He tore panels away from the escalator in order to get at the seat of the fire but no sooner did he achieve a degree of success than it flared up again. Three times they attacked the fire but it was to prove a lost cause.

All the while, passengers were alighting from main line trains and heading down into the subways, ignorant of what was about to hit them. A group of five British Rail engineers arrived at St Pancras station from Derby at 7.39 p.m. Three minutes later, they arrived at the Underground ticket hall, only to find their way barred by a closed set of gates. Through the gate, they noticed a bluey-white smoke. People were running everywhere. Suddenly there was a blast of hot air and brown oily smoke. They decided to get out as quickly as possible and headed back for St Pancras. The oily smoke caught up with them along the perimeter subway but cleared as they descended the short flight of steps leading into the St Pancras subway. However, as they reached the steps up to St Pancras, the smoke rapidly turned from brown to dense black. They ran for their lives up the stairs to the St Pancras station concourse.

Designer Jeremy Asquith had gone to meet his wife off that same Derby train. As they reached the Underground ticket hall, they too faced a closed gate. They turned to their right to use an adjoining entrance but Mrs Asquith was having difficulty breathing. She paused at the exit from the St Pancras subway. Her husband looked into the ticket hall and, although it was smoky, he saw no obvious outward signs of panic. The calm was shattered by a cry of 'Get out!' He wasted no time in retracing his steps and as he turned, he saw black billowing smoke racing towards him. He managed to make his way to the St Pancras subway where he caught up with his wife and they escaped to the main line station.

Among the first passers-by on the scene were two cafe workers, Brendan Gallagher and Ian Edwards, from a restaurant opposite the station. Between them, they pulled out at least a dozen people.

Black with grime and smoke, Brendan Gallagher told reporters, 'I only went to the top of the escalator to get some tobacco. There was a terrible smell of fire and then I noticed this woman lying there at the top of the stairs. I went to her and at once smoke billowed up and even more people came staggering over. I carried her to the top and called my friend Ian before going down for others. By now it was a black hell. You could hardly see. The smell was horrible and people were fighting each other to get away. I saw one man, blinded by the smoke, run into the wall.'

Ian Edwards added, 'I carried up five or six people. There was sheer panic. People were pushing and shoving – they didn't know where they were.'

There were many heroes that night, in and out of uniform. One who was to receive special praise from the coroner was Sheffield businessman Anthony Palmer, who chanced upon the fire after stepping off a train at St Pancras. Noticing a crowd gathering at the Underground subway exit outside King's Cross station, he went over to investigate and could see smoke pouring out of the stairway, followed by several dazed people with blackened faces. They were choking and gasping for air. Other passengers had fought off the smoke by wrapping scarves over their mouths.

'Suddenly there was a roar,' he said, 'followed by a thick black jet of smoke that billowed from the exit. I noticed a further person trying to get out of the stairwell. At this point, I couldn't tell whether it was male or female. I got hold of his right hand and could feel it was red hot. Some of the skin came off in my hand. I got hold of his right arm and started to lead him from the smoke. I went back to the Underground entrance and at the top of the stairwell a woman was semi-crawling. She was obviously very seriously injured. I put my arms around the woman's back and assisted her from the stairwell. I tried to get down into the stairwell but I was driven back by the smoke and the heat. I then asked a fireman for permission to take a rope from his vehicle, tie a loop at the end of it and throw it down the stairwell. I threw the rope in several times, but to no avail.'

Below ground, Leading Fireman David Flanagan and Firefighters Robert Moulton and Stuart Button made a gallant attempt to re-enter the ravaged ticket hall in breathing apparatus. The heat was so great that at first they were driven back until Robert Moulton entered again, this time with two colleagues using their hoses to spray his back and thereby keep the temperature bearable, albeit for brief periods.

At 7.49, Assistant Divisional Officer Shore of Euston Fire Station arrived. He was told that three officers – Colin Townsley, Roger Bell and Peter Osborne – were missing. Shortly afterwards, crawling along by the steps leading up to the Pancras Road exit, crews made the discovery they had been fearing – the body of Station Officer Colin Townsley. He died less than 30 yards from the street, at the foot of the steps. His uniform and body were virtually unburnt and lying close beside him was the badly burnt body of a woman passenger. Some witnesses recounted seeing a fireman wearing a white helmet moving across the concourse just before the flashover, and someone with a torch exhorting passengers to get out. This would appear to have been S.O. Townsley. Typically, he had delayed his own escape to help the injured passenger. He had been trying to lead her to safety when he himself was overcome by smoke and fumes.

By 7.53, there were eight pumps at the scene. Seven minutes later, the officer's report read: 'Dense smoke emitting from lower level of station. A large number of people are believed to be involved.' At 8.04 the number of pumps attending had risen to twelve, and by 8.19 it was up to twenty. The firefighters had to work in atrocious conditions, their efforts hampered by the intense heat and by debris from parts of the station which were in danger of collapse. Electrical cables, dislodged by the blaze, caught on the firefighters' breathing apparatus. The booking hall area was strewn with charred bodies, not that the crews could see them through the dense smoke. Gingerly, they felt their way along the floor on all fours, dreading any obstruction which could denote another hapless victim of the inferno. As they crawled among the bodies, aiming water jets at the flames, they could feel the searing heat taking the skin off their foreheads. They tried to spray the subway with water to lower the temperature but still they were beaten back. As fast as they sprayed the water, it turned to steam which blew back in their faces.

One firefighter recalled the scene of devastation. 'There were some bodies in the concourse but we left them. We were looking for live ones. The escalators looked like a volcano – there were sheets of flame around us. The ceiling tiles were falling on us and every time a train went through the station, the fire would roar up all over again. There were bodies in the exit corridors, the ticket hall and at the top of the escalators. We found someone in one of the corridors. We were just about to put a cloth over him like the rest of the bodies and somebody said, "He's still alive." '

Every firefighter in King's Cross that night was dicing with death. Sub Officer Vernon Trefry was crawling through the smoke-filled booking hall concourse when he collapsed and lost contact with the hose which he had planned to follow in order to find his way out. He thought he would die. Reliving his experience, he told the subsequent inquiry: 'We had to proceed on our stomachs. I could see approximately six inches ahead. I noticed a pile of burning clothing in a corridor which I thought initially might be a casualty, but in fact it was simply somebody's jacket on fire. I also heard a series of small explosions, which I now believe were wall tiles coming off, in the ticket concourse. Reaching the booking hall, I slithered down the stairs on my stomach and immediately found a casualty to my right. I checked the body quickly and noticed that life was extinct. The body was charred, almost beyond recognition.'

After twenty minutes, the warning whistles began to sound on the B.A. sets and he sent the men back, using hoses to guide them. He then went back to change his own B.A. set. Returning below ground, he went to the other side of the booking hall where there were a number of bodies slumped on the ground. Before long, the air on his B.A. was almost used up once more. 'I couldn't stand up because of the heat. I turned round squatting and at that point, my legs gave way under me. I fell over and managed to get squatting again.'

He collapsed again, rolled over and fell on his back. Then someone leaned over him and turned on his distress signal unit. 'I then realised I was in serious trouble. I couldn't walk. My legs kept giving way under me and I was having difficulty breathing. I was concerned that I might die.'

Sub Officer Trefry remembered being helped up the stairs before passing out. He was suffering from heat exhaustion and was treated for burns inside his nose.

The first ambulance had arrived at King's Cross at 7.59 and as the extent of the tragedy became apparent, University College Hospital and St Bartholomew's were put on red alert. Surgeons at University College Hospital said the injuries included some of the worst flash burns they had ever seen. Other casualties had horrific burns to the hands, the result of placing them on the burning rubber handrail of the escalator. Yet the number of injured was relatively small for such a major disaster, simply because so few survived to reach hospital.

The firefighters' task was hindered from the start by the lack of detailed plans of the station. These were kept in a box which had to be broken open with an axe and a pair of bolt-cutters, wasting valuable time. And even then the map omitted the subway link to the Midland and City Line, a vital source of access which could have enabled the crews to tackle the blaze from a different direction. Indeed the Midland and City passageway should have offered the safest exit from the station but the exit gates were locked at the end of the rush hour. Police and petrified passengers were forced to try to tear them apart with their bare hands until a station cleaner eventually arrived with a key.

The badly injured Richard Bates was one of those whose evacuation was delayed by locked gates. 'Two policemen tried to get me out of the station,' he recounted, 'but the gates were locked. After five minutes, the keys were found. Then we came to another set of gates. These too were shut. There followed twenty minutes of shouting, rattling and kicking gates by policemen as frightened and confused as me. I was walking around in circles, screaming with the pain from my hands. I imagined the fire snaking its way down the tunnels and there I was with my back to the wall. I thought I was going to die. And then, thank God, someone with the keys heard our desperate shouts for help.'

At last, Richard Bates was taken outside and put into an ambulance. He remembers another casualty already in there, his face covered by an oxygen mask. 'In hospital a few weeks later, I suddenly realised I hadn't seen that man again. He had died – seventy per cent burns and the lung-destroying smoke had proved too much.'

At 8.35, fire officers reported that the fire appeared confined to the Piccadilly Line escalator. The search for survivors continued at the bottom of the escalators and in the corridors leading from the platforms. Every few minutes, the crews were still being blasted with scalding air. The heat sapped their strength but they pressed on.

The death of Colin Townsley was a devastating blow to the firefighters. Some, emotionally and physically exhausted, were seen sitting sobbing against a wall at the top of a subway. But the Fire Brigade is a highly professional unit and the loss of a colleague would not deter them from resuming the quest for possible survivors. The grieving would be done later. For the nation's firefighters, death is an occupational hazard.

From time to time, officers would call for total silence to determine whether any cries for help could be heard. A couple were rescued taking refuge in the staff toilet. Roger Bell, also feared to have been lost, was found in the area at the foot of the escalator. Peter Osborne was also located safely. The last casualties were removed at 9.08 but there were still bodies to be hauled out, a process which lasted well into the night. By 9.11 there were 30 pumps and over 200 firefighters present from as far afield as Millwall and Hendon. There were some gruesome finds among the charred debris. While clearing up, one firefighter stumbled across a human foot. In the booking hall, the digital clock offered a painful reminder of the event which had claimed so many lives, for it had stopped at 7.45, the exact moment of the flashover, its mechanism destroyed by the sheet of flames. At 1.30 a.m., it was confirmed that 30 people had been killed in the blaze, with eleven seriously injured. One of those was to die later, taking the toll to 31. It could have been even worse. Many more firefighters might have been killed by the flashover, had they not been outside at the time donning their breathing apparatus sets. At 1.46, the 'stop' message was relayed to Brigade headquarters, indicating that the King's Cross Underground fire was finally out.

The body of Neville Eve was identified the following afternoon by his watch and dental records. His body had been burnt beyond recognition. Every death hid a tragic story. One man died because he went for a drink with a colleague after work on the way to the station; another had swapped his shift to visit his nephew that night;

and a woman was passing through King's Cross on her way back to Germany after attending her grandmother's funeral. In every case, their only mistake was that of being in the wrong place at the wrong time. John McClintock, a lecturer at Reading University, was luckier. He stepped off the Newcastle train at King's Cross to see smoke pouring out of the subway. If the train hadn't been late, he would have been caught in the midst of the fire.

The inquest was told that the fire had probably been started by a match discarded by a smoker. It had fallen down a gap at the side of the old wooden Piccadilly Line escalator and ignited the mixture of grease and fluff which had built up over the years. Most of the victims died from inhaling the hot fumes. Some died after the smoke and toxic gases given off by burning plastic fixtures and tiles torched their throats which then swelled up and closed their air passages. Others succumbed to carbon monoxide poisoning.

The public inquiry into the fire pinpointed considerable slackness and negligence. Experts examining the wreckage estimated that there was as much as half a ton of grease beneath the escalator that went up in flames. London Underground staff had little or no experience of fire safety training, nor had they been trained in emergency procedures for evacuating the station. More damning even than the hidden map of the station was the fact that a fire hydrant, with two 100 foot hoses and other essential firefighting equipment, was locked and concealed behind a temporary hoarding, only yards from the top of the Piccadilly Line escalator. Unaware of its existence, those first fire crews on the scene had to send for jets from their appliances. This wasted crucial, life-saving time. At that stage, the fire was still 'small and innocuous'. Had the equipment been to hand, the fire might well have been extinguished without any loss of life. Fire chiefs themselves calculated that another three minutes could have averted the fatal flashover.

Twenty firefighters were given bravery awards for their heroic deeds that cold November night. But the overriding feeling was that they should never have needed to earn them.

Among the heroes was 44-year-old firefighter Paul Hale, who went down into the heart of the fire on six separate occasions and brought out six bodies. On one descent, he had seen a man crying for help, his face apparently burnt off. He received three bravery awards for his efforts, but the horror of King's Cross – the crawling over bodies, the feelings of disorientation which convinced him that he was going to die – had left him so traumatised that in 1991 he had to retire from his job. He kept experiencing hallucinations and reliving that awful night. He was eventually awarded damages of £147,000 for the trauma he suffered. Making the award, Mr Justice Olton said: 'Mr Hale is probably one of the most courageous men I have ever had, or shall ever have, the privilege of meeting. On that terrible night, he showed devotion to duty at a level not only expected by the London Fire Brigade and the public, but well beyond it.'

*   *   *

A hospital patient blew himself up in March 1996 when he lit a cigarette next to his oxygen mask. Unable to resist the urge, he slipped under the bedclothes for a furtive smoke while nurses' backs were turned. But in doing so, he created an oxygen 'tent'. For the moment he flicked his lighter, a fireball erupted. He was rushed from hospital in Llanelli, South Wales, to a burns unit.

*   *   *

An Early Alarm Call

The Scandic Crown Hotel was one of Edinburgh's finest, a plush, modern city-centre venue popular with businessmen and tourists alike. Situated in the Royal Mile, it was built in 1990 and had been designed to blend in with the historic buildings in the street. In December 1992, it housed the Danish and Dutch delegations who were in town for the European Community summit. But just ten days later, on the morning of Sunday 20 December, it was the scene of a dramatic evacuation as fire raged through parts of the building, threatening to engulf guests and staff alike.

The seven-storey hotel was only two-thirds full that weekend but there were still 190 guests. Many had spent the Saturday evening taking in the sights and enjoying the amenities of the Scottish capital, whether it be the theatre, the cinema, restaurant or bar. Others preferred to relax in the lounge after a hard day's shopping.

By 3 a.m., the hotel was quiet. The last of the late-night revellers had succumbed to fatigue and retired to their rooms. Those who weren't checking out in the morning were looking forward to that small luxury which a Sunday can bring – a lie-in.

At 5 a.m., they were rudely awoken from their slumbers by the sound of the hotel fire alarm. In one room, a middle-aged woman pulled the covers back over her head, convinced that it was nothing more than a false alarm or a masochistic manager's chosen time for a fire drill. Nothing was going to deprive her of her much-needed beauty sleep. Fortunately, her husband was more cautious and decided to investigate. Wiping the sleep from his eyes, he stepped out of his room to see hotel staff busily knocking on doors to evacuate the guests. People in pyjamas and nightdresses were scurrying down the corridor.

There was no time to waste.

'What's all the commotion?' demanded his wife. 'I'm trying to get some sleep.'

'There's a fire,' he replied, urgently. 'Come on, let's get out.'

With that, he pulled the covers back off the bed and dragged his wife, still half asleep, reluctantly towards the door.

'What about the suitcases? I'm not leaving behind all the clothes I've just bought – not that lovely black evening dress . . .'

The husband was becoming more agitated. 'I'll buy you a new one. Just get out before we both fry.'

She barely had time to grab her slippers before he had yanked her out of the door and down the corridor towards the fire exit.

The alarm was raised with the Fire Brigade at 5.03 and they were on the scene two minutes later, by which time the blaze had already reached serious proportions and was spreading from the roof of a 300 foot wing on to the floors below. It was thought to have started in the machine room on the fifth floor of the hotel. At first it was mainly smoke, but within a few minutes flames were shooting through the roof.

One guest, a Surrey businessman, said, 'I was in bed when the alarm went off and I grabbed my coat and went outside. Within minutes, the roof at the back of the hotel had flames coming through it. But everyone was remarkably calm – there was no panic.'

The smoothness of the evacuation was directly attributable to the speedy and efficient action of the hotel staff and the fire crews. In what looked like a fashion parade of nightwear, the guests were led out into the high street. It was bitterly cold. Some had managed to snatch up their coats and shoes, some even their trousers. One woman still had her hair in curlers. A head count was arranged. Ten people were missing, including the hotel pianist. As the remaining guests were taken to the warmth of a neighbouring hotel, where they were given emergency clothing and a cooked breakfast, teams donned breathing apparatus in readiness to search the building for the missing persons.

The fire was becoming increasingly dangerous. Pumps were called in from as far afield as Penicuik. A turntable ladder was summoned from Fife in case of any emergency elsewhere in Edinburgh that morning. Hoses were trained on the upper part of the hotel where the fire was at its fiercest. The fifth floor, where the fire had started, was burning freely but the crews battled to prevent it spreading to the rest of the hotel.

Inside, the crews made their way up to the danger area. They proceeded with extreme caution. Suddenly they heard a rumbling above their heads and they leapt clear just as a 120 foot section of roof caved in and landed perilously close to where they had just been standing. They dusted themselves down and made a swift exit. The entire roof was now unstable and orders were given for residents from a nearby youth hostel and a block of flats to be evacuated due to the threat of the roof collapsing.

The missing ten were soon accounted for. All were safe and well. The firefighters emerged unscathed, although one was taken to hospital for treatment to burns on his arm. Gradually the fire was brought under control although it took 100 firefighters three hours before it was finally extinguished. The hotel's sophisticated fire precautions had greatly assisted in confining it to one area. The fifth floor was wrecked beyond repair. All 30 bedrooms there would have to be demolished and rebuilt. Many of the guests lost their possessions. The lovely black evening dress never did make it out of the bag.

* * *

A faulty microwave oven which set fire to a Christmas pudding brought more than twenty firefighters to the Tower of London on Christmas Day 1993. The oven had failed to switch off after cooking pudding for the Tower's Yeoman warders.

* * *

History Repeating Itself

The Sealed Knot Society, who specialise in re-enacting battles from the English Civil War, pride themselves on their sense of realism, but at one contest in August 1994 the heat of battle was a little too realistic for comfort.

A crowd of over 1000 had gathered at Witney, Oxfordshire, to watch members of the Sealed Knot recreate the little-known battle of Windrush Valley. The pageant was a riot of colour, and everyone – participants and spectators alike – was having a great time until it all went horribly wrong.

It is believed that a piece of burning wadding from a seventeenth-century cannon ignited dry stubble. The resultant fire spread quickly through the ranks of both Roundheads and Cavaliers. Sealed Knot members fought to put out the fire but it had taken too strong a hold. The battle was abandoned for the day as Cavaliers on horseback and Roundheads on foot helped people to safety.

The strong winds blew the flames towards the spectators' area and the car park. One witness said: 'I couldn't believe how quickly everything went wrong. The cannons started firing and we saw something smouldering on the ground. Then the fire just started moving. It was a very frightening experience – a wall of flames coming towards us.'

As people fled the scene, the Fire Brigade arrived and within 30 minutes the fire was under control. Seventeen spectators were treated for injuries. Some had been hurt in the rush to escape, others had been overcome by smoke. Three special constables also suffered minor injuries and a total of 30 cars were destroyed or damaged. Several dogs trapped in the cars were treated at the scene. Two Roundheads suffered burns from trying to extinguish the fire but lived to fight another day.

*   *   *

Firefighters at Crownhill Fire Station, Plymouth, received an unusual visitor in the shape of two-year-old Christopher Wain. For Christopher came complete with a cake tin jammed under his chin like a collar. It took them 45 minutes to free him. 'We tried bolt-cutters but had to resort to a hacksaw,' said one of the crew.

*   *   *

Disco Inferno

The narrow streets and passages leading off London's Charing Cross Road are home to a myriad of clubs of varying respectability. The area really comes alive at night when customers pour out of the pubs in search of late-night drinking, music and women. Two such establishments were situated in the same three-storey building at 18a Denmark Place, a scruffy alleyway off Denmark Street. On the first floor was a South American gaming club called Rodo's and on the second a Spanish drinking club known as El Hueco – The Hole.

Friday night was usually the busiest night of the week for both of these unlicensed clubs. Few of the patrons had to think about work the next day so they could merrily drink away into the early hours and beyond. Indeed, El Hueco was in the habit of staying open serving drinks until eight o'clock in the morning. The Spanish club certainly lived down to its nickname. It consisted of nothing more than one extremely modest, claustrophobic room with a bar, a jukebox and half a dozen small tables. Stringfellows it wasn't.

The ground floor of the building was home to a hot-dog trolley park, where street vendors would return their trolleys after an evening wooing London's threatregoers with extra ketchup. So there was a constant stream of hot-dog sellers in and out of the building right up until around 2.30 a.m. The only link between the first and second floors was via an external iron fire escape which had been enclosed by a makeshift hardboard surround to shield guests from the rain. There was an internal staircase connecting the two floors but for some reason this was invariably blocked off.

The Friday night of 15 August 1980 saw the two clubs more crowded than usual. There were believed to be over 100 people inside. This was partly because a nearby restaurant, El Rodadero, a favourite haunt of South Americans, was closed for redecoration at the time. Many of its customers, including the manager, Eduardo Arbelaez, chose to go to Rodo's instead. Also, the club was staging a private farewell party for a Colombian woman who was due to return home in the next few days. Someone decided that the party should go with a bang.

The two clubs were no strangers to controversy. The police had been watching them for some time. To put it mildly, some of the clientele were a shade dubious. Consequently, loud altercations and threats of retribution were a regular occurrence in Denmark Place.

That night had been particularly volatile. Witnesses remembered a man becoming exceedingly irate after being refused admission to the clubs. Eventually he had gone away, muttering to himself, and the incident seemed to have blown over.

It was coming up to three o'clock on the Saturday morning. Inside, the clubs were in full swing. The air was heavy with smoke and alcohol. Drinks were ordered, toasts were made, songs were sung, and some even found room to dance. And in darkened corners, lovers were furtively whispering terms of endearment.

One man, in his early 50s, was trying to convince his mistress that he was finally going to leave his wife. She had heard it all before. They had been having an affair for six years and he had repeatedly promised that he was going to tell his wife everything. He was supposed to have told her that very day, but hadn't. It wasn't the right time, he insisted. Next week, maybe. That would be better. His girlfriend was furious. She accused him of stringing her along. She wanted nothing more to do with him and stormed off in a huff. As it turned out, her timing was immaculate for her Latin temper almost certainly saved her life.

Out in the street, all was not well. Witnesses saw a man throw a petrol bomb through the letterbox of 18a. He was then seen running off down the alley. Maria Delaney, the night manager of the trolley park, was preparing to pack up when she spotted flames shooting from the first floor. Her son Mark immediately tried to break down the door but fierce flames licked out and forced him back. There seemed to be a liquid on fire on the staircase.

A Turkish passer-by ran to the rescue but his efforts were also in vain. 'I must have kicked that door fifty times,' he said later, 'but I just could not get it open. Flames were coming right out of the windows and I could hear these terrible screams. I tried . . . but that door wouldn't budge.'

The manager of a fast-food shop in adjacent Charing Cross Road saw the flames and called the Fire Brigade. As appliances sped to the scene, the fire roared through the two packed clubs at such a rate that many people simply had no time to escape. The first they knew was the sound of an explosion. People started shouting, 'It's a bomb! It's a bomb!' Those in Rodo's on the first floor ran to the door leading to the ground floor and the street but flames were already pouring up the stairs and through the door. Panic stricken, they fought their way over to the windows and started smashing them with their elbows.

From there, some managed to jump on to a ledge before leaping to the ground. Others were trampled underfoot or couldn't reach the windows in time and were swallowed up by the fire's voracious appetite. One man was just about to jump when he was pushed out of the way and plunged back into the flames. This was no place for even a split second's hesitation.

Some cowered under tables in the hope that the fire might somehow pass them by. It showed no such mercy. As it spread, the fire burnt plastic fittings, creating fumes of toxic smoke. People were paralysed in sheer terror at the approaching flames. They wanted to escape but their bodies were unable to move.

Eduardo Arbelaez escaped with burns but lost two close friends in the blaze. 'Before I tried to get out of the window, I went back in to find my two girlfriends. They were clutching each other, completely petrified. They were terrified and couldn't move. As the flames reached them, they started calling my name, asking me to help them. But there was nothing I could do. I felt so helpless.'

The flames rapidly fanned upward so that by the time the Brigade arrived, the top floor was already alight. Soon flames were leaping out of the roof. The firefighters faced a daunting task. Not only was the fire burning wildly but the alleyway was too narrow for their appliances. Everywhere, people were jumping. The Colombian woman, in whose honour the party had been arranged, escaped by making a drop of 20 feet to the ground. Several of her guests never managed to reach the windows and perished in the inferno.

The screams rang out across Soho. Every available window was being smashed. One man, unable to get near the windows at the front, fought his way clear of the flames to make his escape from a back window. Jumping from there, he landed on a sloping roof. Another leap and he was down into the central well at the rear of the building. He spotted the door of an adjoining property but it was too hot to open. The perspiration pouring down his face, he managed to force an entry into Rhodes Music Store in Denmark Street. He ran through the shop, dodging the drum kits and organs, and tried to open the front door to reach the safety of the street. But it was locked. He knew there was no turning back so he decided to smash the window. In desperation he looked around for something with which to break it, until his gaze settled on an expensive electric guitar. In Pete Townshend mode, he lashed the guitar at the glass. It duly gave way, only for him to find, to his horror, that the shop window was protected by a security grille. There was no way out. Furiously, he banged at the grill, using his last gasps of energy in a cry for help. Above the mayhem, a fire crew heard him, broke down the door and dragged him out.

Meanwhile, firefighters were doing their utmost to prevent the blaze devouring adjoining premises. As crews poured in from across central London, they doused the building with gallons of water from high-pressure hoses. All too aware that there were people trapped inside, teams in breathing apparatus made their first tentative steps. For the 37 people who died in the fire, it was too late – the majority had been swamped by flames within a couple of minutes. The crews were not prepared for the sickening sight which awaited them in the two clubs. Several burnt bodies were found still seated in the charred remains of their chairs. Perhaps the alcohol had slowed their reactions or, more probably, they had not been able to get out in the crush. More bodies were stacked on top of each other where people had tried to escape through a door leading down from the first floor – a door which, according to witnesses, was always kept locked. One of the firemen lamented, 'Normally we find fire victims asphyxiated but these people were roasted where they sat.'

When the fire was eventually put out, both clubs had been gutted. Rescue workers were left with the unenviable task of sifting through the blackened remains. Amidst the rubble, they discovered two human hands welded to a table by the heat. The final bodies were not removed until the Sunday and four pathologists and four dentists spent the whole of that day trying to identify the victims from what little remained of them.

Twelve survivors were taken to hospital with varying degrees of burns. The rest fled into the night, not wishing to be part of any police investigation into the causes of the blaze. The rapid spread of the fire pointed to the use of an inflammable liquid and, to support that theory, a plastic container was found near the downstairs doorway. Furthermore, those survivors who were willing to talk spoke of a distinct smell of petrol, followed by thick black smoke. A man was subsequently charged with murder.

A similar tragedy took place in London two years later, on 18 July 1982, in the heart of the city's Chinese community, Gerrard Street, Soho.

A three-storey building at 39 Gerrard Street housed a shop called Loon Fung Oriental Provisions, but the basement was given over to a well-known gambling club. The club was invariably full with anything up to 50 punters.

At eleven o'clock on the night of the 17th, the police were called to a fight near the club. It appeared to concern the non-payment of £500. Then at 1.30 a.m., petrol was poured into the basement and the place set on fire. The explosion ripped through the club and wrecked the shop front. People fled for their lives into the surrounding streets. But for some there was no escape.

Firefighters in breathing apparatus struggled for hours to combat the smoke and flames, all the while keeping a watchful eye out for collapsing masonry. At one stage, the fire seemed to be under control, almost to the point of being extinguished, when crews were rocked by a second blast. One firefighter and two policemen were injured. A chief superintendent sustained back injuries and a punctured lung caused by flying glass which hit him in the back of the chest and led to serious bleeding. A doctor saved the officer's life by holding together his damaged arteries.

When the fire was finally put out, crews found seven bodies in the charred remnants of the basement. The club had been reduced to nothing more than a burnt-out shell. The Chinese community adopted an inscrutable silence, and the only help the police received was from a European witness. Nevertheless, within a month three Vietnamese men had been charged with murder.

2 Air Disasters

Twenty Seconds from Safety

Dr John McCrea and his wife Josephine had enjoyed their week's holiday in London. He had treated her to a night at the ballet. But now it was time to return to their home in Belfast. It was normally a routine 70-minute flight from Heathrow but on this Sunday evening, 8 January 1989, British Midland Flight BD 092 was to claim the lives of 47 passengers.

There was a certain amount of tension anyway as the 118 passengers assembled in the cheerless atmosphere of Gate 47 at Heathrow's Terminal One. For just eighteen days earlier, 270 people had been killed when a terrorist's bomb blew apart a Pan Am 747 in mid-air over Lockerbie, Scotland. As a result, extra security checks were in operation at the airport, all of which served to delay the departure and heighten the apprehension. So when the passengers finally stepped out into the misty drizzle to board the twelve-week-old Boeing 737, they were eager to get home as quickly as possible.

The McCreas took their seats in Row 15 by the left wing. The flight was scheduled to depart at 19.30 but the security precautions meant that it was 19.52 before the Boeing was airborne. Powered by two strong engines which enable it to climb quicker than most other jets, the 737 quickly rose above the thick cloud cover. Take-off safely accomplished, the passengers began to relax. In the darkened flight deck, Captain Kevin Hunt, a man with 25 years' flying experience, and his co-pilot, David McClelland, monitored the glass display panels. They glowed blue, orange and grey, indicating that the plane was heading smoothly over the Home Counties on its journey north.

Ten minutes into the flight, Dr McCrea was reading a magazine while the cabin crew started serving a light supper of pork salad. Suddenly he felt a shudder and, looking out over the left wing of the plane, saw flames and sparks flashing from the port engine. The cabin staff stopped serving meals and walked to the front of the plane. In the cockpit, the pilot had also felt the vibration and sensed a smell of hot oil and hot metal. Looking round the cockpit, Captain Hunt saw a trail of smoke which appeared to be coming through the cabin door. He took control from David McClelland and disengaged the auto-pilot. At 20.05, he called British Midland's operations department at East Midlands Airport, describing what his instruments told him and reporting that he had an engine vibration problem and smoke on the flight deck. He asked David McClelland which engine was causing the trouble. McClelland replied: 'It's the le . . . it's the right one.' He was told to throttle it back. Forty-three seconds after the first vibration, the pilot, knowing that the aircraft could fly safely on a single engine, ordered him to shut down the troublesome engine. The Boeing was flying at 30,000 feet but the pilot was reluctant to continue climbing to the planned cruising altitude of 35,000 feet. Instead he was instructed to divert to East Midlands Airport, near Castle Donington in north-west Leicestershire, just west of the busy M1 motorway.

The crisis appeared over. After the right-hand engine had been throttled back, the vibration, smell and smoke receded. Captain Hunt reassured the passengers that they were not to be unduly concerned. He said there had been some trouble – a fire in one of the engines – but that the engine had been closed down and they were diverting to East Midlands. But Dr McCrea could still see flames pouring from the left-hand engine. He was not alone in his concern. Two girls, also spotting the flames, began screaming. The cabin staff tried to calm the girls down and then started to collect up the meals and store them away. The aircraft commenced its descent towards East Midlands Airport. Below them in the distance, the passengers could see the lights of the M1. Knuckles were turning white. The soothing voice of the public address system announced that they hoped to land shortly at the airport.

Captain Hunt had established the 737 firmly on a glide path to land at Runway 27. The aircraft was travelling at 170 knots and 1100 feet when, less than two miles from the runway, there was another bang and more flashes. Captain Hunt reported to the airport that the second engine was also failing. The cabin crew swiftly removed all the baggage from the lockers. Dr McCrea took out the safety card and told his wife to brace herself. There were further flashes and more of what seemed to the passengers like turbulence. Dr McCrea won-dered whether the faulty engine had started up again. Then the captain came on the PA and told everyone to get ready for an emergency landing. The passengers prepared themselves for the worst, their faces traumatised with fear, knowing they were about to crash. A steward ran up and down the aisle, desperately searching for a place to hide. Almost immediately, Flight BD 092 vanished from radar screens.

Oblivious to the drama unfolding in the sky, Terry Lovett, director of East Midlands Airport, was at home in the village of Barrow upon Trent, seven miles from the airport, reading *Old Possom's Book of Practical Cats* to his five-year-old daughter Amy. It was a typically peaceful Sunday evening. Then, just after 8.15 p.m., the telephone rang. It was the airport's duty manager informing him that Flight BD 092 was coming in for an emergency landing in three minutes. Lovett asked to be called back when it touched down. Two minutes later came the call he was dreading. The voice on the other end said: 'We have an aircraft disaster.'

Just eight seconds after the captain's warning to the passengers, the plane had touched down – not on Runway 27 at East Midlands Airport but on the M1 motorway, a mile south of Junction 24 and just half a mile, and twenty seconds' flying time, from the safety of the runway.

Losing height rapidly, the pilot had somehow managed to steer the jet clear of the village of Kegworth before it belly-flopped into a field at Mole Hill Farm, just above the embankment of the southbound carriageway of the M1. In a last, desperate attempt to reach the runway, Captain Hunt had briefly got the plane airborne again. It sliced through some saplings on the embankment before dropping once more, part of its undercarriage ripping through the motorway's metal crash barriers. By now breaking into three parts, although its wings remained intact, the aircraft careered upward into the 30 foot high wooded embankment of the northbound carriageway where it came to rest at a precarious angle of 45 degrees. The cockpit section, which was almost severed from the main part of the fuselage, nearly made the crest of the hill, over which the airport landing lights could be seen, mapping out an elusive welcome. The main fuselage section lay upward on the embankment. The rear fuselage and tail had been severed and formed an ugly 'V' shape of mangled metal.

Cars, coaches and lorries screeched to a halt on the motorway. By some happy chance, traffic on the normally busy M1 was relatively light that night, and miraculously the jet had managed to cross all six lanes without striking a solitary vehicle. If any vehicles had been hit, death for the occupants would have been inevitable. If something like a petrol tanker had been hit, the consequences would have been too awful to contemplate.

But there were still some narrow escapes. A coach driver brought his coach laden with 42 passengers grinding to a halt just feet away from the wreckage. Other drivers, scarcely able to believe what they were seeing, ducked down in their cars, fearful that the aircraft would hit them. Rachel Meadows, a nineteen-year-old accounts clerk, was driving on the M1 at the time. She described how the jet seemed to make contact with the embankment on one side of the motorway and then bounce across before ploughing into the trees and brambles on the other side. 'There was an almighty flash, but it didn't explode. A lot of cars on the motorway began to brake hard. I thought it was going to be a massive pile-up but luckily it wasn't.'

Remarkably, only minor injuries were sustained by motorists involved in a small pile-up. One passenger from the plane was thrown clear of the wreckage by the impact and landed on the motorway. He was found by a stunned motorist stumbling along the carriageway yet escaped with nothing more than a bruised leg.

Inside the plane, darkness prevailed. The lights had gone out with the crash. There was a strange silence, broken only by the sound of plaintive moans from those unable to free themselves. Someone cried out, 'My legs hurt.' Another begged, 'Please help me.' Dr McCrea's arm was hurting. He checked to see that his wife was alive. The man next to his wife got up but Mrs McCrea couldn't move – she was pinned down by pieces of metal and by a shaft of plastic wedged up against her throat. Dr McCrea was terrified that fire might break out in the fuel tanks at any moment. If that happened, they could all be burnt alive. He quickly undid his wife's safety belt. Within a minute or so, a rescuer smashed through the window over the wing and the man next to Mrs McCrea helped drag off the debris. The McCreas were helped out through the broken window.

From his hospital bed the next day, he recalled: 'I think I was the third person out of the plane. I scrambled down the wing. My wife was put on a kind of impromptu toboggan and slid down the wing to the ground.' Dr McCrea sustained an arm injury while Mrs McCrea suffered a broken left thigh bone and a cracked pelvis. They were comparatively lucky – 44 others lost their lives that night and three more died from their injuries over the ensuing weeks.

The miracle was that there were any survivors at all. That 71 passengers and all eight crew members cheated death was due in no small way to the heroic efforts of the emergency services, aided by residents of Kegworth who had heard the stricken aircraft skim over their village and raced to the crash scene on foot, by motorcycle or by car. As they were on standby ready for the emergency landing, East Midlands Airport's fire crews, including three tenders carrying foam equipment, were on the scene within minutes of the crash. To combat the threat of fire in the fuel tanks, they immediately began pumping gallons of flame-killing foam into the wreckage. Their task was made easier by the quick thinking of an airline engineer who had the presence of mind to close off the taps on the aircraft, thereby preventing aviation fuel from pouring out and greatly reducing the risk of the plane catching fire. Leicestershire Fire Service received its first call on the crash at 8.26 p.m. Six pumps and a foam salvage tender were despatched at once from stations in Leicester, Loughborough and Coalville. By 9.04 p.m., the number of pumps present had risen to ten. Eighteen minutes later, another five were sent from stations in Derbyshire and Nottinghamshire.

The sight that greeted the fire crews was one of total carnage. Pieces of the plane were strewn over the motorway and the surrounding fields. Seats, luggage and clothing, jettisoned from the aircraft by the impact, lay littered along the embankment, the hard shoulder and across the six lanes of carriageway. The authorities closed the motorway for six miles, restricting access to emergency vehicles. Thirty ambulance crews from five counties raced to the scene, along with two medical flying squads from Derbyshire Royal Infirmary, comprising sixteen doctors and nurses. Ambulances were parked in the fast lane ready to ferry the injured to hospitals at Derby, Nottingham, Leicester and Burton upon Trent. Just four months previously, staff at the Queen's Medical Centre, Nottingham, had taken part in a simulated air disaster. They hadn't expected to face the real thing so soon.

Arc lights erected on the motorway lit up the cool night air and helped the crews in the grim chore of searching for survivors. One of the firefighters' first tasks was to tether the precariously hanging tail section with ropes in case the plane should slip down the bank during the rescue. Perched on steel ladders and using special cutting equipment, fire crews hacked their way into the fuselage in the hope of reaching any survivors. Once inside, they found a hideous tangle of metal and human flesh. People had been hurtled forward by the force of the crash and crushed by the sheer weight of their fellow passengers and the wreckage. The overhead luggage bins had broken free, showering the passengers with debris. Many, particularly those in the twisted tail section, were dead, still strapped in their seats. Others were barely alive and were using their last gasps of breath to plead for help.

Once access had been gained, firefighters picked their way gingerly through the wreckage to try and free those who were trapped. The beams from their torches shone into areas of hope. All the while, more foam was being pumped in and hoses were played on the wings of the plane.

Elsewhere, rescuers clawed at the wreckage with their bare hands. Among them was Joe Weston-Webb, a 50-year-old businessman from nearby Sutton Bonington, a village on the flight path to East Midlands Airport. 'I was watching television when I heard this horrendous noise as the plane went over my house. It was obviously in trouble. I went outside and saw it disappearing over a hill and I realised that it had crashed. I went to give what help I could. When I arrived, people were already there and had begun to pull away at the wreckage with their bare hands. There was an eerie silence but people were beginning to scream. The seats had concertinaed forward to the front of the fuselage and passengers were trapped. They all seemed to have smashed ankles and legs. It was a miracle anyone got out alive. I lifted out a baby in a blue romper suit. The baby seemed all right but there was no way of telling where its parents were or if they were injured. I tried to comfort a woman but she just mumbled incoherently.'

The baby, a boy of seven months, survived but his mother died in hospital two weeks later.

Using spades and shovels, fire and police crews dug out a series of steps in the soft mud of the embankment to facilitate the removal of passengers dead and alive. A human chain was formed to take survivors down to the waiting ambulances. The dead were placed on stretchers, covered and laid on the hard shoulder of the motorway before being taken to a hangar at East Midlands Airport which served as an emergency mortuary.

Trees were flattened to improve access to the aircraft. Bodies were found in the adjoining countryside and helicopters equipped with thermal imagers hovered over the fields at the side of the motorway searching for signs of life. Helicopters were also brought in to ferry the seriously injured to hospital. By 10.30 p.m., there were over 100 firefighters on the scene and the rescue effort was reinforced by the arrival of an army team. Doctors were helped inside the aircraft to administer pain-killers to survivors. Surgeons carried out on-the-spot operations, including amputations, and paramedics applied cardiac massage and mouth-to-mouth resuscitation. They didn't all make it. While medical and fire crews toiled around him, desperately trying to free another victim, a priest gave the last rites to one dying passenger.

Two AA patrolmen were among the first to stumble on the scene. One used an axe to chop a hole in the side of the fuselage. The other helped comfort a screaming woman passenger trapped in the wreckage while a surgeon amputated her leg. If her leg had not been removed, she would have died.

Sub Officer Eric Moss from Leicester Fire Station laboured for six hours inside the fallen jet. 'The conditions inside were very difficult,' he said. 'Very tight and very hot. We were taking away layer upon layer of wreckage inside the fuselage. People were underneath; people were alive but I don't know how. At one stage, we all kept quiet and we heard a bloke calling. Part of the fuselage was on top of him. We dug a way through to him for nearly three hours. There were layers of bodies. It was chilling. We used everything to get him out – pliers, screwdrivers, anything we could get our hands on. In all that time, I never even saw his face. He believed we were going to get him out and we did. I can't tell you what a great feeling it was to see him come out alive.'

Two and a half hours after the crash, Captain Kevin Hunt was finally lifted from the wreckage after being trapped by the feet. As firefighters brought him out, he had bloody gashes on his head and a plastic bag over his left foot. He was rushed to Leicester Royal Infirmary but his serious spinal injuries would confine him to a wheelchair.

At 11.05 p.m., firefighters began stripping away the skin of the fuselage where the plane had split to reach those still trapped. But a ruptured wing tank threatened the entire operation. Orders were given to prepare to leave the aircraft because of the risk of fire but the heroic firefighters ignored the danger – and the instructions – and carried on with the rescue mission. One station officer later recalled how his six-man team had been working to rescue a young woman from the tail section. 'We'd been in there two hours and had freed the top half of this girl when we received a message from the Chief Fire

Officer of Leicestershire to be prepared to abandon the plane. Apparently there was fuel leaking from the wing. But whatever happened, there was no way we could leave her – we'd built up a relationship with her. She was relying on us. Within an hour, we'd managed to free her. I only knew her name was Sharon.'

Crews dug a channel to allow the fuel to drain from the tank, allowing the search for survivors to continue through the night and into the early hours. At midnight, by which time there were some 300 rescuers on the ground, ten people were believed to be still trapped in the remains of Flight BD 092.

Black humour and the Fire Brigade go hand in hand, even on such bleak occasions as this. Helping a young man covered in blood – but still conscious – from the seat which had been his prison, one firefighter remarked, 'Never mind, son. There's only passport control to get through now!'

The last survivor, a seriously injured young woman, was brought out at 4.20 a.m. She had been trapped and crushed for eight hours, her spirits sustained by the comforting words of her rescuers. Ten minutes later, the last two bodies were lifted clear of the wreckage and the police and fire crews began to drift away. Their job was done. It was an experience none would forget.

As word of the disaster spread, anxious friends and relatives waited at Belfast Airport for news of their loved ones. For a thirteen-year-old boy, eager to tell his mother and two brothers about his recent school skiing trip to Grenoble, the news was tragic. All three had been killed in the crash. Mercifully, while the rest of the family headed back home to Northern Ireland on the fateful flight, his father had elected to stay over in England on business. For another man and his two children, there was profound relief. They were told that Mrs Kerry Gorman, who was due on Flight BD 092, had in fact caught a later flight.

Among the dead were six service personnel. David Ward and his fiancée Judith Pattison were lance corporals on their way back to duty in Northern Ireland after their New Year's leave. They had spent their leave planning their spring wedding and arranging last-minute details with the vicar in their home village of Bildeston, Suffolk. They had been engaged for two years and had just bought a house. Some of the wedding presents were already stored there. The crash left her dead and him critically injured.

Another service victim returning to Northern Ireland was Falklands veteran David Hastings, a warrant officer in the Army Pay Corps. He had been due to leave the Army after 22 years the following April. Darren Mitchell lost his life after flying all the way from Melbourne, Australia, to visit his aunt in Northern Ireland.

Others, like Dr and Mrs McCrea, lived to tell their tale. Donal Desmond survived but is now an inch and a half shorter because his frame was compressed by the force of the crash. Worse still, he lost his Finnish wife Marya in the disaster. She had been sitting in the seat next to him. He remembered how, after the pilot's final announcement, 'My wife and I clung together and prayed. Those eight seconds seemed to go on for a long time. It was interminable. Your body just can't react.' The crash threw him halfway through the cabin door. When he came round, the first thing he saw was a seat upside down with a dead woman looking into his eyes. Blood was pouring from his arm wound but he knew that if he lost consciousness, he would never wake up. His life was saved by Graham Pearson, a motorist who was on his way to Hull with his children and who used a dog lead as a tourniquet to stem the bleeding from Mr Desmond's shattered arm.

After visiting friends in London, solicitor Mary McHugh and her boyfriend John Loughlin had been booked to travel home on the Stranraer to Larne ferry. However, they missed their train connection and instead went to Heathrow where they were given seats on Flight BD 092. She told reporters: 'I was sitting right where the plane split apart. Behind me was a total abyss. It was just black. The lights went out and there was absolute chaos. I thought I saw a fire start at the front of the cabin. I thought to myself, This is it, we are going to get burnt. People were screaming, going crazy. My boyfriend just disappeared. I could hear him calling – it was terrible. Together with other passengers, he'd fallen into the hole where the aircraft had split. We were only on the ground for three or four minutes before people started pulling us off. But first there was the foam. It just hit us, large amounts of it. I thought, Wow! It was great – it meant we weren't going to get burnt.'

Passenger Gareth Jones recounted the terrifying final minutes in the air as it became clear that there was something drastically wrong with the aircraft. 'The lady next to me, who was very disturbed and weeping almost hysterically, put her head down and waited for the worst. I tried to do everything I could to take her mind off what was happening. She squeezed my hand, held tight for a few minutes, then seemed to be OK. But as the motorway lights came into view below us, there were more sparks and a severe bang. As soon as she saw the second load of sparks flying, she broke down completely. When we hit the ground, there was just a massive crash – like a multiple car accident. Because we were right next to the emergency hatch, I could see outside. I could see a tree so I knew that we had hit the ground. I also knew we had to get out as quickly as possible so I pulled the emergency exit handle and pulled out the lady next to me. I saw we were on the motorway but, as I got to my feet, they immediately gave way and I fell down again.' The young woman, who gave her name only as Emily, covered him in blankets, nursed his head injuries and got his home telephone number. While Mr Jones was being rushed to hospital, she phoned his wife to say that he was alive. Nursing a head wound, Mr Jones concluded, 'I am sure it was because we were seated above the engines that we were saved. They took the full impact.'

Gardener Alastair McCrory from Downpatrick celebrated his escape from the crash by proposing to his girlfriend Pat Miles after nine years of courtship. He decided his luck must be in after just missing two other disasters. He was meant to be on a helicopter which crashed off the Scilly Isles in 1983, killing twenty people, and also on a coach which crashed on the M4 in 1988.

Meanwhile the 5000 residents of Kegworth were just grateful that their village had been spared, particularly in the wake of the eleven who had perished on the ground in the Lockerbie explosion. In fact, the people of Kegworth were warned of a full-scale emergency by the sound of fire and ambulance sirens along the main street while BD 092 was still airborne with one failed engine. Some locals thought it was just another practice drill until they heard the sick sound of the plane overhead.

Peter Wragg watched the approach of the plane from his house. 'It was heading for the airport. Then on its final approach, the engine noise was very much curtailed. Usually you can hear the engines of planes rev up as they go into reverse thrust prior to landing. But here the noise was cut short.'

Another witness said: 'The sky lit up red. I was horrified. There was the sound of backfiring and the plane was swooping lower and lower. Thoughts of Lockerbie came into my mind. For a moment, it looked as though the pilot could possibly have made it to the runway, but he was losing height rapidly. He did really well to avoid the village. It was only seconds away from hitting the centre of the community. It could have wiped out the entire area.'

Student Andrew Pendleton was at a friend's house when he was alerted by the noises from the aircraft. 'I heard a chuffing sound like a train. I believe it was the flames being fanned by the wind. When I looked out of the front window of the house, towards Kegworth, I saw the plane. The engine was on fire and was going in spurts. It looked as though it was coming straight for us. All I could see was the nose of the plane. The nose was down. It was so near that I could make out the British Midland logo. I had never been so scared in all my life as when I thought it was coming for us. I was running around shouting to everybody to get out of the house, especially after Lockerbie. I ran to the other side of the house and could see that the pilot had managed to pull the nose up, which meant that it lost speed but carried further and missed Kegworth. If he hadn't done that, I think it would have hit the village. We watched it go over the hill and as it did, all you could see were flames and smoke.'

The villagers of Kegworth hailed Captain Hunt as a hero but the official report into the crash, published in October 1990, was critical of the pilots. It said the cause of the accident was that the crew shut down the right-hand engine when the problem, a fractured fan blade, lay in the left. When, approaching the airport, Captain Hunt tried to apply additional power from the damaged but still-running left-hand engine, it failed and it was too late to start the fully operational right-hand engine. Captain Hunt told the inquest that he saw smoke coming through the cabin door which indicated, to his mind, that the right-hand engine was on fire. If the fire had been in the left, he reasoned that the smoke would have got into the cockpit through the air-conditioning system which was powered by that engine.

The report said of the pilots: 'If they had taken more time to study the engine instruments, it should have been apparent that the No. 2 engine indications were normal and that the No. 1 engine was behaving erratically. In the event, both pilots reacted to the emergency before they had any positive evidence of which engine was operating abnormally. Their incorrect diagnosis must, therefore, be attributed to their too rapid reaction and not to a failure of the engine instrument system.'

For the passengers on board Flight BD 092, it was a tragic human error.

* * *

Two days after Christmas 1994, Hampshire Fire Brigade were called out to deal with an elderly man who had caused widespread flooding in a Southampton tower block after inadvertently leaving his dentures in the sink with the tap running. As water seeped through the ceiling of the flat below, neighbours had tried banging on his door but he had removed his hearing aid and couldn't hear a thing.

* * *

Suspended in Mid-air

Most of us nurture a secret ambition. It could be to drive a Formula One racing car round Silverstone, swim the Channel or climb Everest. Mrs Gwen Brown's yearning was, on the face of it, somewhat more modest, but it turned out to be every bit as dangerous. For she had always wanted to fly a glider.

Accordingly, she enrolled for lessons at the Southern Gliding Club at Parham Airfield, West Sussex, and on 27 January 1982 she took to the skies for the first time, accompanied by her instructor, Ray Brigden.

But her maiden flight ended in ignominy and near tragedy as the glider plunged into the uppermost branches of a tree close to the airfield and came to rest precariously perched 30 feet above the ground on overhead electric cables carrying 400,000 volts. Witnessing the mishap, staff at the airfield called the West Sussex Fire Brigade.

Waiting for the fire crews to arrive seemed like an eternity for Mrs Brown and her hapless instructor. They knew they had been lucky to survive the crash but their ordeal was by no means over. They dare not attempt to climb out of the glider for fear of electrocuting themselves on the cables. Besides, so delicately was the craft balanced that any sizeable movement would undoubtedly have sent it – and its occupants – crashing to the ground. As it was, whenever there was a mild gust of wind, the wings began to sway ominously. So there was nothing to do but sit tight, be patient and pray.

Eventually a crew from Horsham arrived to assess the situation. From some distance away, they could see the glider perched on the treetops like a huge bird with injured wings. Since it was nesting on live cables, the priority was to get the power supply turned off. Only when that was done could the rescue mission begin in earnest.

The obvious problem was that of how to reach the stricken glider. It was quite a way off the road and was surrounded by branches and cables, making access extremely difficult. Ladders alone would clearly not suffice – it was a job for the hydraulic platform.

Although aware of the need to get the occupants to the ground as quickly as possible – Mrs Brown was in a state of shock and had also sustained facial injuries in the crash – the firefighters proceeded with caution. The hydraulic platform had to be manoeuvred into a position whereby the boom extensions could reach the cockpit. Despite rotating the cage in both directions and trying every possible approach, there was still no clear avenue for the booms through the branches and cables. So a number of larger branches were felled using cutting equipment. At last there was daylight and the cage was raised towards the cockpit. It was touch and go whether it would reach but with the extensions just a few feet from their maximum, the cage was positioned safely alongside.

Mr Brigden was lifted out uninjured and lowered to the ground in the cage. Mrs Brown was given first aid and comforting reassurance by the crews before she too was released from the cockpit and brought down by the hydraulic platform. Never in all her life had she been so glad to be on terra firma. As she was driven off to hospital in a waiting ambulance, maybe she thought of taking up a less strenuous hobby.

* * *

A lady in Arnold, Nottingham, had to be rescued by firefighters after getting her hand trapped in the remote control compartment of her television set.

The unfortunate woman was watching *Neighbours* with her husband when she went over to the set to fetch the remote control. However, when she tried to pull her hand out of the compartment, it wouldn't budge.

Fearful that she would have to spend the rest of her life with a television set attached to her right arm, she began to pull furiously. The more she pulled, the more her hand swelled up. She tried, her husband tried, but the hand was stuck fast. And the swelling was growing by the minute. There was nothing else for it – the Fire Brigade would have to be called.

Accustomed to dealing with such predicaments, the firefighters calmly asked the husband for some ice which was then placed around her hand. The swelling went down and within five minutes, the hand was safely removed.

'It was quite a simple operation,' said one of the modest firemen. 'But I think it probably took longer for the lady to get over the embarrassment . . .'

* * *

Disaster on Flight KT 328

The suntan cream and swimsuits had all been packed, along with the flip-flops, straw hats and other holiday paraphernalia. Now the 137 passengers were ready for their flight to the sun and the mouthwatering prospect of a week or two on the Greek island of Corfu.

It meant an early start, particularly for those from Yorkshire and Derbyshire who had been obliged to leave home in the small hours in order to cross the Peaks in time to catch British Airtours Flight No. KT 328 from Manchester Airport. But few minded – they were just pleased to be getting away from the typically unpredictable British summer weather.

It was shortly before seven o'clock on the morning of Thursday 22 August 1985 that the passengers, among them two babies and a number of children, crossed the tarmac to board the Boeing 737 named River Orrin. Their pilot was 39-year-old Captain Peter Terrington, a man with twenty years' flying experience. As the crew of six completed the standard last-minute checks, for some holidaymakers there was the usual apprehension prior to take-off, notably among those who weren't seasoned fliers. Twenty-year-old joiner Ellis Wardle fell into this category. It was his maiden flight.

Steadily the aircraft taxied around the tarmac, waiting for the all clear. The pilot was cleared for take-off and at 7.13 a.m. the 737 began hurtling along main runway 2406 at 100 mph, ready for its ascent into the skies.

Thirty-two seconds into the take-off run, as the speeding plane swept past the air traffic control tower having covered two-thirds of the length of the 10,000 foot runway, Captain Terrington heard a thud on the port side. For a split second, he thought it might be a burst tyre or a bird hitting the fuselage. But then the flight deck alarm was activated and he realised it was something more serious. He radioed to the tower: 'We are abandoning take-off. It looks as though we have a fire in Number One.' At the same time as the captain had heard the bang, a controller in the tower had seen metal bouncing on the runway in the aircraft's wake, followed by a plume of smoke and flames 'like a blow torch' from the port engine.

Leading Fireman John Sheppard was on duty at the airport fire station that morning. From his vantage point in the observation tower above the garage, where his colleagues waited by their tenders in case of an emergency, he too saw the aircraft trailing smoke and flames.

He immediately punched the crash alarm and jumped into the seat of his Rapid Intervention Vehicle.

Captain Terrington applied the brakes and steered the stricken aircraft to the right in order to get off the runway and as near as possible to the airport fire station. Within 30 seconds and 1000 yards further on, the Boeing slowed to a halt.

The situation was even worse than Captain Terrington had imagined, for the port engine had exploded and chunks from it had burst into the port wing fuel tank and fuselage with the ferocity of an artillery shell. As the plane slowed down, hundreds of gallons of highly inflammable fuel spewed on to its belly.

In the passenger section, panic had already broken out. Hearing the bang, a woman had looked out of a window on the port side to see flames spurting from the port engine. Instinctively she screamed, 'Oh my God, the plane's on fire!'

Suddenly gripped with every air traveller's worst nightmare, other passengers stood up to see what was happening. The sight of flames licking the wing and spreading along the fuselage confirmed their fears. A stewardess with a microphone moved swiftly down the aisle and told everyone to keep calm and remain seated. A sense of order was momentarily restored. But then passengers at the back started screaming as flames began shooting inside the aircraft through cracks caused by the explosion. Parents snatched up their children, husbands dragged wives out of their seats, and everyone stampeded towards the exits. The moment that the aircraft had ground to a halt, the captain announced over the public address system: 'Starboard side passengers off, please.' He repeated the evacuation order twice more but to many his words were lost in the general furore. By now, there was no hope of an orderly evacuation.

Fed by the leaking fuel, the flames were racing along the interior of the fuselage from the back. It was a race to get out alive, very much a question of survival of the fittest. Anyone who hesitated was liable to be trampled underfoot and burnt alive. The crush from the rear of the plane was unbearable, where neither of the exits could be used because of the fire. That area was engulfed in flames. The rear starboard exit door had been opened and the escape chute fully deployed by a stewardess while the plane was still moving, but as the plane veered off the runway the chute had been destroyed by flames licking under the fuselage before it could be used. With no escape from the rear of the plane, the passengers there had little option but to press forward.

Stewardesses manned the other exits in their usual professional manner but the look of horror on their faces betrayed their innermost feelings. There were other problems too. The emergency over-wing exit on the port side was too dangerous to use – anyone leaving the aircraft by that means would have jumped into the very heart of the blaze. And for crucial seconds, the starboard front exit door was jammed. Responding to the captain's orders to evacuate on the starboard side, the purser tried to open that door first but it wouldn't budge. He went instead to the front port exit, opened that door and deployed the emergency chute. The starboard front exit was eventually forced open but it meant that at the start of the mad rush to safety, only two of the six escape routes were fully operational. Without a shadow of doubt, this contributed greatly to the scale of the disaster.

Ellis Wardle and his girlfriend Deborah Wilson were two of the lucky ones. He said: 'We saw a fire in the wing when the plane was moving and people started to panic, but a stewardess calmed them down. We were told to stay in our seats but then I looked behind and I saw that flames were already coming inside the plane. The fire seemed to be coming through the fuselage. There was no way anyone was going to stay in their seat. People started moving forward away from the flames but the fire was getting closer and then a gush of smoke came over all our heads, making it difficult to see.

'I looked around for my girlfriend and she was just behind me. I grabbed her by the wrist and we went down the chute and landed in foam. The Fire Brigade had got there very quickly and we were helped up and someone got us on to a bus. I did not look back. I did not want to see any more.'

By the time the doors had been opened and the emergency chutes released, the crush of passengers had already started to block the escape routes. Anna Findlay was sitting in Row 15 towards the rear of the aircraft. 'We all heard a bang. Everyone stood up immediately and a couple of seconds later I looked out and saw the engine was on fire. At the same moment, people were telling us to sit down, shut up and not to panic. At first everyone sat down but then the flames got worse and some people started to rush for the front. All the windows had cracked within a few seconds. I stayed for a moment thinking that if everyone starts running, we've all had it. But then the push came from behind and I started to climb forward like everyone else over other people. When they moved, most of the people fell down and got trampled on. By the time I decided I was going to move, people were crushed and lying down in the aisles. I went over the seats and just forced my way out. I could hardly breathe because of the smoke.

'There was a piece of rope outside the door and I just grabbed it and people behind me pushed me out on to the wings. I thought I was going to die. The back doors didn't come open. Nobody moved backward – everyone moved forward. The passengers helped kick open some of the doors. It was crazy in there. You looked after yourself with no thought for anyone else at all. If everyone had stayed back and been orderly, I think more people might have got out alive.'

Captain Terrington had succeeded in bringing the crippled aircraft to a standstill just 200 yards from the airport fire station – an amazing feat in the circumstances. Thus, fire crews were able to reach the blazing jet within seconds of it stopping.

John Sheppard's vehicle was first on the scene. It had the capacity to spray foam for 55 seconds from its own supply and was doing just that within 70 seconds of the explosion. A second tender arrived almost immediately, closely followed by Leading Fireman Michael Bradley at the wheel of a large 3000-gallon foam tender, affectionately known as Jumbo One. The last-named tender was capable of pumping foam at maximum speed for two minutes.

The eighteen airport firefighters immediately began to saturate the fuselage with the life-saving, fire-quenching foam. For a fleeting moment, the fire appeared to be under control. The blaze on the port and wing tail and the pools of burning fuel surrounding the aircraft were quickly extinguished, enabling grateful passengers to begin their escape down the emergency chutes. Firefighters clambered on to the wings and two managed to get inside the aircraft with their hoses. But then there was a second explosion. The heat caused oxygen cylinders stored at the rear of the aircraft to explode, thereby igniting the fuel again in a deadly fireball. Leading Fireman Brian Wilson was positioning his hose on the centre aisle when the explosion blew him out of the plane and on to the tarmac. After being given oxygen, he insisted on returning. But by then it was too late.

The fire spread at such an alarming rate, causing so much damage, that just ten seconds after the first foam was sprayed the aircraft broke its back. The tail section collapsed on to the tarmac, sending passengers who were waiting in the aisle to jump to safety through the front doors tumbling back into an inferno from which there was no escape. There was less than a minute between the plane stopping and a time when nothing more could be done for those inside. It is a chilling statistic that most of the 55 people who died in the Manchester Airport fire did so within a mere two minutes of the original engine explosion.

Due to the problems with the exit doors, it was those at the front who had the best chance of escape. They were the first to freedom. Any who hesitated at the top of the long slope were given a helping push by the cabin crew members stationed at the doors. Some were literally thrown down the chutes. This was no time for niceties. But no matter how hard they tried, the crew were powerless to control the crush of fleeing passengers which continued to claim innocent lives. A woman and her young daughter were holding hands near one of the exit doors. The mother was encouraging her to push through. But in the jostling and shoving, their hands were forced apart. The mother got out. The little girl didn't.

Those at the rear of the plane stood little chance. As passengers near the front waited to plunge down the chutes, all they could see of the back was thick smoke, pierced by constant screams.

One survivor, 21-year-old Mike Mather, admitted: 'We knew there were people in there who had no chance of getting out alive. Anyone who was left in there after me didn't stand a chance. I'm just glad to be alive.

'You could see the flames shooting past the windows but we all thought the fire would go out when we stopped and they got the extinguishers going. But the smoke and flames started coming into the cabin. It was mass panic as people started queuing to get out. People were falling over each other and the heat was tremendous. Flames were coming out of the engines and we thought it was going to blow up. Smoke was coming along the roof inside the cabin and getting through that smoke was like trying to go against a brick wall. There were about thirty people in front of me and as I went down the chute, I felt this blast of searing heat. It hit the back of my throat and tasted like acid. I didn't know my girlfriend had got out until I saw her on the tarmac wandering away from the wreckage.'

Once the fire started, the cabin filled with thick smoke and fumes in a matter of seconds. No one could breathe. The lack of visibility also hampered their efforts to find the exits. They could hardly see the person in front of them. It was a case of follow my leader and hoping that you somehow made it into daylight.

Survivor Keith Middleton remembered: 'Everyone got pushed into the aisle trying to get out of the aeroplane. There was a lot of pushing and jostling. I couldn't see past the middle of the plane because of the smoke but I could hear terrible screams and shouting. The flames were billowing into the plane and I couldn't breathe. It was just a thick black, smoke-filled aeroplane. I tried to hold my breath as long as possible. We could hear the pilot trying to say something over the intercom but he was drowned out by the screaming and shouting. People were falling on to the floor and getting trampled on. Finally a steward grabbed me and threw me down one of the chutes.'

Twenty-two-year-old Debra Whalley from Preston was travelling with her boyfriend and two other friends, both of whom were killed. 'We were sitting right next to the wing which was on fire. For ten or fifteen seconds we didn't do anything. I remember how the smoke hurt when you breathed in. I got pushed through the door. I took one breath and I thought my number was up. We were just like sardines.'

In company with her colleagues, stewardess Joanna Toff did her utmost to evacuate as many passengers as possible in the horrifyingly short time before the aircraft was totally engulfed in flames. Seeing a small, helpless girl being trampled on by her fellow passengers, she reached in to the throng and plucked the child to safety. Then she pulled a young boy from a mêlée of passengers. Through the ever-thickening smoke, she spotted a man slumped in his seat. She reached across and dragged him out by his collar before pushing him down an escape chute. After rescuing an unconscious woman, she found herself clear of the fire but still returned to the inferno in the hope of saving others and began crawling along the cabin floor to check for survivors. At the subsequent inquest into the disaster, the coroner rightly praised her. 'You acted magnificently that day,' he told her. 'It is clear that a good number of the people who are alive today probably owe their lives to your actions.'

Two of her fellow stewardesses perished in the fire. Both had ample opportunity to escape but chose to stay and help people trapped in the smoke-filled rear of the aircraft.

Some passengers managed to escape by climbing out on to the wings of the aircraft. Michael and Hilary Loftus were on the plane with four-year-old daughter Joanne and two-year-old son Daniel. Mr Loftus carried Joanne out on to the wing and managed to get down on to the tarmac. After taking her to safety, he then returned to make sure his wife and son had got out. He found them sitting on the wing. Mrs Loftus said: 'There wasn't a chute on our side of the plane. The door was open but I couldn't see anything but foam from the firemen. I had Daniel in my arms and when I got on to the wing, Michael appeared out of the foam below and shouted: "Jump!" So I closed my eyes and jumped and he grabbed us.'

Royston Metcalf, a dental technician from Chesterfield, lost his fiancée in the disaster. He recalled how, after the initial bang, the plane's nose went down and the duty-free bottles rattled in the bins as the aeroplane veered from side to side under extreme braking. 'There was a tremendous fireball, fifteen feet high. It was too big for just an engine. As the plane stopped, tongues of flame like fingers were coming through the windows and shooting to the ceiling. Smoke poured in with the flames. People's clothes were on fire. You could feel your skin creeping with the heat.

'The aircraft stopped. Within four seconds, it was as black as night. The smoke was so thick it was drowning the noise of the flames roaring across the ceiling as the fireball travelled up from the back to the front of the plane. I turned to get my fiancée out. She said, "What about my handbag?" I told her to forget about the blessed thing.'

Arm in arm, they struggled to move forward along the aisle to the front exit doors. 'People on fire were running forward. I passed out at some stage. I woke aware of a burning in my mouth. I put my finger in and brought this filth out. It was like an Oxo cube. Chunks of black muck were in my eyes, nose and ears too. I'd lost my glasses and so I took a handkerchief out of my shirt pocket, dragged it across my eyes and saw a chink of light, the size of a postage stamp, down to the left. I went for it and managed to get out.'

Passenger John Beardsmore experienced a similar struggle. 'I checked the emergency over-wing exit but realised it was next to the burning engine and was therefore of no use. At that time, I knew I wasn't going to get out. The smoke was absolutely choking. I knew if I took a second breath I would die. I fell into a row of seats from where I glimpsed daylight through the smoke. I just staggered towards the open exit door.'

Other passengers spoke of the horror of being inside a skidding, fast-moving aircraft, the fuselage of which was burning inside and outside. One said, 'There were loads of kids on board but everyone was trampling over everything and anybody to get out. It was like being in hell.'

Even after the oxygen cylinders had exploded, the airport fire crews strove manfully to put out the flames. By then, they had run out of foam and had to resort to using hand-held extinguishers. Four back-up appliances from Wythenshawe Fire Station were still five minutes away. They had received the alarm at 7.15 and arrived at the prearranged Rendezvous Point North at 7.21. However, as the aircraft burned furiously, they had to wait a frustrating three minutes until police vehicles arrived to escort them on to the airfield. Within ten minutes of their arrival, the fire was out. As it transpired, the delay was probably not critical in this case. The fire had spread with such speed and ferocity that most of the victims were dead long before the back-up appliances arrived.

Robert Docherty, Divisional Officer of the Greater Manchester Fire Brigade, had been on the scene within a minute of the alarm being raised. He battled his way inside the blazing jet, but although he managed to help one passenger through a front door, he found dozens of bodies piled up against the emergency exits.

The chances of finding anyone alive seemed remote but as long as there was a chance, no matter how slim, firefighters were prepared to risk their own lives by scrambling into the burning, smoke-filled fuselage. Then suddenly, through an emergency exit, Firefighter Eric Westwood spotted an arm waving. It was that of a thirteen-year-old boy. Firefighter Westwood remembered: 'I saw an arm waving over a body already slumped in the starboard over-wing exit. I climbed on to the wing and hauled out the boy who had been pinned beneath a pile of bodies. When I was getting the boy out, I could see there were lots of bodies piled up in the side of the plane. I then tried to drag out the man slumped in the exit door but I had to retire when the smoke and fumes affected me.' The man was already dead. The boy survived although his mother and sister were killed in the blaze.

As firefighters continued to tackle the blaze, the 83 survivors were put into buses and ambulances and rushed to nearby hospitals. The vast majority were ferried to Wythenshawe Hospital two miles away although those suffering the most serious effects of the fire were later transferred to Withington Burns Unit. Wythenshawe had been notified of the fire at 7.22 a.m. and it was a rare stroke of good fortune on such a wretched morning that the first busload of 26 casualties arrived at a time when the night and day shifts were changing over. Consequently, there were twice as many staff as usual to deal with the emergency from the outset. The hospital also had an abnormally large number of empty beds because of the holiday period.

The seventh and last ambulance arrived at the hospital at 8.45, bringing the final patients from the scene. At the height of the emergency, over 50 nurses and 25 doctors were treating patients. Dazed and bewildered, those casualties who were not seriously hurt wandered around the hospital looking for friends and relations. Some left in tears, having been informed that their families were not on the list of those admitted.

With the last flames extinguished, it was time to discover the full horror of the fire. Inside the blackened, broken jet, its tail section slumped to the ground and the roof of the main cabin area ripped open, rescue workers were reminded yet again of the terrible toll which fire can exact. The rear section in particular was crammed with charred bodies, barely recognisable as human beings, piled on top of each other as much as three deep in the aisles. Among them, near the closed rear starboard door, was one of the hostesses. Some of the dead were still strapped in their seats – they simply hadn't been able to react quickly enough to the stampede for the exits. A little girl was found still sitting on her mother's knee in their seat on the plane. Both were dead. Victims had to be identified by dental records and belongings which had survived the blaze. One woman was identified by her designer shoes.

Rex Brearley, Manchester's director of airfield services, was full of praise for Captain Terrington. 'It was a miracle anyone escaped,' he said. 'If the aircraft had come to a halt any further away and if the tenders hadn't been there to meet it as it came to a halt, I don't think anyone would have got out alive.'

The inquest into the tragedy revealed that it was started by a failure in the combustion chamber of the aircraft's port engine. It emerged that the port engine had been giving problems prior to the accident and that repairs had been carried out on it throughout the night before the fire. Only nine victims were killed purely by the effects of the heat. A total of 26 died as a result of breathing in smoke and toxic fumes and the remainder succumbed to a combination of effects. Experts described how the flames spread along the fuselage at a rate of 68 feet per minute, exceeding a temperature of 1000 degrees Centigrade. Some 250 gallons of fuel escaped from the ruptured tanks each minute to feed the fire. When the jet was on the runway, the smoke and the flames were blown backward from the aircraft but when it turned right off the runway, the wind drove the fire on to the fuselage. The final position of the aircraft was partially cross-wind and that unfortunately contributed to the spread of the fire from port to starboard.

It was a terrible accident but one which was described as 'wholly survivable'. It was the speed of the fire and the widespread panic among passengers which were principally responsible for the high death toll. Nevertheless, some of the emergency procedures carried out that fateful morning gave cause for concern. The shortage of foam was particularly alarming. The airport fire service was carrying 8220 gallons of foam, 50 per cent more than was legally required by the Civil Aviation Authority. The fact that supplies were exhausted so quickly suggested that the figure needed to be urgently reviewed.

To make foam requires water. When they needed fresh supplies of water, firefighters discovered that three hydrants on the airfield were dry. One firefighter spent three vital minutes testing three separate hydrants before driving his foam tender back to the airport fire station. There he spent nearly ten minutes refilling his vehicle before finally being able to return to the blaze. On his way back to the aircraft he saw that one hydrant which he had not tested, assuming that it was on the same feed line as the others and would therefore also be dry, was now being used by another tender. The problem with the hydrants wasted time and kept essential manpower away from where it was most needed – at the aircraft. If the hydrants had been working correctly, the most effective way to have tackled the fire inside the cabin would have been with hoses connected directly to them. At the time of the disaster, outside contractors were engaged in upgrading the hydrants but it was claimed that they had not told the airport fire service that part of the supply was being turned off.

Finally, the inquest was told that smoke hoods would have saved many lives on board Flight KT 328. The provision of these was among the safety measures recommended to ensure that there was never a repetition of the Manchester Airport disaster.

The horror of that August morning will probably never be forgotten by those who lived through it. For Ellis Wardle and Deborah Wilson, the nightmare haunted them for months afterwards. Recalling the effects of the Manchester fire, he told the *Sunday Times* magazine: 'It didn't sink in for days. Then I started turning the whole thing over and over again in my mind. Some nights I couldn't sleep and when I did, I dreamt about the plane and the fire. I was moody and became irritable for no reason. The smell of any sort of smoke reminded me of the pungent fumes from the burning aircraft.'

The memory of Manchester reared up again a year later when they took their first holiday since the abortive trip to Corfu. They went to the South of France and promptly found themselves witnessing a forest fire. Whereas most of the other passengers on the coach were captivated by such excitement and started taking photographs, Wardle and Wilson were terrified.

'When the coach stopped moving because of a traffic jam, I felt trapped,' said Deborah. 'There were bushes on either side of the road and I kept thinking that if the fire got closer, there'd be nowhere to run.'

Ellis Wardle added: 'I remembered the black smoke, the pitch darkness and I thought I was going to die again.' They cut short the holiday.

* * *

Toddler Sophie Cotterill had to be rescued by Nottingham fire-fighters after getting her head stuck in a toilet seat. She tried on the plastic seat for size at the Ring A Ding babywear shop in Sherwood, only to find that she couldn't get it off again.

Her mother, Nicola, from Keyworth, Notts, was contemplating buying the toilet seat when she asked 21-month-old Sophie to hold it for a minute. 'She likes hats and is always trying things on,' said Mrs Cotterill. 'She will put most things on her head but this time the seat would not come off. At first it was funny but then I realised it was stuck. It was embarrassing but I was more worried about Sophie because she was screaming.'

The Fire Brigade were alerted when one of their appliances was flagged down in the street, but it wasn't carrying the necessary equipment and another vehicle had to be summoned. Staff and customers battled to keep a straight face as the firefighters tried in vain to squeeze the seat off Sophie's head with washing-up liquid. Eventually they resorted to a small hacksaw and cut the seat in half.

Sub-officer Bryan Gray said: 'I've been in the fire service seventeen years and have never dealt with a job like it. Sophie was very upset. I think the sight of five firemen frightened her so we bought her a chocolate bar to keep her calm while we got to work on the seat.'

After the ordeal, Sophie's mum admitted, 'I don't know if I will be buying the seat in case she keeps trying it on.'

* * *

3 Explosions

An Underground Blast

For the villagers of St Michael's on Wyre in rural Lancashire, it was to be a pleasant evening out and an opportunity to allay their fears.

In 1981, the village (population 500) had suffered serious flooding when the nearby River Wyre had broken its banks after heavy rain and there had been sporadic, less serious waterlogging in the intervening three years. The villagers were convinced that the flooding was caused by the transfer of water by the Abbeystead outfall pumping station from the River Lune to the River Wyre. Eager to provide reassurance, the North-West Water Authority agreed to a request from St Michael's parish council for a party of villagers to visit Abbeystead to watch a demonstration. It seemed a good PR exercise. The trip was arranged for the evening of 23 May 1984.

Abbeystead is some twelve miles from St Michael's and is situated in the Forest of Bowland, an area of outstanding natural beauty. The plant is surrounded by a 1000-acre estate belonging to the Duke of Westminster, and in those days the estate was a popular retreat for members of the royal family keen to escape the prying lenses of Fleet Street. In order to appease locals worried that such a building would be a blot on the landscape, Abbeystead was constructed to blend in with the surrounding countryside. It was built underground and any above-ground structure was suitably camouflaged. To outsiders, the waterworks appeared nothing more than a large grass-covered mound.

The outing to Abbeystead had been advertised in the window of the village shop at St Michael's for some weeks. There had been plenty of interest and children were encouraged to go as well as adults. Abbeystead wanted to be seen to be opening its doors to whole families. The subject matter may not instantly have appealed to them but the prospect of a trip out on a pleasant May evening and the opportunity to stay up late was sufficient to entice a few youngsters. Ten-year-old Stephen Hogarth had been looking forward to it. He was going with his eight-year-old sister Catherine, mum Linda and dad Frank. But shortly before they were due to leave, Frank discovered that Stephen hadn't done his homework and, as a punishment, the family stayed at home. Stephen had to watch enviously as his friend, twelve-year-old Mark Eckersley, set off with the party. He would never see Mark again.

The 30 villagers departed from the car park of the Grapes public house at St Michael's at 6 p.m. in a flotilla of cars and minibuses. They stopped off at Garstang to pick up another group of twelve who were touring the plant that evening, and arrived at Abbeystead in good time for the 7.15 start. Everyone was in good spirits. They admired the countryside and some even said they wouldn't mind a bungalow on top of the works.

On arrival, the visitors were warmly welcomed by Water Board officials and made their way into the underground station at 7.20 p.m. The party soon became strung out. Some lingered near the entrance door talking to officials, while others were led further into the plant to wait for the demonstration. District manager Alan Lacey duly telephoned a pumping station on the River Lune and asked for water to be pumped through for the demonstration. As some of the party stood on the metal mesh floor craning their necks to get a good view, Mr Lacey told them that when the water came gushing through, the noise would be so great that they wouldn't be able to hear themselves speak. They all waited a few minutes, making polite conversation, but nothing happened. Mr Lacey couldn't understand why the water wasn't coming through, so eight minutes later he phoned again and suggested using a larger pump.

Suddenly, at 7.30 p.m., there was an almighty roar and a huge explosion. Before they had a chance to take cover, people were engulfed in flames and the roof of the building was blown away. Bodies were catapulted into orbit and the force of the blast threw 30 two-and-a-half-ton concrete roof beams of the underground building soaring upward through tons of topsoil before they collapsed back into the devastated valve house below, smashing through the heavy duty metal grille and killing or injuring those who had been standing there watching the demonstration. A hole five metres square was blown out, like a large crater.

One of the party, John Holmes, staggered from the blast to raise the alarm. 'I saw people who had all their clothes ripped off by the flames. Then I looked down and saw that mine had gone too. I borrowed some car keys from one of the others and managed to drive to the nearest houses. I knocked on the door and told the person that answered, "For God's sake get us some help. There's been an explosion!" '

The sound of the blast was heard some miles away and locals raced to the scene. Among the first to arrive were farmer Peter Entwistle and his wife Tizzie, a nurse. 'We saw about twenty people lying around,' he said. 'All were burnt – most had lost their hair and clothes. People's skin was singed and had been peeled back. Some were crying. One man had been thrown a tremendous distance by the blast. My wife freed another man who was trapped under a car while I ran to dial 999.'

Divisional Officer Chris Guinan of Lancaster Fire Brigade was the first senior officer on the scene. He had been at home when the alarm was raised and had hurried through the winding lanes to Abbeystead in his own car, arriving at the same time as the first two pumps and emergency tender. The stench of burning flesh pervaded the air. 'There were casualties everywhere, crawling around the grassy embankment like ants. Others, clearly in a state of severe shock, had wandered off into the surrounding fields. Their clothes were burnt and hanging off their bodies and their flesh was burnt. They were helpless. I tried to find out what had happened. There was only one person who seemed a little bit coherent but I couldn't get much out of him. Everybody else I saw was either dead or injured. I had to assess the situation quickly and from the evidence at hand, I decided that an explosion had occurred in the building used as a valve house.

'Inside, the scene was one of utter devastation. Normally Abbeystead was spotless, like heaven. I couldn't believe what I saw.'

As more appliances arrived, farmers and neighbours brought tea and blankets. The shocked survivors were wrapped in blankets and rushed to hospital by ambulance. To speed up the process, roads across the lonely moorland were closed to all but emergency vehicles. Above ground, cars were badly damaged. One bonnet was later found several hundred yards from the rest of the vehicle.

In the underground chamber, some of those caught in the blast were lying mutilated or dead on the partly collapsed metal grille, their bodies trapped beneath the heavy concrete beams. Others had crashed through the floor into 27 feet of water below and were left floundering about in the cold swirling torrents, pleading for help.

Two men were spotted, half submerged in the water, clinging to pipes. They were in bad shape and barely conscious. One had a broken leg and severe burns while the other was badly burnt and blue with the cold. They needed to be pulled out of the water as quickly as possible but they were in the far corner of the area and could not be reached simply by lowering a ladder through the shattered grille. So Leading Firefighter David Saville and Ambulanceman Michael Able clambered down the ladder and, defying the freezing waters, swam across to the injured men. Ropes were tied around the pair and the rescue workers swam with them back to the ladder where they were hauled to safety.

The Royal Lancaster Infirmary was notified of the explosion at 7.50 p.m. and told to expect numerous casualties. The first three injured arrived fifteen minutes later, driven to hospital by a local rescuer. They were suffering from severe burns. Their hair was badly singed and most of their clothing had been burnt off. They were distressed, in severe pain, and shocked.

Back at the plant, the rescue mission was fraught with danger. The entire structure was unstable and liable to give way at any minute, and there was the constant fear that the fallen roof beams might inflict yet more damage. Orders were sent out for heavy lifting gear to be brought from Lancaster to remove the beams. In the meantime, the search for the injured and dead continued until the Chief Fire Officer decided that the building was in too dangerous a state. He called off the search until the crane arrived to secure the roof. It was obviously going to be a long night and, as darkness descended, floodlighting was set up to steer the crews through the gloom. By now, there were over 150 emergency personnel working among the piles of rubble.

When the crane arrived, the 30 roof beams were removed, enabling the firefighters to reach further casualties. The blast had caused widespread flooding within the plant and at midnight crews began to pump out the various underground chambers to ascertain whether anybody was still trapped down there. Eventually, three bodies were discovered lying in silt at the bottom of one chamber, forcing firefighters to wade through the deep silt and mud to recover the corpses. The dead trio had been blown into the water by the force of the explosion.

The pumping operation went on through the night. The following morning it was decided to empty the chambers either side of the river.

A team of firefighters wearing breathing apparatus was also sent in to check the four pipes, each little more than 3 feet in diameter, which connected the works with the river. They endured these claustrophobic conditions for half an hour before being able to give the all clear.

Sixteen people were killed in the explosion, among them manager Alan Lacey. Stephen Hogarth's friend Mark Eckersley died along with his mother, Pauline Eckersley. Mark's sisters, Julie and Susie, had backed out of the Abbeystead trip at the last minute. Julie had decided to stay at St Michael's and play cricket while Susie chose to go to Girl Guides. There could have been many more victims but for the fact that St Michael's Bowls Club was playing a match that night. Fortune also smiled on villager Elizabeth Tyson. She would have been among the Abbeystead party if she had been able to get a babysitter. David Kellett, chairman of St Michael's parish council, played his part in keeping down the death toll, bravely dragging two men to safety after they had fallen through the metal floor into the icy waters.

In hospital, survivors described their ordeal. St Michael's villager Pat Kaylor and her party were standing just inside the pumping station's main doors at the start of the visit, talking to Water Board officials when she was suddenly engulfed in a ball of fire. 'Some went through another doorway but I never got that far. There was this dull sort of thud and a big ball of fire came out of the doorway and blew us out of the entrance. Pieces were blown off cars in the car park fifteen yards away. People were lying everywhere. I couldn't recognise many of them because they were burnt like me and their hair was fused together. People with their clothes on fire were rolling on the ground. We could hear others groaning and calling for help from inside. I think I only survived because I was near the main entrance.'

Maureen Burgess, a senior clerk with the North-West Water Authority, had gone to the plant that evening to help with refreshments. She recalled: 'There was a sort of roaring noise from the right-hand side and just heat and noise. There was a flash of light from my right and I went down and closed my eyes. I sat up and turned towards the entrance and within a few seconds, the roof collapsed in front of me. I managed to climb out through the top.'

The official inquiry revealed that the blast had been caused by methane gas which had built up in the tunnel and been pushed to Abbeystead by the onrushing water.

A month later, picturesque St Michael's on Wyre was in the full bloom of summer. Of course, the villagers still mourned their dead but, as one pointed out, they are a resilient bunch. After such an appalling disaster, they needed to call on all their reserves of strength and courage.

* * *

In June 1989, Kent Fire Brigade had to deal with a blaze caused by the sudden explosion of a pit full of pig carcasses. The landowner of the former farm at Hempstead decided to light a bonfire, unaware that buried in a covered pit beneath the pyre was a heap of old pig carcasses. Gasses given off by the carcasses were quickly ignited by sparks from the bonfire, resulting in instant roast pork and a spectacular underground blast which sent sods of earth flying through the air.

* * *

A Time Bomb, Ticking Away

At 11.40 on the evening of Friday 8 July 1995, Police Constable Richard Parkin was driving with his car window open along Cotman-hay Road in the Derbyshire town of Ilkeston when he became aware of an overpowering smell of gas. He stopped to investigate but, unable to trace the source of the smell, he radioed in to alert British Gas before being sent off to deal with an all-too-familiar closing-time pub brawl.

Further examination of the area revealed what appeared to be a major gas leak and the emergency services were called in to begin a hasty evacuation of local residents.

Among the first on the scene was Ilkeston Station Officer Mick Peacock. 'We knew we only had a matter of minutes in which to evacuate the area,' he said. 'The tarmac on the road was rippling with the pressure of escaping gas – the whole lot could have gone up any second. It was a very dangerous situation. When we were helping with the evacuation, we could not use our radios in case they set off an explosion.'

The road was shut off and firefighters and police officers rushed around, knocking on windows and doors. There wasn't a moment to waste. Some residents could leave under their own steam; others, particularly the elderly, had to be helped out. Many people were fast asleep and it took valuable time to wake them up. And all the while there was this time bomb in the back of the rescuers' minds, ticking away. They knew that every door they knocked on could be their last.

Around 100 people were evacuated to a nearby school, including locals at the Hand and Heart public house and most of the residents of Glover Court, a two-storey block of eleven flats. Alan Dunmore, manager at the Hand and Heart, could smell gas as the pub was closing. When his wife Gail looked out of the window and saw the road bubbling up, Mr Dunmore dashed outside to try and stop the traffic.

Crews were in the process of getting the last people out of Glover Court when, at 12.36 a.m., the place erupted. A massive explosion ripped through the flats. The roof was blown into Cotmanhay Road and within seconds a fireball swamped the building in flames.

Two policemen were thrown to the ground by the force of the explosion. One was leading out an elderly lady at the time. He managed to scramble to his feet, scoop up the old lady and take her to safety. Every window at the Hand and Heart opposite the flats was smashed.

As they took in the full impact of the explosion, the crews' immediate thought was to get out anybody else who was still in the block. Firefighters battled their way in to rescue two people while another resident jumped from a window.

Acting Police Sergeant Steve Dawson was caught up in the blast. He recalled: 'There was a loud bang, a loud rumbling sound and then an almighty bang. The first gave me a hint that something much more serious was to follow. So I took refuge behind a wall and then the second large bang and the fireball that came with it blew me off my feet. There was a shower of broken glass and debris. The whole of the block of flats was engulfed in flames and the road was split open by flames. There was a huge crater – it was just like a war scene. I thought my time had come. I remember thinking, This is it – I'm not going home again.

'Perhaps in retrospect it was a risk to go back and get people out, but that's not really something you think about. I remember seeing one family with a baby – you just have to get them out.'

Most of the residents had been rescued in time. One witness, Michael Holmes, said, 'I don't know how they managed to evacuate everyone so quickly. It was like a fireball, like something out of *London's Burning*. Flames were even coming out of the tarmac on the road. That explosion was like a direct bomb hit – you wouldn't think anyone still in there would have had a chance.'

Another passer-by, Ian Bower, added, 'The blast could be heard all over Ilkeston. You could see that all the sky was lit up – there was an orange smoke in the air. When I got there, I saw glass and window frames all over the place and it had thrown the whole road up. It was a scene of total devastation.'

Wayne Ward, 21 and unemployed, lived in a flat at Glover Court with his pregnant girlfriend, seventeen-year-old Becky Cotton. He woke to find the bedroom on fire. 'I was in bed and my girlfriend woke me up and all I can remember is opening my eyes and being surrounded by flames. I had to jump out of the window which is on the second floor and then they rushed me to hospital. Firemen had to put a ladder up to get Becky because she is heavily pregnant.'

As he watched firefighters sift through the rubble the next morning, he moaned, 'All my stuff's gone. I've got nothing. All I have left is the clothes I'm standing in.'

Mr Ward's 28-year-old sister Janet lived in Flat 9. She suffered slight head injuries in the explosion. She too was in bed at the time. 'I just heard shouting and then I was showered in glass,' she said. 'The door blew off and I heard screaming and then a neighbour came in and helped me to get out.'

The street was littered with broken glass, window frames and rubble. Windows in neighbouring streets had also been blown out. A team of 50 firefighters worked through the night to put out the fire which had torn through the flats and was sending flames shooting 30 feet up into the night sky. The fire was finally extinguished at 6 a.m. although it continued to smoke for some hours afterwards.

By daylight virtually all that remained of Glover Court was a pile of rubble. Exhausted crews began the grim task of searching through the debris. At first, three residents were feared missing, trapped in the rubble, but one was found staying with friends and it emerged that another had moved out some time ago. However, the dead body of the third, a 37-year-old ice cream salesman, was pulled out of the rubble at 10.45 on the Saturday morning. His two children, a boy aged nine and a girl aged seven, were in the habit of staying with him every Saturday night and occasionally on Fridays too. Happily, this week was not one of those occasions.

With all persons accounted for, JCBs moved in to start clearing the rubble, but not before a grey and yellow cockatiel had been pulled out safe and well and been reunited with his owner, 21-year-old Ruth Price. She and her boyfriend had been in her ground-floor flat at Glover Court at the time of the blast. 'I was going to turn off the TV when we heard a huge bang,' she said. 'It was like a nightmare. We could smell gas, rubble was falling into the flat, and it was pitch black. I was thinking, Just get out, get out. We just fled. A man living nearby gave me some clothes and took us back to his home. Almost everything we owned was destroyed. Then when I went back to the scene the following morning, a firefighter handed over Pricey, my cockatiel. Somehow he'd survived the blast. I'd completely forgotten about him in the panic.'

A total of five people were treated in hospital for injuries while many others suffered severe shock as well as cuts and bruises.

Station Officer Peacock summed up: 'I've never seen an explosion like it. We were really lucky – a few minutes earlier and the explosion would have wiped us out. We knew we were all risking our lives evacuating the homes but we have to take that risk for the public. That's what we're here for.'

* * *

Richard Morgan and Andy Thomas were two public-spirited lads. Richard's mum, Gaynor, had reported seeing rats in their home town of Pentre in the Rhondda Valley, Mid Glamorgan, and so the two 24-year-olds set about flushing the sewer vermin out of the town's drains. They thought they would be doing everyone a favour.

After inspecting the area where Mrs Morgan said she had seen the rats, the modern-day pied pipers sent a ferret down the drain but the trusty creature returned empty-pawed. There was no sign of any rats.

But the pair were not going to give up quietly. In an act of supreme desperation, they decided to drop a blazing petrol-soaked rag into the sewers in the hope of burning the rats alive or at least driving them out into the open. Alas, things didn't quite go according to plan. The flames ignited a hidden pocket of methane gas, blasting manhole covers into the air and shattering the windows of nearby houses.

Gladys Cilias was showered with glass when her terraced house caught the full force of the blast. The puzzled pensioner said, 'I was sitting at my dining-room table when there was a terrific explosion and my window suddenly shattered. There was glass everywhere.'

Sent to investigate the case of the boom town rats, Mid Glamorgan firefighters discovered no vermin, just two embarrassed amateur catchers. One of the fire officers said: 'There must have been a lot of petrol on the rag to cause a blast like that. It was a miracle no one was injured or killed. We advised the lads that next time they should call in the experts.'

While Richard and Andy adopted a low profile, Mrs Morgan remained unrepentant. 'They were just trying to help me get rid of the rats,' she insisted. 'And it looks as though they succeeded – the rats seem to have disappeared . . .'

* * *

Buried for Six Hours

Built in the 1930s, Newnham House was a large private residential block of flats situated in the quiet side-street of Manor Fields off Putney Hill in south-west London. The three-storey block was home to single people and families alike, many of whom commuted to work in Central London. For them, Newnham Court, with its relative proximity to East Putney tube station on the District Line, was an ideal base.

Living at 9 Newnham Court were two sisters in their 30s, Eva and Karen Krejci. They were very close and worked together as gaming inspectors in the casino at the Clermont Club, Berkeley Square. Thursday 10 January 1985 was their day off.

Shortly before seven o'clock that dark winter's morning, Gerrit Gellissen, warden of the Manor Fields Estate, went to deliver a parcel to the Krejci sisters. Being a friendly sort, he stood chatting with them for a minute or so and they asked him whether he could smell gas.

'The smell of gas was obvious and very strong,' he said later. 'I began to walk back to the office building where I intended ringing the gas board, but before I had a chance to pick up the phone, there was a massive explosion like an atom bomb. It blew me off my feet. I picked myself up, ran outside and saw this ball of fire in the darkness. It was chaos. There was debris everywhere. People were standing around crying. I couldn't make out the words but they were mumbling and obviously in terrible pain.'

The explosion ripped out the heart of Newnham House. The centre section of six flats was reduced to a pile of rubble 10 feet high. Residents were thrown from their beds, bricks and shredded timber were flung hundreds of yards down the hill, and scores of windows were shattered. People living 100 yards away had their windows blown out. Many were spared injury from flying glass by the fact that it was not yet daylight and so their curtains were still drawn and acted as a shield.

The force of the blast could be felt up to three miles away. Ian Connors, a fifteen-year-old paperboy, was doing his round in Putney Hill when he was knocked from his bicycle. Recovering in hospital from cuts and bruises, he recalled, 'There was a vivid blue flash and an explosion. It seemed like the trees were disintegrating.'

It was the suddenness of the explosion which was the biggest shock for the residents of Newnham House. One moment they were lying in bed, taking a shower or having breakfast, conducting their usual early morning routine, the next walls and ceilings were caving in and they were being hurled about their flats. One little girl was asleep in bed when a bookcase toppled on to her. Luckily, she escaped unscathed. Shaken by the blast, a couple in another flat snatched up their three-year-old daughter and ran out of the front door, completely unaware that the explosion had demolished their landing. As they went through the door, they stepped into thin air and crashed to the rubble beneath. They too escaped serious injury.

Firefighters from Putney Fire Station were quickly on the scene but the rubble had already settled and no bodies were visible, either dead or alive. Dazed residents were wandering around helplessly, unable to take in what had happened. Parents hugged their children, so relieved that they had managed to get out alive but all the time wondering whether any of their neighbours were buried under the rubble. A lone Christmas card fluttered in a tree, wedged there after being blasted from a Newnham House mantelpiece.

As ambulances arrived to take nine of the injured to St Mary's Hospital, Roehampton, it seemed increasingly likely that some people were trapped beneath the mountain of debris. It was clearly a major disaster. The fire chief at the scene likened the explosion to that of a 50 lb bomb. Pumps were made six and subsequently ten and a thermal image camera, one of only twelve then in use in London, was brought in to use its heat-detecting properties to locate any persons hidden under the rubble. These cameras were designed principally to enable firefighters to spot the hot seat of a fire through dense smoke but they proved to be of such value in the aftermath of the Putney blast that their uses became more widespread, being particularly effective where people were believed buried.

The long search for bodies began. The building was too unsafe to risk using mechanical excavating equipment so fire crews had to claw away at the tangle of wood and masonry with shovels, sledgehammers and bare hands. While they did so, the second floor landing of Newnham House, parts of the roof and a fallen lift shaft swayed ominously above them, liable to collapse at any minute. But they dare not demolish them until they were absolutely certain that everyone had been rescued. Another problem was that the mains gas supply couldn't be cut at first, so crews were unable to communicate with each other by short-wave radio in case the sets sparked a new explosion.

Although the advent of daylight helped the search, it was still an onerous task. Human chains were formed to remove the rubble in buckets but the mountain was diminishing painfully slowly. And the dust and grime made it an uncomfortable process for the rescue workers. Every few minutes, they called for total quiet and put their ears to the rubble to listen for any signs of life. All they could hear was the sound of silence.

Then a slab of concrete was removed to reveal a human hand. Frantically, the crews dug away at the surrounding rubble. It proved a futile gesture. The victim was already dead. As the morning wore on, others were recovered from beneath the tons of brickwork. All were dead. Spirits were beginning to fade as the prospects of finding anybody alive grew increasingly slim. It was now four hours since the flats had crumbled to the ground. Surely nobody could survive in there for that long. The state of the remaining walls was becoming ever more dangerous. It was time to consider demolishing them.

First, another call for silence. Nothing. Then, just as the crews were on the point of resuming their manual excavations, one of the firefighters heard a faint tapping sound.

'Quiet! I heard something,' he whispered excitedly. 'Like somebody tapping.'

Others put their ears to the debris and listened intently. The sound was repeated.

'There! Did you hear it?'

They had. The search recommenced with renewed vigour and optimism.

It was a race against time. Brick by brick, they edged towards the tapping sound, praying that whoever was in there would be able to hang on until they worked their way through. It took the best part of two hours. Finally they found a young woman. It was Eva Krejci. Her legs were trapped by a huge concrete pillar but she had been protected beneath the fallen rubble by the cast iron bath she had been standing beside at the time of the explosion. The bath was acting like an arch over her head, propping up a large section of wall and preventing her from being buried alive. It was a miraculous escape.

There was still plenty of work to do before she could be freed. It was decided that the best way to reach her was to dig a tunnel in the rubble through which she could be pulled clear. But first they needed to ascertain her physical condition. Depending on her injuries, any movement could make things worse. So she would be examined by a surgeon before any attempt was made to bring her out. Not surprisingly, she was greatly distressed. She kept asking about her sister, Karen. How was she? They had been in different rooms at the time of the explosion. Was she safe?

As yet, there had been no trace of Karen. She was to be one of the eight people killed in the explosion.

Slowly but surely, their hands red raw and their arms weary with the exertion, the teams carved out a tunnel 6 feet long and 18 inches high, just big enough for someone to crawl through. Every extra inch was needed, for the chosen surgeon was Mr Barry Powell, a senior registrar at Roehampton who stood 6 feet 4 inches tall and weighed in at 17 stone.

Mr Powell made himself as flat as humanly possible and crawled in on his stomach to reach her. Three times he made the perilous journey. On the first occasion, he took her a blanket and a drip containing plasma substitute. He was unable to reach her arm to fix it and spent fifteen minutes attaching the drip to her hand instead. He returned twice more to examine her before deciding that she should be pulled out feet first. Miss Krejci was very frightened but didn't ask for any pain-killers.

Moving her was a delicate operation. She had broken her back and her right leg, and the crews had to exercise great care. They took over ten minutes to pull her out so that by the time she finally tasted fresh air, it had been six and a half hours since the explosion. Once she was free from the rubble, rescuers formed a human corridor to pass her down to a waiting ambulance. She was wrapped in thermal foil to conserve heat. Her frilly nightdress in tatters, she was able to whisper to the firefighters, 'Thank you very much for getting me out of there.'

The discovery of one survivor suggested a possibility, however remote, that there could be more. So the search carried on under arc lights through the night, with its sub-zero temperatures, and into the next day.

It was then that there was very nearly a second catastrophe. A team of twenty firefighters were clearing the rubble when a fire safety officer saw a chimney stack beginning to topple. He blew his whistle – the warning for immediate evacuation – and seconds later the chimney, weighing several tons, crashed to the ground precisely where the crews had been searching. Three firemen were injured by falling masonry as they made their escape but after being released from hospital that same day, they insisted on returning to the search. Fire Officer Brian Clark admitted: 'It was a split-second business. If our safety officers had been less alert or if the men had been slower to react, we could have had a new disaster.'

The search for a possible ninth victim continued until finally, after 36 hours, senior fire officers concluded that nobody else was buried. It had been a long, hard operation but the moment when they pulled Eva Krejci out alive made it all worthwhile.

*   *   *

Firefighters were called to Newport Police Station on the Isle of Wight after a prisoner got his head stuck in the peep-hole of his cell door. They soon managed to free him but the police refused to name the victim in order to spare him further embarrassment.

*   *   *

Saved by a Mattress

The six-storey tenement building in Guthrie Street in Edinburgh's Old Town was much sought after by students from the nearby university seeking cheap accommodation. Nineteen-year-old Dawn Howbridge lived in a flat on the top floor . . . until on the morning of 4 October 1989 when her world literally collapsed around her.

It was shortly before 7.30 a.m. and most of the students were still in bed. The first lecture of the day was still a couple of hours away so there was no great rush to wipe away the cobwebs. Suddenly there was a mighty explosion and all six floors were instantly reduced to a mountain of debris and dust.

Firefighters using thermal image cameras quickly began searching through the debris for survivors. They found the body of a 21-year-old girl student but had no idea how many people could be trapped in the rubble. Since the building was sub-divided into flats, nobody knew how many people actually occupied the place. There was also a suspicion that the basement may have provided shelter for vagrants. They could be buried beneath the masonry.

One person definitely safe was Dawn Howbridge. She had plunged 60 feet to the ground from her bed but got away with only minor injuries after landing on her mattress. A member of the fire team revealed: 'She was very fortunate because she was in the top-floor flat which doesn't exist any more! She came all the way down and her fall was cushioned by her mattress. Also, because she came from the uppermost floor, she landed on top of all the debris and so avoided being buried.'

Firefighters climbed turntable ladders into the remains of the building and saw 'just feet and legs' protruding from the rubble. 'It was quite horrible,' remarked one. 'I don't think anything ever quite prepares you for something like this.'

The search for survivors continued throughout the morning. While anxious to remove the debris as quickly as possible, crews were reluctant to use digging machinery for fear of causing further injuries to those trapped. So much of the excavation was done by small tools or by hand. It was a painstaking process but it would continue as long as there was a chance that somebody might still be alive in there.

Three hours after the blast, the crews got their reward when nineteen-year-old Martin Baptie was pulled out alive from the rubble. He was taken to hospital with crush injuries, his life having been saved by the fact that he too had been in bed at the time of the explosion and had fallen between two mattresses.

But then the weakened roof of the collapsed building started to sag dangerously, presenting a major threat to the rescue teams. After much deliberation, senior fire officers ordered the search to be halted while the roof was demolished, even though it would then crash down on to the rubble where further survivors might still be buried. 'It was an agonising decision,' admitted Edinburgh Firemaster Peter Scott, adding that the roof was brought down in a controlled manner so that it would not add significant pressure to the pile of debris and those possibly beneath it.

As searchlights were introduced to steer the crews through the night, a second body was brought out from the rubble at 10.15 p.m. A total of five casualties were taken to hospital and by the following morning, it was apparent that there were no more bodies buried beneath the rubble. The search was over. Firefighters had seen enough of student digs.

* * *

In 1993, West Sussex Fire Service announced that teddy bears were to be added to the equipment on their fire tenders to comfort distraught children involved in fires.

* * *

The Curse of the Internet

Fireworks are potentially lethal weapons. Every year, the nation's fire services are inundated with calls on or around 5 November following accidents sustained while playing with fireworks. Some victims are burnt, some are maimed for life, others are killed. The message is rammed home year after year but the injury list goes on.

A sixteen-year-old Wiltshire youth can testify to the dangers of fireworks after losing a hand and suffering severe leg injuries while endeavouring to make homemade devices. Apparently, he had been following instructions on the Internet.

Emergency crews were called to the house at Corsham at 9.10 p.m. on Sunday 29 October 1995 where the youth was found to be seriously injured in the wake of an explosion. The house received blast damage. While the boy was taken to Frenchay Hospital, bomb disposal units were called out to make safe a number of similar devices. Fire crews remained at the scene until 8.30 the next morning.

The boy's father was naturally distressed and, through Wiltshire Fire Brigade, issued a warning about making or experimenting with homemade fireworks or explosive devices at any time of the year.

Two Wiltshire Fire Brigade appliances also attended a fire started by an exploding aerosol. They were called to a house in Chippenham where a bedroom blaze was caused by the heat from a nearby radio passing to a pressurised aerosol deodorant which dramatically exploded. The bedroom walls were blown out by seven inches and doors and plaster were blasted away. The rear of the house sustained serious structural damage and debris was scattered over a distance of 70 yards on to surrounding roofs. The subsequent fire was put out by the occupier with a carbon dioxide extinguisher and luckily none of the occupants of the house suffered anything more than shock.

A further reiteration of the potential hazards of aerosols occurred on 29 December 1995 when a can of deodorant given to a boy for Christmas exploded in his bedroom, blowing a hole in the wall, another in the ceiling and starting a fire which engulfed his possessions. The blast also tore off the bedroom door and blew out windows. The fourteen-year-old had made the mistake of leaving the aerosol near an electric fire at his foster parents' home in Tipton, West Midlands, before going cycling.

*　*　*

In April 1996, a family returned to their home in Hucknall, Nottinghamshire, after a power cut to find a fire in the kitchen. They had forgotten to turn off the oven and it had started a blaze when power was restored.

*　*　*

4 Animal Rescues

Curiosity Nearly Killed the Cat

Kittens are a law unto themselves. Utterly fearless and with little sense of self-preservation, they will venture into the tiniest nook or cranny, the most inaccessible hole, all in the name of adventure. The harder it is to get back out again, the more they seem to like it. And hang the consequences! They're just being playful, cute and kittenish – it's their owners' responsibility to rescue them, even if it means demolishing the entire house to do so.

David Tedder, a 25-year-old Sunderland postman, very nearly did just that when the family's fourteen-week-old kitten Jess disappeared during the evening of 21 October 1993. Jess, named after Postman Pat's famous black and white cat, had been a present for David's two-year-old daughter Megan and in her short time at the house had already proved to be a bundle of mischief.

So when Jess vanished that Thursday evening, David and his wife Lorraine assumed that she had somehow managed to escape and had gone walkabouts. Any minute, they expected to hear a plaintive miaowing from outside, begging to be let in. At 11 p.m., they did hear a plaintive miaowing, but to their horror, instead of coming from outside, it was coming from behind the lounge wall. Jess was up the chimney.

While David had become fond of Jess, his immediate concerns were for his daughter. He knew that little Megan would be absolutely heartbroken if anything were to happen to her pet kitten and so he resolved that no effort would be spared to bring Jess down safely. Furthermore, he didn't want to worry Megan unduly. Therefore, he left her to sleep while he put Plan A into action and began removing bricks from the lounge wall – as carefully and as quietly as possible. The idea was to create a hole large enough for Jess to escape but one which wouldn't completely wreck their living quarters. Once Jess caught a glimpse of daylight from her darkened tomb, they felt sure she would spring back into the living world.

No such luck. They waited and waited, but there was no sign of the errant Jess. Clearly this was a problem which needed sleeping on but before David and Lorraine retired for a well-earned rest, they put into operation Plan B. A bowl of Jess's favourite food, tuna fish, was placed beneath the hole in the hope that it would lure her out.

They hardly slept that night with the worry. They kept listening out for further miaowing, any indication that Jess had emerged from her hiding-place. But when they went downstairs in the morning, the tuna had not been touched. The only consolation was they could still hearing miaowing, from behind a wall in the dining room.

There was only one thing for it – Plan C. With a certain degree of reluctance, David set about demolishing the dining room wall. Jess remained conspicuous by her absence.

By the Friday evening, her miaows seemed to have shifted to a bedroom wall. Plan D was immediately put into effect and David began knocking down the relevant partition. He was left with a pile of rubble and an unsightly hole – but no cat.

The entire street was now on full alert for Jess. It was the most intensive animal hunt since Shergar. Even Megan had been told of the drama. Everyone wanted to know the latest bulletin and neighbours popped round to offer comfort and suggestions, ranging from laying waste to most of Sunderland to David dressing up as a mouse.

Come late Saturday afternoon and David had almost run out of walls to demolish – any more and the house would fall down. So, after lengthy discussion with Lorraine, he decided to implement Plan E. He called the Fire Brigade.

'I felt a bit daft calling them,' he admitted later, 'but it was the only option left. We couldn't bear to leave her to die. We hadn't been able to eat or sleep because we could hear Jess crying.'

No job too small, the Fire Brigade duly sent out two appliances. From time to time, one had to go off and fight a fire but it always returned to the real action. And one crew stayed there throughout. They called for quiet and listened intently. The miaows could still be heard but the precise location remained intangible. Precious little progress was made until, shortly before midnight, the firefighters concluded that the gravity of the situation called for Plan F. A third appliance was sent for, one which came equipped with, an instrument primarily designed for locating earthquake victims. The arrival of the third crew meant that, in the course of the evening, no fewer than fifteen firefighters had been involved in the seach for Jess.

The extra manpower, but more importantly the new equipment, did the trick. As Saturday became Sunday, Jess was finally located – in the chimney of the adjoining house.

David's neighbour may not have been too thrilled about being woken at midnight but she allowed the crews to go into her house, remove the fire and gently lift Jess to freedom, a move which was greeted by spontaneous cheers. Outside, the welcome was even louder. Sensing an imminent result, a crowd had gathered, and hailed Jess's appearance with a roar not heard in Sunderland since the FA Cup was paraded through the streets in 1973. David burst into tears.

Young Megan was thrilled to have her pet back. Covered in soot and suitably chastened by the experience, Jess was taken home for a good clean-up. And David set about rebuilding his house.

* * *

The day that Smudge the hamster decided to investigate a water pipe proved to be a traumatic one, for himself, his owners and Wiltshire Fire Brigade.

Smudge toppled down the pipe at his house in Swindon on 6 November 1995. His owners called the Fire Brigade who calculated that Smudge's journey would have taken him under the foundations of the house to a point below the front garden. So, armed with spades, two crews of burly firefighters began digging a trench in the garden.

By now, the police, the RSPCA and assorted onlookers had gathered to watch the dig. As discarded earth piled high, adding little to the decor of the garden, the firefighters disappeared further and further below ground. Eventually, at a depth of 6 feet, they located the pipe. And, after removing a section of the pipe, they found Smudge, wet and bedraggled but otherwise a remarkably healthy hamster.

* * *

A Breath of Fresh Air

After fighting a fire in a flat in Birkenhead, crews were clearing away their equipment, opening windows to get rid of the smoke and making sure that everything was sound structurally, when the elderly lady occupant suddenly burst into tears.

One of the men went over to comfort her. 'There, there, luv, it's OK,' he said, putting an arm around her shoulder. 'You're still in one piece and a bit of decoration and the place will be as good as new. You haven't lost anything you can't replace.'

'I have, I have,' she sobbed, pointing at a bird cage on a stand in the corner of the room. 'My budgie's dead.'

Deeply disturbed by the revelation, two of the crew went over to the stand. Sure enough, there was the budgie lying on the bottom of its cage. It looked pretty lifeless. To all intents and purposes, it was no more. It had gone to meet its maker. It was an ex-budgie.

Perhaps it was merely stunned, overcome by shock. The lady was so distraught that they felt awful just leaving it there.

'How about we give it a whiff of oxygen?' said one.

'It could work, I suppose,' replied his colleague. 'Bit of a long shot, but it's worth a go.'

So they lifted the bird out of its cage, placed one of their oxygen masks near its head and turned on the supply. Unfortunately, they turned it on too quickly and the budgie was blown out of the open window like a bullet. It was last seen heading over the Mersey towards Manchester, still rising.

The firefighters bade a hasty and sheepish farewell to the old lady, who was still gazing out of the window in stunned disbelief.

A couple of years later, the incident was resuscitated more successfully than the budgie, as a storyline in an episode of *London's Burning*.

*　*　*

Preparing to travel from Newport Pagnell to Aylesbury, a woman loaded her suitcases on to the roof rack of her car. She then drove off, unaware that also attached to the roof rack was her cat. It wasn't until she arrived in Aylesbury, fifteen miles away, and went to take down her cases that she discovered the horrified cat hanging on for dear life.

She tried to lift the cat down but it had been so terrified by doing 60 mph on the open road that it had dug its claws in deep to the rack and could not be moved. Buckinghamshire Fire Service were called out to deal with the incident and, showing great patience and kindness, they managed to prise the poor cat, its legs rigid with fear, from the rack. It has never watched an episode of *Tom and Jerry* since.

*　*　*

Sheep Dip

The summer drought of 1995 left water levels in North Yorkshire dangerously low. Many ponds were completely dry so that sturdy metal pipes which were usually submerged well below the surface now became exposed. Such was the case at a pond near Catterick village, and it resulted in firefighters spending three hours trying to free a sheep which had got stuck in a pipe.

Quite what possessed the sheep to wander into the pipe in the first place is anyone's guess. Perhaps it was attempting to find a spot of shade, out of the glare of the midday sun. More likely, it was just stupid, sheep not exactly being renowned for their intelligence. After all, when was the last time you saw one on *Mastermind*?

Anyway, having climbed into the pipe, which had a diameter of just under 2 feet, the animal found that it couldn't get out again. There was no room to turn around and it wasn't terribly good at reversing. Not that it could move in either direction because the more it struggled, the more firmly wedged it became.

Luckily, a member of the public heard its bleating and, spotting its plight, called the North Yorkshire Fire Service. Equally fortuitously, the old adage about sheep following each other blindly did not apply in this case, otherwise crews could have been dealing with anything up to half a dozen sheep jammed nose to tail in the pipe. Maybe even the rest of the flock sensed that this particular individual was one row short of a jumper.

One of the firefighters volunteered to try and pull out the woolly prisoner. But even with tunics off, paraphernalia removed and breath held firmly in, there was no way that any of them could squeeze into the narrow pipe. And the sheep was too far in to be reached from outside.

The pipe was partly buried beneath the ground so the crews decided to dig away the surrounding earth and then slice through the pipe. However, the ground was so hard under weeks of baking sun that manual excavation proved impossible. Therefore, a request was put out for a mechanical earth-mover to be brought over. The specialist Incident Support Unit was also summoned since they had pneumatic cutting equipment which would be required to break through the pipe.

The crews waited patiently for the back-up to arrive. Neither they nor the sheep were going anywhere. Taking care not to damage the pipe and in the process its occupant, the earth-mover shifted huge mounds of soil. When the cutting gear arrived, marks were made on the pipe indicating where the machine was to operate. The cut had to be made sufficiently far beyond the sheep so as not to injure it (mutton was not on the menu) but near enough so that the firefighters could then stretch in and pull the animal out.

Steadily the equipment scythed through the pipe. By now, there were over a dozen firefighters in attendance. At last the section of pipe snapped off and one of the crew was able to reach in and drag the creature out by its legs.

As the crews packed away, the sheep trotted off to join her colleagues and tell them how, throughout her ordeal, she had managed to keep calm by counting firemen.

*   *   *

Nottinghamshire firefighters answered an emergency call to free a pet goldfish which had become stuck in an ornamental boot inside its bowl. For once the razor-sharp cutting equipment wasn't needed and after a little careful manipulation, the fish was able to swim away.

*   *   *

Within These Walls

Sixteen-year-old Samantha Hamnett was pining for her cat Sooty. By the morning of 29 November 1995, her pet had been missing for two and a half weeks and she was beginning to wonder whether they would ever be reunited. Assisted by family and friends, she had searched high and low near their terraced home in Blythe Bridge, Staffordshire, but without success.

Yet Samantha never gave up hope and her faith was rewarded early on that Wednesday morning when she was just able to make out the weak and pitiful cry of a cat. She raced to investigate where the sound was coming from and discovered that Sooty was trapped between the gable ends of her own house and the next door neighbour's. It seemed that Sooty may have climbed on to a flat roof at the rear of their house, jumped down on to another sloping roof next door and then slipped into the narrow gap between the two houses. There was no way Samantha or any of her family could reach Sooty so they decided to call Staffordshire Fire and Rescue Service.

The call was received by Fire Control at 1106 hours, indicating that a cat was trapped between two walls. The station officer from nearby Longton Fire Station was mobilised to the incident and was met at the scene by the worried Samantha. After discussions with a local builder, it was decided that the best plan of action was for the builder to cut a small hole into the brickwork from inside the fireplace of one of the properties in order to gain access into the gap. With that, the fire crew returned to the station.

However, at 1314 hours, a call was received by Fire Control from the RSPCA, requesting that the crew reattend the incident since the builder's efforts had proved unsuccessful. Following further consultation between the station officer and the RSPCA inspector, the water tender ladder from Longton was mobilised at 1348 hours.

Using short extension and roof ladders, the firefighters managed to climb on to the lower pitched roof and from there they could see one rather sorry-looking cat. Sooty was not only very weak but extremely frightened, and the crew's initial rescue attempts met with little joy.

Eventually, a little bit of firefighter ingenuity saved the day. An RSPCA animal handling pole, complete with noose, was extended by using the neighbour's washing-line prop and firefighters' personal belt lines. Then it was lowered between the gable ends. With the handling pole in position, firefighters, the RSPCA, Samantha and assorted neighbours all did their utmost to coax Sooty into the noose. After much persuasion and a lot of patience, Sooty began to make feeble movements towards the target. When the cat edged within range, the firefighters secured it in the noose and, grabbing hold of its skin and the fur at the back of its neck, lifted it to safety at 1415 hours.

Thanks to the Fire Brigade, Sooty and Samantha were reunited. So impressed were the RSPCA with the efforts of the Longton crew that they planned to award them a Certificate of Merit.

* * *

Responding to an emergency call, Norfolk firefighters arrived at a house in King's Lynn to find an Alsatian puppy with its head stuck in the garden wall. The dog was chasing a bird. The bird flew into a specially designed hole in the ornate concrete wall and the puppy followed it in, oblivious to the risk. The bird promptly flew out the other side but the puppy was unable to extricate itself from the hole and was left to reflect on its folly until the Fire Brigade turned up. With a vet in attendance to ensure the puppy did not suffer any undue distress, firefighters used cutting gear to saw through the wall and free the hapless hound. It would be a while before he chased birds again.

* * *

Tiger, Tiger, Burning Bright

Malcolm Burt and his wife Sue enjoyed studying wildlife. They were also keen photographers and reckoned that the perfect place to combine their two hobbies was Longleat Safari Park, near Warminster, Wiltshire.

They had been to Longleat a number of times in the past, and once again, on 10 August 1994, they made the short journey from their home at Westhay, near Glastonbury, and joined the holiday crowds. Longleat, home of the Marquess of Bath, attracts some 350,000 visitors a year. It first became famous for its lions but is now also home to gorillas, giraffes, monkeys, elephants and tigers. The safari park is divided into four enclosures with locking gates, guarded at all times by the park wardens. On arrival, all drivers are issued with safety instructions, particularly regarding breakdowns. In certain sections, drivers and passengers must not leave their cars under any circumstances. If in trouble, they should sound their horn to alert one of the wardens.

As regular visitors, the Burts knew the ropes and had absolutely no intention of stepping out of their car in the lion or tiger compounds. After seeing the giraffes, the Burts moved on to the monkey zone. The monkeys are notorious for clambering all over visitors' cars and trying to get in, so Malcolm Burt decided to put on the central locking system.

Next it was the Bengal tigers, great favourites with the couple, who liked the idea of the animals being free to roam instead of being shut away in cages. The concept of the safari park allows the animals to wander right up to the cars. They become used to seeing vehicles drive through their home every day. Whereas a tiger in the wild would probably run off at the sight of a car, the Longleat tigers prefer to investigate. They have no fear.

As they drove through the gates into the tiger compound, Sue pondered aloud. 'Wouldn't it be terrible if we broke down? What would we do?'

The Real Blue Watch

Malcolm's reply was straightforward and to the point. 'Signal for help, I suppose. The wardens would come and rescue us. It's nothing to worry about.'

The tigers were at their most impressive. They strode majestically around the roadway, sizing up the passing cars. Malcolm stopped the car as one of the tigers, Sonar, came right alongside. He was only 2 to 3 feet away. From the passenger seat, Sue was eagerly taking photographs to capture the moment when they had been so close to a beautiful but deadly creature. For handsome as Sonar was, the Burts were grateful for the pane of glass between them and those piercing green eyes.

Their photographic assignment complete, the Burts prepared to move off. The car in front had also stopped and Sue was aware of a pall of light smoke drifting across the bonnet of their car. She attributed it to the exhaust from the car ahead. But with Sue turning around to gain a last glimpse of Sonar, Malcolm realised something was wrong. The smoke was getting thicker and was beginning to pour from the front of the vehicle.

'There's something up with the car,' he said.

Sue thought he was joking after her earlier comments about breaking down and didn't even bother to turn to look.

'No, I'm serious,' he insisted. 'This is no joke.'

The urgency in Malcolm's voice convinced Sue that he wasn't fooling about.

Malcolm switched off the ignition. Smoke began to drift into the car. Although naturally concerned, he was not panicking because the car wasn't on fire. A warden's pick-up truck was standing just 20 yards away and so Malcolm tried sounding the horn to tell them that he was in distress. But the horn wouldn't work. He tried flashing his headlights, and the warden, sensing that they were in trouble, immediately drove up alongside.

The warden told them to stay in the car as long as possible while he arranged for the tigers to be shepherded away. But then flames started shooting out of the front of the car. It was time to evacuate – tigers or not.

Malcolm pressed the switch to unlock the doors. Nothing happened. The doors wouldn't open. Nor would the windows. Nor the sun-roof. The electrics had failed, and they were locked inside a burning car.

Sue's brother was an ex-fireman. 'I was so scared when I realised we couldn't get out,' she said. 'My brother used to come home with tales of people being burnt in cars and I could see this happening to us.'

By now, 8 foot flames were leaping out of the front of the car and up from the wheel arches. Malcolm, a martial arts expert, made one last desperate attempt. He gave the steering lock an almighty thump and, to his immense relief, the blow did the trick. The car was unlocked.

The wardens had managed to move two of the tigers away but the third, Sonar, was still out there somewhere. Malcolm got out and stood at the back of the car to guard Sue's exit to the pick-up truck.

'I knew the tiger was there somewhere,' said Malcolm afterwards, 'but I dare not look behind me. I could almost feel his breath and his claws sinking into my back.'

But Sonar kept his distance and Malcolm and Sue were able to climb into the truck and be driven out of the compound. They had only travelled 100 yards when their car exploded into flames. They had got out with just seconds to spare.

The three tigers were subsequently ushered into their night-quarters to allow Wiltshire Fire Service to enter the compound safely. There was precious little for them to do. The car was burnt to a cinder.

Reflecting on his ordeal, Malcolm confessed: 'When I realised the car was locked, I was more worried about us being burnt alive than being eaten by the tigers. The whole of my life just flashed before me. To be trapped in a car on fire is dreadful enough, but to be trapped in a car on fire in a tiger reserve is unbelievable. It is the stuff of which fiction books are made.'

* * *

Firefighters in Avon had to deal with a bull which had got its head stuck in a hole in the trunk of an oak tree! No amount of tugging could release the mighty bull so crews decided to hack out a hole in the tree around the bull's head and pull him out that way.

'It took us about two hours to get him free,' said one of the crew. 'The farmer was there throughout and the bull was quite calm. More importantly, with its horns wedged in the tree, its dangerous end was out of action.'

* * *

Scatty by Name . . .

Never was a cat more aptly named than Scatty. The friendly feline was popular with customers at her home, the Wych Way Inn at Gosport, Hampshire, but had a reputation for getting into scrapes. Her most spectacular escapade occurred on 4 January 1994 when a team of firefighters had to free her from the pub's pool table!

The pool table was always in use and the only time the landlord could remove the money box was in the morning before the pub opened. That morning, he unlocked the table as usual, took out the box and went away to count the cash contents. A few minutes later, he replaced the container and locked the table. What he didn't know was that, in his absence, Scatty had elected to crawl inside the table, presumably in search of a warm place on a cold winter's day.

As the day wore on, there was no sign of Scatty, not even at mealtimes. The staff began to get worried and hunted in every corner of the pub for the year-old cat. The pool table saw plenty of action and nobody noticed or heard anything out of the ordinary. There were no reports of the black ball miaowing as it went down.

Come the evening, and a couple of lads playing on the pool table thought they could smell something funny.

'There's a strange smell over here,' called one, to nobody in particular.

'You sure it's not that curry you had last night?' piped up one of the regulars at the bar.

'No, there really is an odd smell coming from the pool table – sort of musty.'

The landlord went over to investigate. As he did so, a plaintive miaowing could be heard. It had to be Scatty, but where on earth was she? They looked under chairs and tables but the noise seemed to be coming from inside the pool table. The landlord was puzzled. It couldn't be. But the miaowing grew stronger. She was definitely in there.

The table was unlocked but Scatty did not emerge. She was clearly somewhere inaccessible. So Hampshire Fire Service were called out.

A crew member said: 'We thought it was a wind-up when the call came in. But customers had noticed a funny smell near the pool table and we could hear the cat miaowing when we arrived. We took the table apart, thinking she was stuck where the balls go, but found her trapped behind the money box.'

After spending nearly twelve hours trapped, Scatty was finally released. Everyone was delighted to have her back – even though she had managed to get on the pool table without putting her name down first.

* * *

Nottinghamshire firefighters were sent to free a pet python which had escaped from its tank and become trapped behind a radiator. As well as finding the warmest place in the house, the snake had also discovered the narrowest in which to slither, leaving crews with no option but to remove the radiator. The snake was duly returned to its living quarters and the owner advised to improve security in order to prevent a repetition.

* * *

Trapped in a Mineshaft

Like all of his breed, Mott the Border Collie enjoyed nothing more than a good walk across rolling countryside. But one day at the end of July 1993, Mott disappeared while out for a walk at Meliden mountain, near Prestatyn, Clwyd. The dog's owner searched everywhere – it was most uncharacteristic behaviour for Mott to go missing – but was eventually forced to return home alone, utterly dejected.

The days passed and the dog still hadn't been seen. His owner was convinced that Mott had suffered some terrible accident and was probably lying dead somewhere.

Then on 8 August, nearly two weeks after the vanishing act, a potholer discovered Mott at the bottom of a 40 foot disused mineshaft. The potholer managed to climb down to the base of the shaft but the dog was bigger and heavier than he had anticipated. He thought he might have been able to tuck Mott under his arm, leaving both hands free to concentrate on his own ascent, but this was clearly impossible. And he had no harness with which to strap the dog safely on his back. So, bidding farewell to Mott for the time being, the potholer returned to the surface and called the Fire Brigade.

A team of five firefighters arrived and, after assessing the situation and discussing conditions inside with the potholer, set about climbing into the shaft. They then proceeded to form a human chain, the five plus the potholer all wedged inside the shaft. The one at the bottom gently lifted Mott from the floor and passed him to the man above. And so it went on, slowly but steadily, until Mott was brought to the surface. The whole operation took some twenty minutes.

The appropriately named Leading Fireman Stanley Ruffley commented: 'It was a delicate operation, passing the dog from hand to hand, but one we usually have to do with humans. We were just glad to be able to help rescue the Collie. All things considered, he was in remarkably good condition. But he was pleased to see his owner and was very hungry.'

* * *

A Bristol family were delighted with their new kitten. But no sooner had they got it home than it landed them with a bill for £84.

As is their wont, the kitten was busy exploring its new surroundings. The owners were keeping a watchful eye to make sure it didn't do itself any damage, but for a few seconds their attention was diverted. When they looked back, the kitten had disappeared. But they knew it wasn't far away because they could hear agitated miaowing coming from outside the conservatory. And there indeed was their pet – with its head stuck between the wall of the house and the soil pipe which led down from the bathroom.

The gap was so tight that they couldn't possibly pull the kitten out. Besides, it was young and they were afraid they might hurt it in some way. So they were obliged to call out Avon Fire Service.

Fire crews arrived, to be greeted by the embarrassed owners. They'd only had the cat five minutes . . .

The firefighters examined the problem from all angles, but there was no easy solution. In the end, they had to saw away the pipe with hydraulic cutting equipment. The owners were left with a mischievous new member of the family and a bill for £84 for a replacement pipe.

* * *

Within a Whisker of Death

Cambridgeshire firefighters sprang into action to rescue a cat which had travelled half a mile trapped in the suspension of a car.

A Rover owner from Peterborough had made the short Sunday

afternoon journey, totally oblivious to the fact that he had an extra, unseen passenger. It was only when he reached his destination, the town's Orton Centre, and got out of the car that the awful truth dawned on him. For as he went to lock the door, he began to hear frantic miaowing.

It was immediately apparent that the noise was coming from his car but he struggled to pinpoint the precise location. At first, he thought the cat might have clambered into the back – a case of puss in boot – but that search proved fruitless. He checked all around the vehicle – in the engine, behind the seats, even lying on the ground to peer underneath – but the cat's whereabouts remained a mystery.

The miaowing grew louder, convincing the driver that it was coming from the suspension and brake workings. Determined to effect a release, he proceeded to jack up the car and take the wheel off. The cat was definitely in there but still the driver couldn't manage to get him out. So, reluctantly admitting defeat, he called the Fire Service.

A crew from Stanground Fire Station responded to the call and, after sizing up the situation, removed the front brake pipes to free the frightened ginger tom.

The cat was slow to show his gratitude to his rescuers. Leading Fireman Peter Burton said: 'He was hissing and spitting, covered in dust, and was a bit bald on the head where he must have been dragged along the ground.'

The firefighters took the cat to a local veterinary surgery where, until his owner was traced, he was christened Sparky. The vet said, 'It's a miracle that he escaped relatively uninjured apart from bruising and shock. I've seen cats in similar accidents lose their tails.'

Cambridgeshire crews obviously have a winning way with cats. In 1994, they freed a cat which was trapped between two walls at St Ives. After demolishing one of the walls to get it out, they found that nobody came forward to claim the pet as theirs. The stray is now living with the firefighter who rescued it.

* * *

Elvis the hamster was one that got away, for despite the efforts of six Nottingham firefighters, who removed a gas fire and ripped up floorboards, the doughty rodent evaded capture.

The alarm was raised after seven-year-old Lauren Archer's pet crawled behind the gas fire at her home in the Bulwell area of the city in March 1996. The family called the Fire Brigade but a team from Stockhill Station were unable to locate Elvis, who had been a birthday present for Lauren.

Leading Fireman Prad Verma could not disguise the crew's sorrow. Clearly none of them had a wooden heart. 'We tried everything to get him out. We put water and food down for him under the floorboards, but still he didn't show. All the lads are disappointed that we couldn't find Elvis.'

Happily, a week later the *Nottingham Evening Post* was able to report that, contrary to worldwide rumours, Elvis was alive! He had emerged from his hiding place behind the gas fire and was spotted by Lauren's sisters while they were watching television. Elvis was OK, although the experience had left him all shook up.

* * *

Bullocks

Cornwall firefighters could be forgiven for expressing their exasperation after having to go out on three successive days to rescue a young bullock with a death wish.

The drama began late on the afternoon of 11 March 1996 when the 8-hundredweight animal was reported stuck on a cliff at St Just. Firefighters arrived to find that the bullock had wandered from its field down on to a narrow ledge at the top of an 80 foot cliff overlooking the rough seas of the Atlantic.

The position was precarious for both beast and Brigade. It was clearly distressed and they didn't want to risk frightening it in case it panicked and toppled over the cliff. Nor was there much room for them to manoeuvre – the beast really had chosen a thoroughly inconvenient spot. A third problem was the rapidly fading light at the end of the day. This was a job which was obviously going to take some time and it was going to be impossible to complete it in daylight. Since there was no way that the crews could operate in such a precarious location at night, they decided to secure the animal to the top of the cliff face by ropes and then return first thing in the morning.

They duly went back at first light, 5 a.m., the next day, only to find the bullock hopelessly tangled up in the ropes. Throughout the morning, they struggled to extricate it so that it could be put in a harness and airlifted by helicopter back to its field at the top of the cliff. They pulled and shoved, shoved and pulled, but the animal's weight presented a formidable obstacle. It was not until 2 p.m. that a naval helicopter was finally able to deposit him safely in the field.

The Cornish firefighters must have hoped that was the last they would see or hear of the wayward bullock. How wrong they were. On the following morning, 13 March, just as they were about to settle down for lunch, a call came in to report that just such an animal was stuck on a cliff at St Just. Instinctively, they knew it would turn out to be the same animal.

Sure enough, they arrived to find their old friend trapped on the same stretch of cliff, 40 feet below the path which runs along the top. Bolstered by the experience of the previous day, they were able to resolve the problem themselves this time without needing outside help. In an operation lasting some two hours, they used winches and a cattle harness to lift him off the cliff face and return him to his field.

A few days later, the newspapers were full of stories about Mad Cow Disease. Members of the Cornwall Fire Service could be forgiven for thinking they had been dealing with a prime example.

* * *

All too often, firefighters have to deal with heartbreaking cases of cruelty to animals. In 1995, neighbours in Birmingham could hear an animal crying from somewhere below ground of the house next door. But it was impossible to determine precisely where. So they notified the RSPCA and West Midlands Fire Service.

The firefighters listened intently for the yelps and eventually tracked them down to a pipe running beneath the garden patio. It transpired that someone had flushed a mongrel puppy down the lavatory but, mercifully, the dog had survived in the pipe.

Crews took up the paving slabs and dug away the layers of sand and soil so that they could gain access to the pipe. Carefully pinpointing the puppy's position, they then broke open the pipe and pulled out one small, wet and confused dog. It was a particularly satisfying day's work for the firefighters who handed the puppy over to the RSPCA for care and attention.

* * *

A Soggy Moggy

Any gardener will confirm that cats love to roll in earth, particularly where expensive seeds have just been sown. A garden with plenty of hiding places is like a huge adventure playground for cats, and they will romp around in muddy soil, quite forgetting that they have a reputation for being among the cleanest of animals.

Naturally, children like to join their pets in the fun and games. Four-year-old Stephanie Lefevre from Widnes was no exception, and on 6 October 1994 she had a great time playing in the garden with her seventh-month-old kitten Oscar. However, when it was time to go in, she was horrified to see that her once perfectly groomed pet had muddy paws. Having observed the way that her mum managed to get all her clothes nice and white, she decided to follow her example and pop the cat in the automatic washing machine.

Wanting to make sure that Oscar emerged in pristine condition, Stephanie put the machine on full cycle and it quickly began to fill up with water. Luckily, at that moment the girl's mum ran to investigate the noise and saw the cat's head peering through the glass door, surrounded by bubbles. She immediately switched off the machine to stem the flow of water which would otherwise surely have drowned the cat. However, since the machine was in operation, the automatic door would not open, so she had to call out Cheshire Fire Service.

Neighbouring curtains twitched as the big red appliance pulled up outside the house. Nobody had seen a fire. Stephanie's mother was terribly embarrassed about the whole thing but the good-humoured firefighters told her that it was all part of the job and went on to list some of the other odd 'shouts' they had been asked to attend. Meanwhile, Oscar was still looking forlornly out of the washing machine door, vowing never to get muddy again.

Putting down plenty of cloths to soak up the water, the crew proceeded to dismantle the machine and safely remove one damp but sparklingly clean cat. Oscar was certainly a lot fluffier after the experience and was left to reflect that he now only had eight lives left.

5 Road Traffic Accidents

Pile-up on the M6

At 9 a.m. on Monday 21 October 1985, an express coach set off from St Andrew Square coach station, Edinburgh, on its daily scheduled run to London. The passengers paid £11 per head for the journey which, all being well, would see them arrive in London at 6 p.m. Not all of those on board relished the prospect of a nine-hour coach journey but it had the advantage of being considerably cheaper than travelling by train.

The coach cut through the Borders and on to the southbound carriageway of the M6. It was a bright, sunny autumn day as it by-passed Lancaster and headed towards Preston. The traffic was not too heavy, enabling the driver to stick to his schedule. But there was a problem up ahead. A few miles north of junction 32, the M55 turn-off to Blackpool, two lanes of the southbound carriageway had been coned off for repairs, part of a £15 million scheme of road improvements. Only the fast lane was open. The southbound traffic was at a standstill because of the congestion but the coach, with its 42 passengers, failed to slow down and ploughed into and mounted two stationary cars. The impact with the coach ruptured the petrol tank of one of the cars, spewing a stream of burning fuel across the motorway. Seconds later, the coach burst into a ball of flames which were sucked in through its shattered windscreen. The burning mass slid along the carriageway, careering into a van which in turn hit another car. Both of these caught fire. Meanwhile, a car containing two people crashed into the rear of the coach and instantly went up in flames. The mayhem was followed by several other knock-on collisions. In total, thirteen vehicles were involved.

Van driver Patrick Davey, a married man with two teenage daughters, had been stationary in the queue on the southbound carriageway when he saw the coach behind him catch fire. He immediately called his firm on the van radio. He said people were trapped, cars were on fire and the carriageway was blocked. He told them to ring the emergency services straight away.

John Laverty was also in the stationary queue. He suddenly felt a bump from behind. When he looked in his mirror, he saw the coach sliding across the road and then another car hit him. 'I got out and saw the coach just burst into flames. It was across the first and second lanes but was still on its wheels. The driver was trying to break the window to get out. At first, the fire was just at the front of the coach but it quickly spread through the entire vehicle.'

Traffic on the northbound carriageway slowed right down as drivers paused to take in what was happening. Lorry driver James Smith made a more positive contribution. A former ambulance driver travelling north, he leapt from his cab, vaulted the central barriers and dashed to the aid of the stricken passengers in the blazing coach. After switching off the engine, he battled through the flames and the choking smoke given off by the burning upholstery and fittings and dragged a man to safety. He dived back in again and found the driver slumped in his seat, with blood pouring from a head wound. He had no pulse and had stopped breathing. Using his medical knowledge, Mr Smith began pounding the driver's heart until another rescuer took over.

'I went back into the coach,' said Mr Smith. 'I found another man and pulled him out. The bus was on fire and I couldn't see. I got out, and seconds later the bus went up.'

He then attempted in vain to rescue the couple from the car which had smashed into the coach but his heroism had already saved at least three lives. He later collapsed from the effects of the smoke.

Most of the passengers on the coach had managed to escape via the rear emergency door. Any who hesitated at the 4 foot drop were unceremoniously pushed out. But some were still trapped inside. The fire ripped through the chassis unchecked and the heat caused the coach's glass panels to explode. Patrick Davey bravely fought his way into the coach through the emergency exit and found a man unable to get out. But as Mr Davey climbed aboard the coach, the door slammed shut behind him. Now he too was trapped. Overcome by the thick smoke, he fell unconscious but was rescued by another passer-by who pulled him to the side of the motorway.

Police Inspector George Lustey had been a passenger on the coach. As he scrambled clear, he too saw the burning car with people screaming inside. He tried to force open the passenger door but it was jammed. PC Alan Bond, one of the first policemen on the scene, desperately tried to extinguish the flames. He said later: 'The screams of the people inside became louder as the fire progressed towards them. The whole car became engulfed in flames in just two minutes.'

Fellow rescuers then made an unsuccessful attempt to pull the woman in the passenger seat out through the shattered windscreen. But it was too late to save her anyway. She had been incinerated where she sat. The impact had reduced the car to just one-third of its original length.

Witness William Robson, who was travelling behind the coach, echoed the feelings of many drivers on the motorway that lunchtime. 'It all happened so fast. One minute we were travelling along at a nice steady 55 mph, the next the car was upside down. I crawled out of the driver's side window and helped out my wife and ten-year-old daughter. I saw people trying to get the coach doors open and then I saw two people trapped in a car which was on fire. It was just terrible watching them trying to get out. They were screaming in agony, but nobody could have saved them.'

Other passengers did manage to clamber out of their vehicles relatively unharmed, many assisted by motorists immediately behind the crash who left their cars to help the injured.

The emergency call from Patrick Davey's firm had been received by Hutton Police Headquarters, South Preston, at 1.24 p.m., just a minute after the pile-up. Four police patrol cars were sent out at once and fire and ambulance services were also notified.

The crew at Fulwood Fire Station, on the northern outskirts of Preston, were just finishing their lunch break when the bells went down. While the duty man ran to the watchroom to get the message, the rest of the crew dashed to the appliance parked in the yard. The message read: 'M6, North, Southbound carriageway, Box 7616B.' They checked the box location on the map and roared off towards the motorway, two-tones wailing and lights flashing. As they turned on to the northbound carriageway of the M6, they could see the object of their attention – a huge black tower of smoke rising into the clear blue sky. Someone from the back shouted: 'Whatever it is, it's a big 'un.'

The traffic ahead was slowing down as drivers craned their necks for a view of the accident. This was potentially disastrous news for the fire services who needed to get there as quickly as possible. The Fulwood driver was left with a choice between the fast lane and the hard shoulder. He chose the former but even then they had to weave in and out of the traffic which by now had ground to a complete halt. On a couple of occasions, one of the crew jumped out and acted as a runner to disperse cars which were obstructing the Fire Brigade's progress. The driver of the appliance was also searching anxiously for a crossover point so that he could move over to the southbound carriageway. Luckily, there was a break in the crash barrier of the central reservation at the accident site so he was able to swerve across, without much reduction in speed, and stop the engine near enough to the fire. In the meantime, a second appliance was on its way from Garstang, racing south along the hard shoulder.

The Fulwood crew arrived at 1.34 p.m. They were faced with a wall of flame – a line of vehicles, including the coach, stretching right across the southbound carriageway. Nearly all were ablaze. The three doors of the coach – the driver's, the passengers' and the emergency exit – were all open. Two people, those in the burnt-out car, were already confirmed as dead. A policeman on the scene reported that everyone who could be released had been and that those still trapped inside vehicles were now beyond salvation.

Lancashire Fire Officer Les Leckie confirmed: 'Everyone who had a chance of getting out was already out. There was nothing we could do to rescue the others. There were also two cars embedded under the coach and it was apparent almost immediately that there was no way of rescuing the people in there. It made the job very difficult for the firemen. They were there to rescue people, but we knew some were already dead.'

The embankment on the southbound carriageway was littered with people. Some were lying on the ground injured, others were staring blankly into space, still in a state of shock. They were joined by a large number of spectators which made life difficult for ambulance-men who were waiting to ferry those who needed treatment to hospital. In the end, they found it easier to label those who did not require attention rather than those who did.

With no hope of saving any lives, the priority for the firefighters was to put out the fires which were still burning fiercely in the coach and four other vehicles. It was clearly a task for more than four men and so the order went out to make pumps four. The nearest water source was found to be a mile away – too far for the hoses – so water was transported to the accident site in a fire engine. The fire on the coach was tackled with gallons of foam.

As more pumps arrived, their progress speeded up by the fact that the police had closed the motorway in both directions between junctions 32 and 33, the fires were swiftly brought under control. To complicate matters, the down-draught from the police helicopters, which were hovering overhead, was fanning the flames of the burning vehicles as well as blowing blankets and papers all over the motorway. The police had no option but to wave them away.

In one burnt-out vehicle, firefighters discovered two hot gas cylinders. These were cooled down with sprays, identified and gently placed in a makeshift water-filled trough to prevent an explosion.

Once the fires had been extinguished, the shells of the vehicles were searched. Three bodies were found on the coach, those of people who simply hadn't been able to get out in time.

Then came the unenviable task of opening up the two cars which had been flattened against the front of the coach. Special heavy lifting gear had to be used to prise the bus away before the cars themselves were cut open. One distressed firefighter likened the operation to opening sardine tins. In each of the crushed cars, they found the charred bodies of two adults and two children, taking the overall death toll to thirteen. At the time, it was Britain's worst motorway accident.

A total of 38 people were hurt in the pile-up, some suffering from smoke inhalation, and they were taken by a fleet of eleven ambulances to the Royal Preston Hospital and the Royal Lancaster Infirmary. Others had sustained head injuries and burns to the face and hands. Those killed in the smash were so badly burnt that identification took several days. The subsequent inquest revealed that seven of the victims died from burns, the remainder (including the four children) from head injuries.

Back at the accident site, fire crews helped the police in their efforts to reopen the motorway. Fire Officer Les Leckie emphasised: 'It was vital that we got the motorway opened as quickly as possible. In situations like that where traffic was building up, more accidents inevitably happen.'

The accident was eventually attributed to driver error. The coach driver was fined £200 and banned for three years for driving without due care and attention.

For people like Fred Williams, the memory of the M6 crash will probably never fade completely. An ambulanceman by profession, he was travelling from Tyneside that day on his way to Blackpool for a holiday with his wife, child and two cousins. As he approached the roadworks, the car behind him slowed down but the coach carried on and rode over the two ill-fated cars. Mr Williams' car, just three weeks old, was then hit by a van and another vehicle. His family escaped serious injury but he was treated for shock. 'It was horrific,' he said. 'The worst part was seeing the two people trapped in that car. They were trapped by their seatbelts and I watched them screaming and dying. I will never forget that scene.'

Motorway Mayhem

Two years to the month later and just eight miles south of where the M6 crash occurred, there was another horrific motorway accident. And once again it involved a heavy vehicle ploughing into stationary traffic which had slowed down for roadworks.

This second smash happened at Walton-le-Dale near the new junction 9 of the M61, about a mile south of where that motorway joins the M6. Roadworks on the M6 were creating a tailback of stationary or slow-moving traffic on the M61 and traffic on the M61 was funnelling into two lanes. There were plenty of signs in advance to warn motorists of the problems ahead. A flashing matrix display began three miles back, warning vehicles to slow down to a maximum of 60 mph. Subsequent displays reduced the speed to 40 mph and finally 30 mph. There were also police boards warning of the roadworks and possible delays.

Wednesday 28 October 1987 was a bright sunny day. Visibility across Lancashire was excellent. It was half-term for many schools in the area and families were making the most of the autumnal weather. Some were heading up to the Lake District for a long weekend; others had decided on the spur of the moment to go to Blackpool or Morecambe for the day. But for many more, it was simply another working day with deliveries to be made. So traffic was slightly heavier than normal that day and by 1 p.m. there was a three-mile build-up of northbound vehicles on the M61 waiting to join the M6 south of Preston.

Travelling north that day was a tanker carrying 17,000 litres of diesel oil. When he saw the first speed restriction sign, the driver reduced his speed accordingly and continued to do so until he was travelling at

30 mph in the slow lane. The traffic ahead was also slowing down as it encountered the tailback. Immediately ahead of the tanker was a Ford Fiesta carrying a family from Bolton – man and wife, sons aged nine and ten and nephews aged nine and fourteen. All was going smoothly until another car tried to cut over to the slow lane, forcing the Fiesta to brake sharply. The tanker driver slammed on his brakes but was unable to stop in time. The tanker rammed the Fiesta from behind, crushing it with its sheer power, before cannoning into a newly built motorway bridge. As it spun around, it ruptured the fuel tanks of cars and lorries in the two outer lanes, creating an instant fireball.

In the space of just seven seconds, the fireball swept through seven vehicles – three cars, two vans and two lorries. All were completely burnt out. Thirteen people died, including the entire family of six in the Fiesta which had been used as an involuntary battering ram by the tanker as it careered helplessly into the bridge.

One man who witnessed the awful chain of events said: 'The tanker cab went right under the bridge and set the whole place alight. It was appalling – sheer carnage. Cars went up in flames in seconds. I couldn't believe that fire could move so fast. Those who couldn't get out of their cars straight away didn't really stand a chance.'

Drivers further ahead in the traffic jam heard the crash and saw the flames in their rear-view mirrors. They immediately abandoned their vehicles and ran to see whether they could help. Shielding their eyes from the heat, they tried to open car doors to free those trapped inside. Through the odd gap in the flames, they could see the contorted, anguished faces of passengers begging to be saved. But the door handles were too hot to touch and the fierce heat drove many of the rescuers back.

A few managed to save themselves. With flames licking all around her, one woman realised that the only way out was through the windscreen. Bracing herself and protecting her eyes as best as she could, she dived through the windscreen, landing on the car bonnet. She was injured but managed to stumble to safety. Meanwhile, her companion in the car had succeeded in forcing open the door on his side and he too was able to climb to safety.

The driver of the tanker came to in his blazing cab. His trousers were on fire and there was blood in his eyes from a head wound. He said later: 'There were flames all around in the cab and I just saw a gap in front and threw myself through it.' His injuries prevented him from fetching a fire extinguisher from the rear of the tanker.

By amazing good fortune, the tanker's load remained intact. Had that too leaked on to the road, the scale of the fireball would have been even greater, with a corresponding rise in the death toll.

Eight fire appliances rushed to the accident site, including four water pumps, a light rescue tender and a foam unit. Within minutes of the crash, 40 firefighters from across Lancashire were spraying gallons of life-saving foam on burning cars and people alike.

By now, the underside of the bridge was engulfed in flames and beginning to disintegrate. As it did so, it showered lumps of burning concrete down on to the motorway. Throughout the rescue, fire crews had to watch out for the falling masonry, adding another hazard to what was already very nearly mission impossible.

Before long, there was nobody else to be rescued – it was merely a matter of prising the dead from the metal envelopes which were once their cars. Four hours after the crash, firefighters were still cutting bodies from the mangled vehicles. The charred bodies they recovered were so unrecognisable that they could only be identified by clothing or belongings.

*   *   *

Fire crews in Nottingham went to a house at Bestwood, in the north of the city, to find a man dressed as Batman, chained up and unable to break free. With no Boy Wonder to bale him out of such a tricky situation, the Caped Crusader had lost much of his Kerpow! by the time the men arrived to set about solving the riddle of how to release him. He must have feared the worst was yet to come when he saw the team brandishing a pair of bolt-cutters, but before you could say 'Holy firefighter!' he had been removed from his shackles and was free to continue fighting crime. It could be that our hero was a little lost, for the village of Gotham actually lies six miles to the south of Nottingham. Holy Ordnance Survey Map . . .

*   *   *

The Girl Who Came Back From the Dead

Each year in mid-summer, thousands of music fans from all over Britain and Europe make the pilgrimage to Somerset for the Glastonbury Festival. All ages go although the audience is mainly composed of people in their late teens and twenties. Not all go for the music.

The Glastonbury Festival is an experience in itself and so many tag along to soak up its unique atmosphere and to take the opportunity to sample a free and easy weekend far removed from the office, factory or Job Centre.

The 1986 festival lived up to expectations and so it was with great reluctance that the throng bade farewell to their little corner of Somerset on the Monday and set off back to their daily routine. For most, there was always next year. But for nine of the festival-goers from 1986, there would be no next year.

On that Monday morning of 23 June, the nine loaded into the blue Ford Transit van which they had hired in Surrey the previous Friday, ready for the journey back along the M4 to South London. It was a case of gross overcrowding. The vehicle, a commercial goods van, was designed to carry only three passengers, for whom seats were provided in the front. There were no seats in the back yet this was where most of the passengers were crammed, sitting on the floor, shoulder to shoulder.

That same day, a family of five were returning home to Wiltshire along the westbound carriageway of the M4 in their large Subaru estate car following a two-week holiday in France. The parents sat in the front, with three girls, ranging in age from ten to eighteen, in the back.

By 12.45, the Transit van was heading towards junction 8/9 near Maidenhead. It was travelling in the fast lane when the driver suddenly had to brake to avoid a motorcyclist. The van went into a skid, spun out of control, flipped over the crash barrier and, after revolving wildly through 180 degrees, rolled to a standstill on its side in the middle of the westbound carriageway directly in the path of the oncoming Subaru. The driver of the estate car had no chance of avoiding the van and ploughed straight into it. Seconds later, a Cortina also smashed into the van which lay spreadeagled over the middle and fast lanes of the carriageway. The Cortina driver had slammed on his brakes but had been unable to prevent his car adding to the pile-up. The three occupants of the Cortina, including an 82-year-old grandmother, were saved by their seatbelts. A Vauxhall Astra, following close behind, also hit the van but again the passengers were not seriously injured.

Those in the Transit were not so lucky. The force of the crash ripped away the side of the van, spilling its passengers out on to the motorway. Bodies were left strewn over the carriageway. Many were hideously mutilated. The few who were still clinging to life were screaming in agony.

Fire crews and ambulances took fifteen minutes to reach the scene, having been sent to the wrong side of the motorway. When they did get to the accident site, firefighters were scarcely able to comprehend the horror before their eyes.

Assistant Divisional Officer Frazer Gunn of the Berkshire Fire Brigade said: 'At first I thought the ground was strewn with wreckage from the vehicles and tents and sleeping bags. Then I realised it was dead bodies that I was stepping over. The carnage was absolutely staggering. There were bodies strewn all over the motorway, mingled with bedding and canvas. My men were sickened and numb.'

With bodies scattered far and wide, firefighters used thermal image cameras to search for human forms over a wide area of the motorway embankment. Meanwhile crews armed with heavy cutting equipment tried to break into the Subaru estate car to discover whether anyone could possibly have survived such a terrible crash. Carefully they cut away the roof and sides of the car so that ambulancemen and doctors could tend to those inside. The signs were not good. The mother and father in the front seats were both dead. There appeared to be two girls in the back and they too had been killed. However, when the crews moved in on them, they found another girl trapped underneath. Amazingly, she was still alive.

The eighteen-year-old survivor, an art student named Samantha, was rushed to hospital with two broken legs and injuries to her back. So badly disfigured were the other passengers in the estate car that both her step-brother and a friend had orginally identified Samantha as being among the dead.

Thirteen people died in the M4 crash, nine from the van and four in the estate car. It took the emergency services five hours to cut the victims from the wreckage and clear away the debris. Only then was the westbound carriageway able to be reopened. As details of the crash appeared on news bulletins, the relatives of thousands of people who had attended the Glastonbury Festival rang police stations and hospitals, desperate to know whether any of their family were among those killed.

It had been a long, traumatic day for all of the firefighters, not least for A.D.O. Gunn who was unable to wipe from his mind the horror of what he had seen. 'When I returned home, I couldn't sleep and could only hear the screams of a woman who was dying by the side of that decimated van.'

* * *

Afternoon lessons at a junior school in Stafford were interrupted when firefighters turned up in force to free a boy who had got his hand stuck in an old-fashioned style radiator. After arranging for the heating to be switched off, they tried lubricating his hand but it was firmly wedged. So they decided to use an angle-grinder to slice through the radiator. As a precautionary measure, a block of wood was inserted between the boy's hand and the top of the radiator. To keep him calm throughout the twenty-minute ordeal, firefighters wrapped him in a blanket and brought a smile to his face by putting one of their helmets on his head and telling him jokes.

* * *

Day Trip to Disaster

For 44 American and Canadian tourists, it was to be the trip of a lifetime. Some had saved up for years to come to Britain in the late autumn of 1993 and see our national treasures in the flesh, instead of merely glimpsing them in establishing shots of old episodes of *The Persuaders*. From their London hotel base, they did the rounds of the Tower of London, Buckingham Palace, Big Ben, Windsor Castle and many more. The weather wasn't great but it couldn't dampen their enthusiasm for English history.

The itinerary for Wednesday 10 November (three days after their arrival in Britain) took them down to the Garden of England, Kent, for a visit to Canterbury Cathedral and then on to Leeds Castle, near Maidstone. It meant an early start but all felt that was a small price to pay for the opportunity to study two splendid historic buildings in the same day.

So by 9.30, the coach party, accompanied by a British driver and tour guide, were already deep in the Kent countryside, travelling east along the M2 towards Canterbury. It was another grey, wet morning but most of the conversation centred around how lovely the fields and trees looked, even in such miserable conditions. An American woman and her two sisters were particularly excited about this green and pleasant land. They were so glad they'd made the trip.

At 9.35, the 53-seater coach was approaching junction 6, the Faversham turn-off, near the village of Ospringe. They were only ten miles from their destination. Then, in driving rain, with the windscreen wipers working overtime, the coach clipped a Ford Transit van travelling in front of it. The coach driver slammed on the brakes but the vehicle skidded on the wet surface, hit the central barrier, spun round 180 degrees and careered out of control for 200 yards before tumbling back first down a leafy embankment where it eventually came to rest on its side, yards from a lane at the bottom.

A lorry driver who had witnessed the accident stopped and ran down the slippery embankment to help. 'It was the most terrible thing I've seen in my life,' he said. 'There were people on the coach with appalling injuries caused by broken glass, and arms and legs were sticking out everywhere. The back window was smashed and bodies had been thrown out. Some of the injured were trying to stand but they couldn't because they had broken limbs.'

Several other cars stopped and soon there was a band of civilian rescuers rushing to the aid of the wounded coach passengers. 'We tried to get out everyone who could move,' said one of the passers-by. 'We moved people very carefully, asking them where they had any pain. About ten of us formed a human chain up the muddy bank to the motorway because it was too slippery to walk up the bank carrying anyone. We tried to staunch their wounds and keep them warm with blankets.'

Another helper had the sense to call the emergency services which were quickly on the scene although the first appliances arrived on the other side of the motorway, forcing crews to run across both carriageways and stop the traffic in order to reach the wrecked coach. As further crews were called out, a more convenient access route was established.

Already, there was a report of one fatality. The team of passers-by had succeeded in pulling out the front window of the coach to tend to the driver. But as soon as they had got the windscreen off, they could see he was dead. Trapped beneath a section of the front of the coach, he had died of crush injuries and a ruptured liver. It was optimistic in the extreme to believe that his would be the only death.

Inside the coach, all was quiet. The silence was almost deafening. There was no screaming, no moaning, just a collection of dazed people, many with their heads and hands covered in blood. Most of the seats were still in place but as the coach had skidded off the road and lurched over on to its side, the passengers had all been thrown to the right. It was those who had been sitting on the right-hand side of the coach who bore the brunt of the crash. Some had been hurled out of the side of the coach as it twisted through the air. Cruelly, it then landed on top of them, instantly crushing them to death. Others had been trapped in their seats by the sheer weight of passengers falling over from the left-hand side of the coach.

Flasks, rucksacks and travel guides lay scattered on the ground. Those who had escaped with minor cuts and bruises huddled up against the fire appliances in the rain. It was a depressing scene. Firefighters, battling against the cold and damp, formed a makeshift bridge across a ditch with a ladder to lead other survivors to ambulances. Once everybody was off the coach, the operation began to reach those trapped underneath the side of it. Nine tourists plus the driver had been killed, all from crush and rupture injuries.

A Catholic priest was called in. He spoke to a 67-year-old man who was worried about his wife. The priest confided: 'He told me he couldn't find his wife after the crash and started to shout her name. He said he felt she was dead.' Sadly, his worst fears were confirmed.

The American woman lost both her sisters. Fighting back the tears, she recounted: 'One minute we were talking about how lovely the countryside was, even though it was grey and rainy, and then we were flying through the air.'

The Faversham crash reinforced the call for seatbelts to be fitted in coaches. Dr Susan Brooks of Kent and Canterbury Hospital, where many of the injured were taken, said: 'Those who died were thrown out of the side of the coach which then landed on top of them. Had they been restrained in seatbelts and therefore kept inside the coach, there is a chance that they would have survived.'

* * *

On 7 December 1990, five people were injured when escaped pigs caused a three-car smash near Scarborough. The accident happened on the A64 near Sherburn at six o'clock in the morning. The driver of a Land Rover braked when he saw the two pigs, which were believed to have strayed on to the road from a nearby farm, and an Austin Mini Metro travelling behind crashed into the back of him. The Land Rover then hit a third car, an Austin Montego, which was heading towards Scarborough. The pigs hit the Montego and were propelled into the Land Rover, causing it considerable damage. Firefighters from Scarborough used cutting gear to free the injured people from their vehicles. They were then taken to hospital but later discharged. Both pigs were killed.

* * *

Hurricane Horror

The night of 15 October 1987 is one which will live long in the memory of the population of southern England. For that night, a hurricane, bearing winds gusting up to 110 mph, swept across the Atlantic unannounced and left a £300 million trail of destruction from Cornwall to East Anglia.

The winds hit the south-east coast at 1 a.m. Within four hours, 15 million trees had been uprooted, 3000 miles of telephone wires had been pulled down, buildings had been demolished, railways and roads blocked and lorries and aircraft overturned. Seventeen people were killed by Britain's worst storm of the century.

In London alone, the Fire Brigade dealt with a record 6000 emergency calls in 24 hours. Throughout the south, alarms were continually going off, activated by wind damage to their circuits. The Fire Brigade, along with the other emergency services, struggled to cope with the unprecedented influx of calls. For all of the crews, it was a long, long night.

For one crew in Dorset, it was also to prove a tragic night. At 3 a.m., the six-man crew had just finished repairing the damaged roof of a factory at Christchurch when they were ordered to another factory where the fire alarm had gone off. They were driving along Lymington Road in Highcliffe when a twelve-ton tree suddenly thundered down on top of their cab. They had no warning of its impending collapse – it just came at them out of the dark night sky. The two men in the cab, Sub Officer David Gregory and Fireman Graham White, were killed instantly. The four men in the back of the appliance were catapulted through the air, sustaining cuts and bruises.

For over an hour, the injured men worked to free the bodies of their colleagues from the crumpled cab even though there was a constant danger that more trees might come crashing to the ground. They were assisted by a back-up crew sent from Christchurch. Only when the bodies were released did the four men go to hospital to be treated for their injuries and shock.

Both of the dead men were volunteer firemen. Mrs White, a nurse, had often begged her husband to give up his retained job but she knew that he loved it too much. 'The odds against the accident must have been a million to one,' she lamented. 'If it had been a split second different, the tree would have fallen in front of or behind the cab.'

Graham White lived for his firefighting and he died for it too. The final sad irony is that the alarm to which the crew were rushing at the time of the accident was yet another false one, triggered off by the hurricane which caused so much heartbreak that night.

6 Domestic Fires

High-Rise Horror

Like so many tower blocks built in the 1960s, Merry Hill Court in the Smethwick district of Birmingham had once seemed the answer to every architect's dream. Build upward was the motto in those days, to create multiple living accommodation without using up acres of precious land.

But for the residents of Merry Hill Court, as with those living in thousands of similar blocks throughout the country, the dream had long since turned into a nightmare. The concept of community spirit where neighbours would pause for a chat on the landing might have been appropriate in the sixties but the subsequent decline in law and order made many tower blocks a haven for criminals instead. The concrete walkways and stairways, often hidden from view by day and poorly lit at night, became the ideal operating ground for muggers, vandals and drug addicts. Residents became terrified to venture out alone. Those who could escaped from their high-rise hell and moved elsewhere. Many blocks were demolished in favour of compact, two-storey developments given appealing names by developers. But some had no choice but to stay on and make the best of things.

There was certainly precious little that was merry about life in Merry Hill Court in July 1990. It too was due for demolition, as a result of which only one third of the 94 flats in the sixteen-storey block were occupied. Vandalism was rife. Following an arson attack six months earlier, anti-vandal barricades had been erected. To many of the surviving residents, Merry Hill Court was more like a prison than a home. The sooner they got out, the better.

One of those left behind was a 41-year-old mother of two. If she had been of a superstitious nature, she might have sensed that, for someone living on the thirteenth floor, something awful would happen on Friday the 13th.

She returned to her flat at around 8 p.m. that evening. There was blood on one of the doors and the rooms were starting to fill with smoke so she immediately telephoned the police. The fire had actually started in the flat next door, yet having raised the alarm the woman opted to remain in her own flat rather than flee to safety.

By the time firefighters arrived, the blaze had begun to sweep through the upper storeys of the building. They were unable to park their appliances as near to the block as they would have liked because of the anti-vandal barricades. In addition, the water main had been vandalised.

Alerted by the sounds of the two-tones, residents hurried down smoke-filled staircases to the street. Crews went in to evacuate the block. Some were totally oblivious to the drama around them and were busily watching television when the firefighters rapped on their door. Eighty people were led to safety down a fire-protected staircase. Windows were shattering with the heat. Glass and concrete came crashing to the ground, forcing crews to take swift evasive action. One ambulanceman remarked: 'It was a real towering inferno job.'

Some people couldn't make it to the stairs – the smoke and flames had blocked their escape route. They ran out on to their balconies and screamed for help. The hydraulic platform, with its long extensions, was positioned so that firefighters could reach the upper floors. As the cage moved nearer and nearer, firefighters shouted to those who were trapped to hang on until they got there. As the cage moved alongside, the frightened residents stepped gratefully on to its floor before being lowered to the ground. In total, eight people were rescued this way.

Meanwhile, the woman who had raised the alarm was seen screaming 120 feet up, from her thirteenth-floor balcony. She was frantically waving her arms, shouting: 'Help! Help! I'm burning!' Flames were leaping out of the side window of her flat. Then suddenly she disappeared from view. One witness described her as having collapsed back into her flat. Smethwick Sub Officer Nick Stuart and Leading Fireman Andy Dickson went up on the hydraulic platform but, even at its full extension, it would only reach as far as the eleventh floor. From there, they climbed over the top of the ladder and jumped on to a balcony on the twelfth storey, just one floor below the woman. Vaulting from balcony to balcony carried a huge risk – one slip would have been fatal.

With the blaze threatening to engulf the entire block, reinforcements were called in from all over the region. Another 600 local residents were evacuated to a nearby community centre as the heat continued to blow out windows. The number of firefighters present had risen to 170. Suddenly the firefighters too were in danger from the rapidly spreading blaze. Nick Stuart and Andy Dickson were not wearing breathing apparatus as they had expected to be tackling the fire from what they thought would be the the safe twelfth floor. However, they now found themselves cut off by fires above and below them.

Andy Dickson said: 'We put the hose out of the window and started fighting the fire from the twelfth floor until the other crews managed to get through to us. There was intense heat and dense smoke.'

Nick Stuart added: 'We were cut off on the twelfth and there were very real fears that we might be overcome ourselves.'

More crews, this time wearing breathing apparatus, tried to fight their way through. Twice they were beaten back by the heat. Finally they made it to their colleagues and up to the thirteenth floor. They managed to get to the woman and passed her down to the men on the balcony below. She was unconscious but still alive. It was touch and go. From there, she was taken down to the tenth floor landing, where she was given mouth-to-mouth resuscitation.

Nick Stuart said: 'She had still got a pulse when we pulled her out of the flat on to the floor below. We tried the kiss of life and cardiac massage for half an hour because the fire was too bad for ambulance crews to get through.'

Despite the valiant efforts of the Brigade, she did not regain consciousness and died from smoke inhalation.

It was some hours before the fire was finally put out and the crews could carry out a floor-by-floor search. Two firefighters needed hospital treatment, one for a gashed arm, the other for an injured shoulder. Considering the seriousness of the blaze, casualties were amazingly light. As A.D.O. Steve Hubball remarked, surveying the extensive damage: 'It is a miracle that no more people were killed.'

* * *

Nife lamps used to be an important part of a firefighter's armoury. They were like small miners' lamps and were worn on breathing apparatus sets. They came with exceptionally long leads.

Crews in Birkenhead had been called out to a fire in a first-floor flat. It had caused widespread damage, the walls and ceiling were charred, and most of the furniture was beyond repair. Among the wrecked items was a gas cooker. Since it was of no further use, rather than cart it down the stairs, they decided to throw it out of the window.

One of the men on duty that day takes up the story. 'The call went out for everyone down below to stand well clear. Then out of the first-floor window came the cooker . . . followed by a guy in his B.A. set! What had happened was the lead from his Nife lamp had hooked itself around one of the legs of the cooker. So wherever the cooker went, he went too. The experience shook him up a bit but he was soon OK. I've never known a fireman get so attached to a gas cooker!'

* * *

Babysitter Saves the Day

Antonio and Ernesta Delduca had enjoyed their evening out. Much as they loved their children – Guiseppe, aged nine, Desolina, five, and the youngest, Alfredo, who was three – it was nice to get away from them occasionally and leave them in the capable hands of their babysitter, Richard Dales. And after an evening out, there was nothing better than a good night's sleep.

So it was that in the early hours of Easter Monday, 1 April 1991, the family were tucked up in their respective beds at their Scunthorpe home. Since they had been due back late, Richard had stayed over.

Then something roused him from his slumbers. It was the smell of burning. He sat up with a start. He quickly went to investigate and saw smoke and flames downstairs. He knew he must alert the family and ran into the Delducas' bedroom to wake Ernesta.

'There's a fire,' he blurted. 'Downstairs.'

At first, Ernesta thought she was dreaming. She was still half-asleep. But Richard was insistent and it was a bit early for an April Fool's joke.

Bleary-eyed, she made her way out on to the landing, but what she saw woke her in an instant. For as she looked over the banister to see what all the fuss was about, a wall of flames suddenly gushed up the staircase.

Her first thought was for the children. She ran into their room.

'Wake up! Wake up!' she cried, shaking them in their beds.

'What is it, Mummy?'

'The house is on fire . . . downstairs. We must get out quick.'

She gathered up the youngest and, helped by Antonio and Richard, guided the other two towards the window. By now, the flames were almost at the top of the stairs. They could hear a series of explosions coming from downstairs. The house was beginning to fill up with choking smoke. If they delayed any longer, they could all be overcome by fumes.

Antonio jumped to the ground, ready to catch the children. Richard and Ernesta took the children over to the window. It was a long drop – all of 30 feet – but their dad was waiting with a welcoming pair of arms. One by one, they jumped into the night sky, and each time Antonio gathered them safely to his chest. Then Ernesta jumped too, injuring her leg in the process. Only when everyone else was out of the house did Richard leap out of the window, very much the hero of the hour.

Scunthorpe firefighters were quickly on the scene. Their hoses brought the blaze under control in a matter of minutes but they were unable to save the downstairs of the house which was totally gutted.

Whilst distraught about the state of her house, Ernesta Delduca knew that the family were lucky to be alive. 'The Brigade said if it had been a few minutes longer, we'd have been dead. We're lucky we weren't turned into charcoal.'

For that they have to thank their vigilant babysitter.

* * *

Teenage brothers Wayne and James Turner were so engrossed in a computer game that they didn't realise their house was on fire. The pair were playing a Sega game at their home in North Tidworth, Wiltshire, in May 1993, when their toast caught fire under the grill and spread through the downstairs area. The boys were unhurt but their mother, Susan, arrived home to £15,000 of damage. She reflected ruefully: 'The moral is, don't leave kids in the house with a computer game.'

* * *

Chip Pan Tragedy

After a night on the town, the young man was feeling hungry. So when he got back to his Nottingham home in the early hours of that August morning in 1986, he decided to cook himself some chips.

Creeping around the house so as not to wake his parents and elder brother who were asleep upstairs, he put some oil in the pan, switched on the gas cooker and sat down to wait for the results. Unfortunately, the rigours of the evening and the lateness of the hour – it was almost three o'clock in the morning – caught up with him and he dozed off.

Unchecked and unattended, the oil started to bubble dangerously. It was rising relentlessly in the pan, getting hotter and hotter. Still the boy slept. Finally it roared up and flowed over the side of the pan, bursting into flames.

The fire raced across the kitchen, swamping everything in its path. The boy slept on. As it moved into adjoining rooms, the crackling, sizzling sound and the burning smell roused the boy. Surrounded by flames and realising he was about to be burnt alive, he smashed the lounge window and escaped into the street.

Neighbours raised the alarm but by the time crews from Dunkirk and West Bridgford Fire Stations arrived, the house was burning freely. The boy was outside with his father who had managed to jump clear from the bedroom window. Both were hysterical, shouting that there were two more people still trapped in the house.

Crews donned breathing apparatus and tried to force their way in through the front door but they had to beat back the flames before they could gain entry. The chances of anyone surviving in such an inferno seemed remote. They knew that people were trapped upstairs but there were no stairs to climb – they had burnt away. So firefighters had to use a ladder to reach the upper floor. They battled their way into the bedrooms where their fears were confirmed. They found the bodies of the mother and her older son.

Sub Officer Dave Thompson was taken aback by the ferocity of the blaze. 'It was one of the most severe house fires I've ever attended. When we arrived, flames were coming out everywhere – upstairs and downstairs, front and back.'

The boy and his father were treated in hospital for shock and the effects of smoke. It took fire crews an hour to control the blaze which also caused smoke damage to adjoining houses. In the end, it was 7 a.m. before they returned to their stations, bitterly disappointed that they had been unable to save two lives.

The menace of chip pan fires never goes away. Ten years later, in the same city of Nottingham, an 88-year-old widow died from severe burns after an overheated pan started a blaze at her home.

After cooking a dinner of sausage and chips, she forgot to turn off a gas ring. Seeing smoke and flames pouring from the house, a neighbour alerted the emergency services. Two firefighters in breathing apparatus forced their way in and found the woman standing in the kitchen, encircled by flames. They managed to rescue her but she died in intensive care two days later.

The inquest heard that chips were the dead woman's favourite food and, although she had been told of the dangers of boiling fat, she continued to cook them twice a week.

After the inquest, Neil Grant, a station officer with the Nottinghamshire Fire Service, warned of the menace which leads to 16,000 chip pan fires every year in Britain. 'The problems happen when people overfill pans with oil, leave the pan unattended while the chips are cooking or forget to switch the heat off. People should use a deep fat fryer with a thermostat.'

* * *

Investigating a cottage fire in Durham in December 1991, firefighters found no fewer than nineteen cats lying unconscious from the after-effects of the blaze. The intrepid crew members brought them round by giving each one a whiff of oxygen.

* * *

Smoke Alarm to the Rescue

In the wake of a series of tragic fires in the city, a Glasgow newspaper ran a campaign encouraging people to fit smoke alarms in their homes. Among those who responded was Janice Barilli who lived with her family in a tenement block in Port Glasgow and who, at the time of the campaign in 1991, was expecting her third child.

The alarm gave her great peace of mind but it was one night two years later that its value was really brought home to her. For without it, Janice Barilli and her three children would probably have been killed.

The drama took place in the early hours of 28 March 1993. Janice, her eleven-year-old son Hugh, seven-year-old daughter Andrea and eighteen-month-old baby Kevin were all sound asleep in their third-storey flat when fire broke out in the home of the pensioner who lived directly underneath. As the fire intensified, thick smoke belched up into the Barillis' flat, setting off the smoke alarm which was situated in the hallway outside young Andrea's bedroom.

Despite its repeated sound, Andrea was the only member of the family who heard the alarm. She immediately ran into her mum's room and shouted that the house was on fire.

Mrs Barilli rounded up the children and, carrying baby Kevin, tried to lead them out of the front door. But as they opened the door, they were confronted by a sheet of flames and smoke. They were driven back into the flat where Mrs Barilli called Strathclyde Fire Service.

By now, smoke was filling the hall so Mrs Barilli shepherded the children into her bedroom, which was still smoke-free, and barricaded the door with pillows to prevent any fumes from seeping through underneath.

Anxiously, they waited for the Brigade. Mrs Barilli tried to reassure the youngsters that the firemen wouldn't be long. It was only minutes but it seemed like hours. Then they heard the reassuring sound of the sirens. After that, the firefighters were quickly able to douse the blaze and lead the Barilli family to safety. And the pensioner downstairs also survived the ordeal.

Little Andrea Barilli was just relieved that she had heard the smoke alarm. 'The moment I heard it, I ran to my mum's room and shouted to her. I knew it was what I had to do. I was very frightened and I was so happy to see the firemen who came to rescue us.'

*   *   *

Hearing the family's pet rabbit scratching at its hutch, 22-year-old Tanya Birch woke up to find that her block of flats at Wisbech, Cambridgeshire, was on fire. Tanya grabbed her two-year-old daughter, Heather, and fled to safety. Sadly, the rabbit died.

*   *   *

For the Love of a Dog

The five year old and his dog, Sly, were inseparable. He used to feed it, take it for walks and play with it constantly. It was an act of mutual devotion. Tragically, this love for his pet was to cost the boy his life when fire ripped through the family home in the middle of the night.

Home was a three-bedroom semi-detached house in Basildon, Essex. There were three children in all – twin boys and a girl aged three. In the early hours of 17 July 1994, the family were asleep when the parents were woken by the smell of smoke and the sound of a succession of small explosions. Even in the disorientation associated with waking up suddenly, it was quickly apparent that the problem was downstairs. The boy's father leapt out of bed to take a closer look. He went to the top of the stairs and was horrified to see flames licking around the hallway.

Despite the shock of seeing his house on fire and the imminent danger it posed to his family, the father kept remarkably calm. He scooped up the three children and took them into the bathroom at the rear of the house. Below the bathroom window was a flat-roof extension, providing an ideal escape route. Firstly, he helped his wife out of the bathroom window and on to the flat roof and then, one by one, he passed the children down to her. From there, they were helped down to the ground where neighbours – who between them had made no fewer than twenty emergency calls to Fire Headquarters – were waiting to help. Finally, the father, having bravely rescued his family, made his own escape.

The fire was reported at 2.20 a.m. and four appliances – two from Basildon and one each from Hadleigh and Corringham – raced to the scene. They should have been dealing with a straightforward house fire with no persons reported, but then events took a tragic turn.

Unknown to his parents, the five year old had slipped back into the burning house in an attempt to rescue his ten-year-old mongrel dog. He had crawled in through a 'dog flap' in the utility room which measured no more than 1 foot high and 9 inches wide. When the boy's father suddenly realised that he was missing and had gone back in, he resolved to go after him. Neighbours tried to restrain him. 'The house was a mass of flames,' said one. 'There was no way I could get anywhere near it.'

But the father would do anything to save his son and, smashing a window with his fist, managed to unlock the back door and pluck the boy from the flames for a second time. He then carried the boy into the garden where he plunged him into a paddling pool. Firefighters too risked their lives, literally going through a wall of flames. Fire crews, the police and the father all tried to revive him, but it was too late. He was already dead.

The father was taken to hospital for treatment to the injuries he sustained when smashing the glass to get back into the house, and his wife was treated for shock.

Numbed by the tragedy, fire crews still had to bring the blaze under control. It took twenty of them, some in breathing apparatus, over half an hour to do so, and one firefighter suffered minor burns to his ears and legs. A family of four in the adjoining house also had to be rescued as smoke from the fire filled their rooms. Basildon Station Officer Martin Hodder went in and carried a two-year-old girl downstairs and the rest of the family followed.

The house where the fire had broken out was gutted. A firefighter described the scene as one of 'absolute devastation'. Crews were sifting through the rubble until 5 a.m. The dog was found dead in the lounge.

Station Officer Hodder summed up: 'It's just tragic. The father had saved all the family in such a valiant rescue but the boy went back in for the dog. He wouldn't have stood a chance – it was an inferno. We all felt quite sick afterwards.'

Three months later, another gallant rescue ended in tragedy, this time in Blackheath, south-east London. A mother and her five children, ranging in age from a three-year-old boy to a fourteen-year-old girl, were in bed in their two-storey council house when neighbours spotted a fire at 8.12 a.m. The mother and the four eldest children managed to escape but the young boy was still asleep upstairs. Defying the dangers, the fourteen year old rushed back into the blazing house in a desperate bid to reach her brother. The smoke was stifling, the heat unbearable, but somehow she succeeded in battling her way through to his bedroom at the back of the house. There, trapped by a blanket of flame, she was overcome by smoke.

Fire crews arrived to learn that there were people inside the house. Putting on breathing apparatus, they fought through the thick smoke and flames to get up the stairs to the back bedroom. They found the bodies of both children and the family dog. The boy and the dog were already dead, but there was just a slim chance that they might be able to save the girl. They dragged her out into the front garden and desperately tried to resuscitate her. But she could not be saved. She had died heroically going back into the blazing house to rescue her younger brother.

The fire was brought under control at 8.50 but by then it had destroyed the house and the family's possessions, including a few early Christmas presents.

The firefighters returned to their stations in stunned silence. The day had been yet another unwanted reminder of the deadly power of fire.

* * *

A group of policemen who arrested a burglar on the roof of a bank in Rainham, Kent, had to be rescued by firefighters after they became stuck. Finding there was no way they could get down from the roof, they had to radio in for assistance and wait patiently for fire crews to arrive with ladders. Embarrassed police and rueful prisoner were then escorted safely to the ground. Stifling his amusement, a Kent firefighter said: 'As far as I know, this was a first!' A 25-year-old man was later jailed for a year at Maidstone Crown Court after admitting burglary.

* * *

The Daring Young Man on the Flying Trapeze

More often than not, firefighters play things by the book. Set procedures are laid down for certain situations, designed not only to offer the best chance of a successful rescue but also to protect the firefighters themselves. For example, when a fire produces thick smoke, crews in the immediate vicinity should wear breathing apparatus sets. It is simple common sense. A firefighter needlessly injured can cause delays to the rescue, perhaps putting the lives of his or her colleagues at risk and even jeopardising the entire operation.

But the job of a firefighter is all about saving lives. And sometimes in order to do that, they have to improvise and invent their own methods of rescue. It doesn't always work, but at Sheffield in the early hours of 27 February 1983, it most certainly did, resulting in one of the most spectacular fire rescues the city has ever seen.

Nineteen-year-old Dawn Lipscombe lived in a sixth-floor council flat in the Broomhall district of Sheffield. At two o'clock in the morning, she suddenly became aware that the flat was on fire. She tried to reach the front door but the fire had caught hold to such devastating effect that the area was already engulfed in flames and thick smoke. Beaten back, she desperately sought an alternative exit. The fire was spreading before her eyes, moving ever closer. She knew that it would be only a matter of minutes before she was caught in its vice-like grip.

With the front door unattainable, the only other way out was through a window. As yet, the kitchen was relatively untouched by the fire so she decided to make her escape through the kitchen window. There was no balcony on the other side to provide a reasonably safe haven while she waited for help, just a narrow concrete ledge, no more than four inches wide. The prospect was scarcely appealing but she was left with no choice. The alternative was to stay in the flat where she would surely be burnt alive.

Gingerly, she climbed backwards out of the kitchen window, not daring to look at the ground below. She knew that any slip would be her last. Her hands gripping the window frame, she lowered herself down so that her forearms were on the ledge outside. And there she hung, sixty feet above the ground, screaming with all the strength she could muster, praying that somebody would call the Fire Brigade.

Her screams alerted neighbours who quickly dialled 999. Fire-fighters arrived to see Miss Lipscombe hanging on for grim death outside her burning flat. They implored her to cling on just a little longer. Safety blankets were positioned to catch her if she fell. Unfortunately, she was beyond the reach of the turntable ladder so they had to find some other point of access.

Aware that she couldn't hang on much longer, Leading Fireman Jeff Yates and Fireman Keith Summerfield decided on a drastic course of action. They broke into an adjoining flat which was empty and, while Fireman Summerfield held on to his legs, Leading Fireman Yates swung out of the window to try and grab the girl. Witnesses described it as 'a sort of trapeze act 60 feet above ground'.

Colleagues below watched in stunned silence.

Suddenly an explosion sent flames shooting through the kitchen window. Miss Lipscombe instinctively threw herself towards the outstretched arms of Leading Fireman Yates and he managed to grab hold of her. For a few perilous seconds, she swung through the air. Then, with Fireman Summerfield maintaining the grip on his colleague, Jeff Yates managed to haul the girl up through the window of the adjoining flat. It was a tremendous feat of daring.

Miss Lipscombe was badly shaken by her ordeal but was otherwise unhurt. The only casualty was a fireman on the ground who was treated for a head wound after being struck by flying glass from the explosion.

As the two men came down to a hero's welcome, Divisional Officer Brian Ellis paid a fitting tribute. 'It was just like a trapeze act,' he said. 'At one stage it was really touch and go, but luckily Jeff is a big lad with arms like ham shanks. It was just good luck that he was the man hanging out of the window. It required enormous strength to do what he did. You will not find that rescue procedure in any manual, but at the end of the day, a young woman's life was saved. The bravery of both firefighters was outstanding.'

Jeff Yates was suitably modest. 'It all happened in a split second. There was a flash and the windows broke. At that moment, she flung herself towards me and I grabbed her and pulled her up. We then managed to get her through the window. I'm just glad that we were able to get her out alive because she had been hanging there for some time. She's a very lucky woman.'

Dawn Lipscombe's biggest stroke of luck was that there were two such heroic firefighters on duty in Sheffield that morning.

*　*　*

On 30 January 1984, Avon firefighter Steve Williams answered an emergency call in Weston-super-Mare, only to find that it was his own house which was on fire. By the time he and the rest of the crew had arrived, his wife Michelle had managed to escape but he was still left with the job of rescuing his sheepdog from the smoke-damaged building.

*　*　*

Prisoners in Their Own Home

Like all too many inner-city areas up and down the country, the borough of Camden in north London is plagued by crime. On the various estates in the district, racial attacks, burglaries and muggings are frighteningly commonplace. Consequently, many law-abiding citizens live in fear and fit window locks and sturdy door bolts to deter intruders. Stringent security measures give residents a degree of peace of mind, but, when taken to extremes, they can also turn the home into a deadly fire trap.

A high crime rate inevitably brings about a high turnover of tenants. Given the opportunity, many people can't wait to move out of the area. While council property remains empty, waiting for the next occupants, another problem surfaces – that of squatters.

Since squatters have no qualms about bashing down a door to break in, many councils are forced to resort to fitting impenetrable steel security doors, just to keep illegal occupants at bay. Camden Council had experienced difficulties with squatters and so when a flat in one particular block became vacant, they erected a heavy-duty door made of steel half an inch thick. The only way to open it from the outside was by means of a small key. Another similarly tiny keyhole enabled the door to be opened from the inside. In short, it was burglar-proof. All vandals or would-be squatters could do to it was daub it with graffiti. It made the flat a fortress.

In time the flat was let to two people – a 56-year-old woman and her daughter, aged 30. The council immediately offered to remove the steel door and fit new locks to a conventional door instead. But the women, fearful for their safety, welcomed the security which the door gave them and insisted on keeping it. Again, the council urged them to reconsider, but the women remained adamant. As far as they were concerned, the door was staying. And the women also thoroughly approved of the metal grilles fitted to windows. They felt confident that nobody would be able to break in.

Their home was their castle and they only ventured outside it for essentials. The pair were virtual recluses. Their local postman remarked: 'You never saw them around the block – they would keep that security door locked and stay indoors. It was very rarely open.'

The council were all too aware that the door posed a real danger in the event of fire and repeatedly advised the women to leave it ajar when they were inside the flat. The women would not listen. The fire risk was tragically underlined in mid-January 1989 when a couple in another inner-city crime hotspot – Stockwell in South London – died in their seventeenth-floor flat following an arson attack. Firefighters trying to rescue the occupants had been delayed because it took them five minutes to batter down a wrought-iron security grille which had been fitted to keep out intruders.

Any message from that fire was obviously lost on the two Camden women because, just two weeks later, they were to die in their fortress home – the flat to which there was no entry and from which there was no escape.

Fire broke out in the flat in the small hours of 27 January. A neighbour heard the terrified pleas for help. 'They were screaming for a long time,' she said. 'Really desperate screams. I woke up and looked out of the window and saw smoke and seven police cars. But they couldn't get into the flat and the screams of the two ladies went on.'

Five police officers arrived within two minutes of receiving the emergency call. They immediately knew that there was no way that they would be able to break down the door so they tried removing the grilles from the windows. That too was impossible.

The London Fire Brigade were on the scene moments later. Armed with sledgehammers, they launched a dual attack on the door and the grilles. Neither would budge. All the while, the screams from inside were becoming more frantic yet at the same time weaker. The occupants' lives were slowly ebbing away.

It took twenty minutes for the firefighters to force an entry. They eventually got in by dislodging the iron bars over a rear window. The flat was full of choking black smoke from where the foam-filled furniture had caught alight. The mother was dead in bed. The daughter was still breathing and was taken to University College Hospital where she died three days later. The younger woman had obviously made a valiant attempt to crawl to the door to unlock it, but through the thick smoke she would have had no chance of locating the tiny keyhole. Even after firefighters had finally broken down the door with sledgehammers, the door itself remained intact. Only the hinges on the left-hand side had given way.

Sergeant Cedric Jones, one of the first policemen on the scene, admitted: 'We were helpless. There was just nothing we could do. It took nearly twenty minutes for the Fire Brigade to get in – and that was with all their equipment.'

The London Fire Brigade said that 'vital minutes were lost' as they struggled to break in. 'It would have taken us less than a minute to enter a traditionally secured home but the heavy steel security door and grilles on the window made it very difficult.

'We can understand and sympathise with people who obviously want to protect themselves in their own homes, but we would urge them to make sure that steel doors are set in wooden frames which we can break down quickly in a fire.'

Alas, as in this case, too many warnings fall on deaf ears.

* * *

Firefighters damping down a house fire at Barnet on 31 August 1989 made a hasty withdrawal after discovering a number of Second World War bombs which had been collected by the owner. Happily, the bombs proved to be inert.

* * *

Death by Candlelight

When everyone else had gone to bed in the family's first-floor council flat at King's Norton, Birmingham, the 34-year-old mother of three liked to stay up and read. It was a chance for a spot of peace and calm at the end of a hectic day. But because she was confined to a wheelchair, she was unable to reach the light switch and so used to read by candlelight instead.

On the night of 28 December 1986, she was reading as usual. Her three boys, ranging in age from four to sixteen, were asleep in their bedroom with their 70-year-old grandmother. Then somehow the candle toppled over and set fire to the sofa. The woman's husband raced in to help and, defying the flames, tried to drag the burning sofa out on to the landing of the three-storey block, but it got wedged in the doorway.

The fire swept through the two-bedroomed flat at a terrifying pace. Neighbours tried in vain to reach the trapped children but were beaten back by the ferocity of the blaze before firefighters in breathing apparatus battled through the thick smoke and flames.

But the fire had engulfed the entire flat by the time they arrived. They found the woman lying dead next to her wheelchair in the lounge and the grandmother and one of the boys dead in the bedroom. The other two boys were rescued from the blazing room but died on the way to hospital. In a matter of minutes, the fire had wiped out three generations of one family.

One of the firefighters said afterwards: 'It was a terrible tragedy. I don't think I've ever seen a fire spread so quickly. The remarkable thing was that none of the other five flats in the block were affected.'

To be caught in a fire is a terrifying prospect for anybody, but all the more so if the person is disabled. For, as the wheelchair-bound woman in Birmingham discovered, escape can be impossible unless there is outside help. In the same year as the King's Norton blaze, disaster threatened a disabled woman in Cornwall.

She and her husband lived in a £150,000 luxury home near Liskeard. She suffered from Parkinson's disease and, in order to assist her breathing, her husband had installed a £5000 rocking bed, one of only 25 in the country.

Up in the loft, a council pest control expert was trying to smoke out a swarm of bees. Somehow the roof caught fire and raged down into the bedroom where the woman lay on her special bed. As luck would have it, the family doctor was at her bedside when the fire broke out. He strapped her to a chair and, with the aid of domestic staff, was able to carry her out of the room quickly before the roof caved in. She was taken to a jeep which then drove her to hospital.

Four fire appliances and an emergency tender were despatched to deal with the blaze but it was well alight by the time they arrived. As they struggled to prevent the fire destroying the entire house, one firefighter was treated after being overcome by fumes. Two workers were also hurt while the pest control expert suffered two burnt fingers. The special bed was destroyed but many priceless antiques and, more importantly, the bed's occupant were saved.

* * *

Seven firefighters spent an hour cutting a puppy free on 11 April 1996 after it got its head jammed in a wheel. The puppy, named Jesse, crawled into the hub of a spare tyre at his master's home in South Shields and got stuck.

* * *

Death Plunge

Fifty-three-year-old Dr Munawar Hussain was one of the country's leading children's eye specialists. He was respected by colleagues for his calm assurance and clear thinking. Yet when he perhaps needed these qualities most, they inexplicably deserted him, resulting in his tragic, needless death.

Dr Hussain owned an eleventh-floor flat in a block at Edgbaston, Birmingham, although it was believed that he was not living there permanently at the time. What is known is that he was at the flat on the evening of 20 July 1992 and that shortly before 10 p.m., West Midlands Fire Service received a 999 call from an office opposite the block, reporting a fire in an eleventh-floor flat.

The doctor was thought to be asleep in the bedroom when the noise and smell of the fire smouldering in the lounge woke him. As he opened the bedroom door to leave, the rush of air caused the blaze to flare up alarmingly. Still not fully awake and confused by the heat, the smoke and the danger, he sensed that the most obvious escape route – via the front door – was cut off by the flames. He opted instead for the balcony and dodged his way through the blaze to reach the fresh air.

But the fire was spreading fast and was threatening to corner him on the balcony. As the fire crews arrived on the scene, he seemed to panic and endeavour to climb down to the balcony below. In doing so, he lost his balance and plummeted 120 feet to his death, landing just 3 feet away from one of the firefighters.

Disconsolate Station Officer Keith Richards said that if the doctor had stayed where he was, the firefighters would have been able to rescue him. 'If he had stopped to think, there were safe places in the flat where he could have waited. He must have been able to see we were there. It's possible that he was trying to swing himself on to the balcony below. That wouldn't have been easy, but it would make more sense than jumping that distance. Having something like that happen is a fireman's worst nightmare.'

* * *

In August 1994, firefighters in Winchester were called out to deal with a flooded house. When they arrived, they discovered that it had been caused by a leaking kingsize water bed from which they subsequently had to pump out 100 gallons of water.

* * *

The Real Blue Watch

Bystander Caught Toddler

For 22-year-old jobless labourer Bill McGowan, Wednesday 27 May 1992 began like any other. It was the usual round of looking for work, interspersed with meeting friends. Yet by the end of it, he was being hailed a hero.

His day was transformed by a lunchtime visit to his aunt who lived in a tower block in Stratford, East London. As he made his way through the surrounding streets, he had no idea that a fire had just broken out in a fifth-floor flat in a 21-storey block close to where his aunt lived. In the flat were a mother and her four-year-old son.

The fire had started at 1 p.m. in a bedroom and had spread at such pace that the family's escape route was quickly sealed off. With flames licking up the walls, the mother weaved her way through the smoky flat and carried her son out on to the balcony.

Seeing the fire, a crowd soon gathered below. Bill McGowan joined them. The mother was shouting to those on the ground: 'Catch my boy, we're jumping.' Fire crews arrived, their progress having been hampered by bollards and fences which had been erected for tenants' security. The fire was growing more menacing by the second. The woman feared that she and her son would be roasted alive. The crowd urged her to jump but a fire officer told her to stay where she was – his men would be able to rescue her in a matter of seconds.

Then, according to some witnesses, the woman tried to swing her son down on to the balcony below, but she couldn't quite make it. Suddenly the flames blew out the kitchen window of her flat and the shock made her lose her grip. The boy plunged 60 feet towards the ground, only for Bill McGowan to leap forward and break his fall. The boy escaped with nothing worse than a broken leg. Seconds later, his mother too fell to the ground but missed a blanket being held by neighbours and was rushed to hospital, having sustained two broken legs and head injuries.

Mr McGowan, who chipped his wrist bone and badly bruised his back in making the rescue, said modestly: 'When I saw the kid fall, I just lunged forward with another bloke. He didn't catch him and the toddler fell on to me. Anyone would have done the same given the situation. I would challenge anyone to sit back and do nothing when a young boy is hurtling towards you like that.'

A doctor at the London Hospital, Whitechapel, where the boy and his mother were taken for treatment, was glowing in his praise of

Bill's efforts. 'If it wasn't for this guy, who knows what would have happened to the boy. He broke his fall when he was dropping at high speed. We think he's wonderful.'

A neighbour added: 'I was watching from my kitchen window and I saw smoke billowing from the flat and the mother standing on the balcony. She was holding her son out and people were saying "Let him go" and were encouraging her to jump. When she let go of him, the youngster grabbed her foot for about ten seconds and he then dropped into the arms of the man below. The impact of the falling child obviously hurt the man because he fell to the floor. He deserves a medal.'

Some residents expressed their anger that the Fire Brigade did not arrive earlier but in fact they turned up within four and a half minutes of receiving the emergency call – and that was allowing for the obstructions to their route. The reason they were not there sooner was because, in the commotion, nobody had actually dialled 999. All of the residents had left it to someone else. A Fire Service spokesperson confirmed: 'Many people assume the Fire Brigade have been alerted when in fact no one has called. Sadly it's a common problem.'

7 Rail Crashes

Derailed by a Cow

Falkirk civil servant David Wallace used to catch the 17.30 rush-hour Edinburgh–Glasgow train two or three times a week. In company with 300 other passengers, it formed his regular journey home from his Edinburgh workplace.

Without fail, he always caught it on a Monday. But on Monday 30 July 1984, 31-year-old Mr Wallace took the afternoon off work to caddy in a charity golf marathon at Larbert and so was nowhere to be seen when the 17.30 pulled out of Edinburgh's Waverley Station. As events turned out, his date with the golf course probably saved his life.

The line linking Scotland's two major cities is understandably the country's busiest. For much of the first part of the journey from Edinburgh, notably the section approaching Falkirk, the track bisects farmland. This had created the occasional problem in the past. In the five years leading up to 1984, there had been two reported instances of cattle straying on to the track.

That evening there was a third. The driver of the 17.15 Glasgow to Edinburgh train saw a cow wandering on the track west of Polmont Station and, accordingly, his assistant informed station staff at Polmont. But before anyone could act on the sighting, the cow had claimed the lives of thirteen people and injured another 44 in Britain's worst rail crash for seventeen years.

The 17.30 six-coach train from Edinburgh, powered by a locomotive from the rear, was packed as usual that evening. The front two carriages were particularly popular with Glasgow commuters, hoping for a swift exit at Glasgow's Queen Street Station. Similarly, Falkirk commuters usually preferred to sit at the rear of the train so that they could alight quickly at their station. At 5.55 p.m., it was travelling at 85 mph as it entered a remote stretch of track about a mile and a half west of Polmont Station. The line was bordered by woodland to one side and farmland to the other. As the train went round a curve, the driver suddenly spotted a cow on the track ahead. He slammed on the emergency brakes but had no chance of stopping in time. The collision was devastating. The cow, weighing between 700 and 1000 lbs, was hurled into space, the impact forcing the leading coach to leave the rails, rear into the air and career along the track for several hundred yards before somersaulting into an embankment where it came to rest on its side with its roof caved in. The second coach also slid along out of control, tearing up the track and demolishing 100 feet of stone wall at the top of a steep embankment before embedding itself in the second-last coach. A fourth carriage was pushed over by the concertina effect with the result that only two of the six coaches, plus the 100-ton power unit, remained upright.

As the train began to veer off the track, passengers held on to whatever they could, anything to prevent them being hurled around the carriage or discarded through windows and doors. One survivor said he braced himself against a table but the force of the crash threw him to the other side of the coach. Another vividly remembered thinking that he would never see his four-year-old daughter again. At that very moment, she was waiting at home for daddy to get in from work. He would never see her grow up. He could feel the tears welling up as the train reeled from side to side. Two hours later, he was at home with his little girl, bruised and shaken but alive.

Meanwhile, a crowded Edinburgh-bound train was approaching the same section of track from the opposite direction at 45 mph. Suddenly up ahead, the driver spotted the twisted, crushed carriages blocking both lines. Horrified, he made an emergency stop and managed to pull up in time before he could add to the carnage. By a stroke of good fortune, the train from Glasgow was running a minute late that evening. Usually the two trains passed at the precise location where the derailment had occurred.

The scene at the crash was one of bloodshed and panic. Passenger June Robinson, a mother of two, described the moments leading up to it. 'The train started to shudder and shake from side to side. People screamed: "We're going to crash." Someone shouted to me to get under the table. I did and just waited for the train to stop moving. It seemed to take ages to stop. When the train halted, there was pure panic. Everyone was screaming because we were worried that the coach would catch fire. To make matters worse, it started filling up with what seemed at the time like black smoke. Luckily, it turned out to be nothing more than dust.'

Those who could walk unaided scrambled out of the coaches as quickly as they could. The alarm was raised by one of the passengers, 24-year-old Ramsay Shields. He had been asleep at the moment of impact. 'I felt a bump and then the whole train shuddered as it left the track and ran along the sleepers. People were yelling: "Keep your head down!" When everything had stopped, I jumped from the train and ran off to seek help. But we were in the middle of nowhere and I had to run over half a mile across fields to the nearest houses.'

Emergency crews were on the scene within ten minutes. As word of the crash spread around the locality, dozens of children dropped whatever they were doing and cycled off to the accident spot. Besides being inquisitive, they wanted to help, and the trail of bicycles acted as signposts for the rescue teams. Adults too raced to the trackside and helped pull passengers from the wreckage, as did those who were not too seriously injured.

Herbert Robinson was travelling in the rear carriage. 'It was just a normal Monday evening journey until I heard this terrible crash. As the train stopped, I jumped out and ran to the front. It was carnage – there were people with terrible injuries. The carriages were like dominoes. We pulled free as many people as we could but some were clearly dead. And others had severed limbs.'

Soon there were 40 firefighters in attendance, from Falkirk, Bo'ness, Larbert and Stirling. Five appliances and two special rescue vehicles were sent out. There was dust, bricks and clothing scattered everywhere. Around the wreckage lay the familiar blue British Rail cushions, stained with blood. Most of the dead and injured were in the front two coaches. The front coach had been torn open and many of the passengers were in a bad way. Amazingly, the driver – whose control cabin was at the very front of the train – survived, although he was taken to hospital with a fractured skull.

Fire crews used hydraulic cutting gear to free those trapped and crushed in the maze of metal. As always in major disasters, priority was given to those who were still alive. The dead were laid out beneath trees on the embankment a few yards from the wreckage, the bodies covered by white blankets. The body of the cow was found further along the line.

Many of the injured were taken to the nearby Answer public house for treatment. The landlord allowed the function suite to be used as an emergency centre. The first casualties were ferried by a fleet of eight ambulances to hospitals in Falkirk and Stirling within 30 minutes of the accident. For some ambulancemen, it brought back painful memories of the previous year when three railway workers died after being hit by a train just a few miles away on the same line.

When the debris was finally cleared and the line reopened, there was much speculation as to how the cow had managed to get on to the track in the first place. People were blamed for removing the fencing at the accident spot, the site of a former level crossing, in order to take a short cut across the track. The fence was repeatedly vandalised. Two days after the crash, the damaged fencing was repaired but a day later it had been pulled down again.

Accident investigators heard that the driver of the Edinburgh train would have seen the cow at a maximum of 513 yards away but, at that speed, he would have needed a braking distance of 1030 yards. There was nothing he could have done to avert the crash. The real concern was how a 300-ton train could be derailed by one stray cow. Following the Falkirk accident, trains in Scotland were fitted with cow-catchers, capable of withstanding a 100 mph collision with a 2000 lb cow.

That evening, David Wallace returned home from golf to hear the news. Deep shock was mingled with immense relief that he had missed the train of death. 'I was absolutely stunned,' he said later. 'I couldn't believe how lucky I had been taking the afternoon off. I normally stand between the front and second carriages and these were the worst affected in the crash. It was frightening to think I would have been on them.

'I travelled home on the 17.30 from Edinburgh the day after the crash and the front coach was empty . . .'

* * *

In June 1994, firefighters were asked to free a man in handcuffs who had managed to get his head wedged under his arm. The man had been arrested following a domestic incident at a house in Kidderminster, but on the way to the police station he put his hands over his head and got well and truly stuck.

* * *

The Salford Oil Train Blaze

As it pulled out of Lime Street Station on the morning of Tuesday 4 December 1984, the 10.05 Liverpool to Scarborough InterCity express was packed with over 300 passengers. Some were only going as far as Manchester, while others were venturing further afield, right across to the east coast.

For Doreen Webster, it was an emotional journey. She was on the way to Scarborough to meet her long-lost sister Sylvia whom she had not seen since they were separated for adoption over 40 years earlier. Ever since she had managed to make contact again after all these years, Doreen had been counting the days to their reunion. Now at last it had arrived and Doreen was heading east with her suitcase and her memories.

The express was not the only train leaving Merseyside bound for Yorkshire that morning. Up ahead, a fifteen-wagon tanker train carrying 30,000 gallons of gas oil was making painfully slow progress on its journey between Stanlow Refinery and Leeds.

By 10.40 a.m., it had crawled as far as Salford in Greater Manchester. Encountering a red signal, the driver stopped the train, jumped down from his cab and called the signal box on the trackside phone for instructions. He was told that it was safe to proceed and so he returned to his cab and began to move off. He had reached no more than 5 mph when he felt an almighty crash from behind. The InterCity, travelling at between 45 and 50 mph, had smashed into the back of the tanker train.

The effect was immediate. The collision ruptured three of the goods train's load of oil-filled tanks and the escaping fuel ignited, causing a huge explosion and sending a ball of flame racing across the adjacent M602 motorway. The engine and front two coaches of the passenger train were engulfed in flames.

Passengers jumped out and ran for cover. One, Kay Brady, said: 'There were screams, and panic broke out in seconds. Nobody could believe what was happening. The crash had sent me tumbling to the floor and my daughter was trying to lift me up so we could get out. Our coach was surrounded by flames – it was orange inside.'

Drivers on the motorway saw a huge ball of fire shoot into the air and thick black smoke heading towards them. As they slowed down, burning debris caused by the explosion showered down upon them. Instinctively, they tried to dodge the wreckage, weaving in and out, but this merely served to cause a succession of minor collisions. Showing commendable initiative, a lorry driver positioned his articulated trailer across the carriageways to prevent any more vehicles going towards the burning coaches.

The first policeman at the crash site was young Constable Michael

Lowe who bravely searched the carriages for survivors when the train was still alight. However, he was unable to get into the front two coaches because of the fierce flames. Christine Grimshaw, a nursing sister at a local hospital, lived nearby and when she heard a loud bang, she immediately went to investigate. Scrambling down a bank, she succeeded in carrying an injured man to safety. Another local resident who raced to the trackside was Brenda James. She crawled under the train to rescue a boy who had hurt his head.

One passenger described the scene in the front two coaches. 'We were bowling along quite nicely and then I felt the brakes go on. The next thing there was a loud bang like a clap of thunder. People were knocked about quite badly. There was just no warning that anything was going to happen. An old lady opposite me hit her head on the table, causing a nasty gash above her eye. I lent her my handkerchief to stop the bleeding from the wound. I was shaken up but otherwise I thought I was OK. Then when I tried to stand up to help the lady towards the exit door, my legs just gave way. By now, we could see flames shooting along the outside. I began to panic. I thought I wasn't going to get out in time. It took me three attempts to get to my feet, but I managed to move along the aisle by grabbing hold of the tops of the seats. I was steering the lady along in front of me. There was a bit of jostling but the evacuation was fairly orderly. Most people were sensible. Eventually we got to the door and stumbled out into the fresh air. As I looked back, I could see other passengers trying to help out those who were more seriously injured. One guy looked a real mess. His face and hands were covered in blood.'

British Rail declared it a disaster area and part of the motorway was closed so that 25 fire appliances could get to the scene. There was good and bad news for the firefighters. The good news was that the tanks had fallen in the opposite direction to the motorway. One, with a laden weight of 100 tons, landed on top of the engine of the passenger train while another lay on its side nearby. But if they had slipped down on to the congested motorway, the consequences could have been catastrophic. The bad news was that the incident had occurred in a built-up area and there was a high risk of further explosion. So the decision was taken to evacuate 400 residents from their homes.

The first thing the firefighters wanted to know was what was in the tanks. That would determine how they fought the fire. The warning markers on the wagons were labelled petroleum, and it was only after twenty minutes that British Rail informed fire officers that the contents were in fact gas oil. In the event, it made little difference to the way in which they tackled this particular blaze.

The order was for foam, foam and yet more foam. By 11.45 a.m., the flames had been smothered by gallons of foam although crews (there were 150 firefighters from four counties present at the height of the blaze) continued to spray foam on to the wreckage for several hours longer. Indeed it was not until mid-afternoon that the danger of further explosions finally passed.

The engine and the front coaches of the InterCity train were completely burnt out. There were two fatalities on the day – the driver of the InterCity who was killed instantly, and one passenger – but a third person was to die from injuries a month later. A total of 68 people were treated in hospital for varying degrees of injuries.

The report into the accident heard that the driver of the express only applied his brakes when he was a mere 180 yards from the tanker train. He was said to have gone through a caution signal as well as a red danger signal at Eccles Station seconds before the crash. The report suggested that he may have missed the two warning signals because his body had not adapted to day working after a period on nightshift.

Doreen Webster was not among the seriously injured. Although the day proved something of an anti-climax for her because she was unable to complete her journey, she was grateful to be alive. And it was merely a postponement. The following day she finally made it to Scarborough for a tearful reunion with her sister. For at least one person, the Salford train crash had a happy ending.

* * *

In 1995, West Midlands firefighters were called out to an industrial estate at Bilston to free a worker whose arm was trapped in a machine for making corrugated cardboard.

'When we arrived, we found that he had been pulled between two large rollers, both about six inches in diameter and made of hardened steel. He was in them right up to his elbow and was obviously in considerable discomfort.

'We couldn't dismantle the machine so instead we brought in four sets of hydraulic jacks to force the rollers apart. After about an hour, the man was able to pull his arm clear.'

* * *

Tragedy at the Level Crossing

The branch line connecting Hull with the seaside resort of Bridlington is one of the quietest in England. Back in 1986, there were just fifteen trains a day on the route in each direction with an extra five on Saturdays when the people of Hull wanted to head off to the coast for the day or the residents of Bridlington and Beverley chose to do some shopping. It is also a line peppered with unmanned level crossings on which there are no gates or barriers, just automatically operated flashing red lights to warn motorists of an impending train.

Such crossings were viewed with deep mistrust by some locals who catalogued a series of 'near misses' over the years. They predicted that one day there would be a terrible accident. Their worst fears were realised on the morning of Saturday 26 July 1986.

Lockington is a small village, some five miles north of Beverley and twelve miles north of Hull. Three-quarters of a mile east of the village, a narrow country lane crosses the railway line at Lockington level crossing. It is a remote spot. The lane itself is exceptionally quiet, leading only to the tiny community of Aike near the River Hull.

In summer, the 9.33 a.m. service from Bridlington to Hull was a popular one with the resort's departing holidaymakers, particularly those who wished to make an early start to their long journey home. Many travelled up from the Midlands or the South and would change at Hull for trains to their respective destinations.

That morning, the four-coach train was carrying 120 passengers – holidaymakers and shoppers, young and old – and was travelling at the permitted speed of 70 mph as it approached Lockington crossing. No more than 250 yards ahead, the train driver saw a small blue van on the crossing. He immediately applied the brakes but the effect was minimal over such a short distance. The train struck the van dead centre, sweeping it off the crossing and tearing it into five pieces. The train careered on out of control for 150 yards before jumping the rails. The front coach, housing the diesel unit, suddenly reared up into the air and the train jackknifed backwards on itself. Passengers were flung clear, only to be crushed to death as the leading coach came crashing down to earth on top of them and then rolled down a 20 foot embankment. The front coach eventually came to rest in a bean field adjoining the badly buckled track. The second and third coaches were also derailed. The van lay at the side of the track, an unrecognisable heap of mangled metal.

Nineteen-year-old Ian Simpson from Driffield was a passenger in the second coach. 'The train started to career to the left and then suddenly it was on its side. The windows had blown through and two of the other three people in my compartment had been sucked underneath the train. A girl flew past me and knocked her head on the seat. She just lay there unconscious.'

People slowly came to their senses and started hauling themselves and others from the wreckage. Everywhere, there was blood and glass. The world seemed to have turned upside down. A father was calling out for his son. They had been sitting separately so that the boy could see out of the window.

'Have you seen my boy? Have you seen my boy?' asked the anxious father.

Dazed passengers shook their heads. He forged on down the carriage, blood seeping from a head wound of his own.

'There was a boy sitting over there,' said a middle-aged man.

There was no sign. The father's heart sank. Then he heard a moaning sound from under a seat on the opposite side of the carriage. It was his son. The crash had catapulted him across the coach. After checking that he was all right, the father pulled the boy clear. Happily, he had nothing more serious than a sore head.

As passengers staggered out of open doors, the train's guard, Peter Sturdy, realised that a train was due in the opposite direction any moment. He ran along the track. Then he saw a train approaching. He waved his arms frantically, imploring the driver to stop. As the train went past him, he breathed a sigh of relief as he heard the brakes go on. The train stopped just 200 yards from where one of the derailed carriages was blocking the line.

Len Robinson was on his way to Hull for a pre-season football match. He managed to scramble clear of the wreckage and then, when he realised the train was not about to explode, he went back to help others. 'People were sobbing and screaming,' he recalled, 'while others were just sitting there unable to take it all in. There was a little boy covered in ballast from the track, and myself and another passenger used our hands to dig him out.'

Christine Beckett had to shield her thirteen-month-old son Craig from flying glass. 'As I climbed out, I saw a dead boy aged about eighteen lying by the side of the track. It was a nightmare. It was a wonder anyone was left alive.'

Firefighters wrestled with cutting equipment to free the trapped. As the injured were rescued, they were taken by ambulance to Hull

Royal Infirmary. In the course of the operation, two firemen themselves had to be treated for cuts. Throughout the day, they searched for bodies. Most of those killed had been travelling in the overturned front coach and there was a fear that there might be more bodies pinned beneath it. So that night, a mobile army crane was brought in to lift the coach clear and check that there were no further casualties.

Incredibly, the van driver – a local cattle dealer – survived the smash but his ten-year-old foster son, who was a passenger in the van at the time, was one of nine who died at Lockington. Among the dead were three members of the same family. A year-old baby escaped unhurt but its mother was killed. Thirty-nine people were treated in hospital for injuries.

It was a mystery how the van came to be on Lockington crossing that morning. British Rail reported that the warning lights were working normally and that, at 70 mph, the train would have activated them some 1280 yards from the crossing. One thing is certain – the tragedy did nothing to ease local suspicions about unmanned level crossings.

*　　*　　*

In 1994, Cornwall firefighters were called out to a nursing home to rescue a man impaled on a chair spring. The elderly gentleman, a resident at the home, had been sitting on the chair when the spring broke through the upholstery and wedged itself up his back passage. The staff tried everything to free him but in the end had to call out the Fire Service. Not surprisingly, the man was in considerable pain but, within five minutes of their arrival, the crew had severed the spring with a pair of bolt-cutters and the patient was on his way to hospital.

*　　*　　*

Commuter Carnage

Sunrise was still the best part of two hours away on that crisp December morning when the bleary-eyed passengers arrived at Bournemouth Station ready to catch the 6.30 a.m. express to London Waterloo. It was a journey which few relished but it was the price they had to pay for choosing to live in rural Dorset, some 100 miles from their London workplaces. The long trek was particularly unwelcome on a winter's Monday morning such as this. After a relaxing weekend, there was an enormous temptation to ignore the shrill tones of the alarm, snuggle back under the duvet and stay in bed for another hour or two.

As the travellers made their way across the car park towards the station entrance, most of the seaside town was still asleep. The silence was broken only by the occasional whirring of a passing milk float, the squeaking of a platform trolley and the chattering of station staff. Sun, sand and Russ Abbot summer seasons seemed a long way away.

Soon, on that morning of 12 December 1988, the plush express (originally the 6.14 a.m. from Poole) was gliding sleekly out of the station and heading towards Southampton, Brockenhurst and Winchester where it would pick up further loads of hardened rail travellers. Those lucky enough to get seats tried to catch up on the hour's sleep they had been denied or buried their heads in a book or newspaper. Others made their way along to the second carriage, the buffet car, to partake of a bacon roll and a cup of coffee – a breakfast they would much rather have had at home. As the train hurtled through Hampshire, cutting a swathe through the south of England on its way to the capital, the number of passengers on board had risen to 468. It was standing room only in all but the first-class coaches. Passengers unable to find a seat or a niche in the buffet resorted to standing in the aisles between carriages with little more to do than gaze out into the darkness.

It was a similar story in the Hampshire commuter town of Basingstoke. The 7.18 train from Basingstoke to Waterloo was a popular one with London office workers and that morning the twelve coaches were crammed with 906 passengers. Among those sitting in the smoking compartment in the rear carriage were a group of four who travelled up together each weekday – Ron Arlette, Helen Briant, Paddy Viney and Phil Waye. They expected to be at their desks around nine o'clock. None had any idea of the drama and tragedy that lay around the corner.

Ahead in London, schoolboy Terry Stoppani was celebrating his twelfth birthday. In his uniform of dark blue blazer, grey trousers and white shirt, he walked to Emanuel School, Wandsworth, shortly after eight o'clock, with his friends Joe Naylor and Peter Pantechi. Trains were part of everyday life for pupils at the school which overlooked the main Bournemouth to Waterloo line a quarter of a mile south of

Clapham Junction, Europe's busiest railway junction. Some 2200 trains pass through Clapham Junction every day. So the thunder of trains through the cutting was a familiar sound to Terry and his pals.

As the day finally dawned to reveal a bright sunny day, the two trains powered towards Clapham Junction. They were on the same line, with the Basingstoke train immediately ahead of the Bournemouth express which was running slightly late. On board both trains, it was business as usual. Passengers began to rouse themselves from their slumbers in preparation for their arrival at Waterloo in approximately ten minutes.

The Basingstoke train was approaching a green light at signal WF47 just north of Battersea Rise road bridge when the signal abruptly turned red. The driver, 49-year-old Alexander McClymont, rightly stopped his train to report that he had run a red light. He clambered down from his cab and used the trackside telephone to get in touch with the signallers in order to find out what the problem was. While he was talking, he suddenly heard a train in the distance. A split second later, before he had any time to react, driver McClymont heard a tremendous bang and the whole of his train shot forward. He immediately asked the people on the other end of the trackside phone to call the emergency services and then he dashed to the back of his train, where the impact had been, to see what he could do to help.

He could scarcely have been prepared for the sight which greeted him. Travelling at 60 mph, the Bournemouth express had ploughed into the back of the stationary Basingstoke train at 8.13 a.m. John Rolls, the driver of the express, had faced only green or amber lights on the signals but as he took a bend, he saw, to his horror, that there was a train stopped on the line 300 yards ahead. At once, he slammed on the emergency brakes but knew it was a hopeless cause. There simply wasn't enough time for the brakes to take effect. Realising there was nothing he could do to avoid a collision, he fled from his cab in a last, desperate act of self-preservation – and also to warn his passengers. It was too late for Mr Rolls and 34 other commuters.

The rear two coaches of the Basingstoke train were hurled into the air and forced diagonally 15 yards up a steep embankment to the left of the track. The impact sent the crumpled front coaches of the express veering off to the right across the southbound track. The front part of the express was reduced to an unrecognisable tangle of metal. Many inside died instantly. Others, thrown clear of the wreckage, were left with an instant decision – whether to go left and try and escape up the steep grassy bank, beneath which was a sheer concrete incline, or go right across the parallel-running track. Tragically, some chose the second option, only to be killed, by a cruel twist of fate, under the wheels of an empty third train, coming in the opposite direction seconds after the crash. As this train, which was on its way from Waterloo to Haslemere, hit the mangled remains of the express, it too was derailed. The guard on the empty train had the presence of mind to run down the line and warn an approaching fourth train which managed to pull up just 20 yards short of the crash. Otherwise, the disaster could have been even worse.

Terry Stoppani and his friends were halted in their tracks by the sound of the collision. 'It was a huge bang,' he recalled later, 'like a bomb exploding. I saw all parts of the train and three or four people flying into the air. We jumped over the railings, scrambled down the embankment and climbed into the train through a broken window. The first thing I saw was a pair of jeans with shoes on. There was no top half of the body. Some people were trapped beneath the train. Inside, people were screaming and too frightened to talk. We started pulling people out through the window as best as we could, sometimes by the arms, sometimes by the legs.'

The pupils were quickly joined by one of their teachers, John Wybrowe, who leapt out of his car, scaled a 6 foot chain-link fence, sprinted down the embankment and then clambered across railway lines which were still electrified. With the emergency services on their way, he organised his pupils into a sort of Kids' Army. They were able to crawl through tiny gaps in the wreckage to reach passengers. Local residents and passers-by who had heard the crash also lent a hand and helped lead scores of dazed passengers to safety up the embankment.

The first London Fire Brigade appliances were sent out at 8.17 and, despite having to battle their way through the statutory London rush-hour traffic, were at the crash site in less than five minutes. A police helicopter, containing two doctors and medical supplies, was flown over from its control point on the M11 to beat the traffic. Twenty-eight ambulances took the ground route to the scene, followed by eleven back-up vehicles. St George's Hospital, Tooting, two miles from the crash location, was prepared in readiness to receive casualties. Little did they know that one of their medical staff was already at the scene. Mr Paul Calvert, a consultant orthopaedic surgeon, had been travelling on one of the trains involved in the crash and put his expertise to use in helping to treat and free injured passengers.

In the back of the Basingstoke train, the four commuter friends were in a state of shock. Helen Briant was semi-conscious. She could see Phil Waye lying in the luggage rack with blood pouring from a head wound. Through the haze she remembered thinking he looked quite peaceful there. She heard the reassuring voice of Ron Arlette saying, 'Helen, there's been a bit of an accident.' She felt bitterly cold and Ron lent her his overcoat. She promptly bled all over it. She could smell the mud which was pressed against the window pane behind her head but, above all, knowing that their train had been derailed, she was terrified that another train would hit them. She did not dare to voice her feelings for fear of upsetting the others.

She later told *The Sunday Times*: 'It was dark because the angle of the train blocked out the light. I couldn't breathe. That was the worst thing. I passed out and when I woke up I realised that I was being crushed, literally, by people. It took me ages to get the words out: "Could someone please move? I can't breathe." Someone said: "We're trying to." Then I don't remember any more.'

Phil Waye had put his teeth through his mouth. He kept thinking of the Zeebrugge disaster and knew that he had to keep awake. He dare not risk drifting into a sleep.

Paddy Viney had landed on top of Ron Arlette. She was determined not to lose control even though she was inwardly shaking. She demanded to know where her make-up bag was. She began searching around for it and put her lipstick on.

Then out of the blue she asked: 'Do you think this is the worst rail disaster ever?'

Stunned, Ron Arlette answered: 'I'll just dangle my head out of the window and ask someone!'

Meanwhile, people were wandering around in a state of shock, unable to take in the enormity of what had happened. Some worried about how they were going to get to work on time, others were just grateful to be in one piece.

Much of the wreckage, crushed and buckled, was barely recognisable as having been part of a train just a few minutes earlier. Five carriages had been flung over on to their sides, their roofs peeled away as if by a giant tin opener. On top of one carriage was a pushchair.

People had been flung 20 feet through the air. Bodies were strewn everywhere. Witnesses described seeing dismembered passengers scattered like rag dolls in the tangle of metalwork. A rescue worker said:

'I saw one man with his leg half off and another passenger, I think it was a woman, whose mouth just wasn't there.'

The first thing one passenger knew of the crash was when he woke up to find himself on the track. He had been asleep and had been hurled through a window. It was an escape bordering on the miraculous.

The majority of the dead and seriously injured were in the front two coaches of the Bournemouth express. There were approximately 70 people travelling in the front carriage at the time of the crash. Among the bodies found there was that of driver Rolls. The buffet coach had taken the brunt of the impact. Those who survived climbed to their feet, looked over the buffet counter and saw that the other side of the carriage had vanished. Now the counter protruded from the debris at a crazy angle.

One of those sitting in the ill-fated buffet car described how she was suddenly plucked from her seat, twisted round and hurled backwards through the air by the impact. 'It seemed to go on for ages, then all of a sudden there was a deathly hush. I opened my eyes and saw blue sky – the roof was peeled back in a corkscrew, like a can of baked beans.' The woman, who suffered a fractured spine in the crash, had her legs pinned down by steel bars. At her feet was a girl who later died.

Among the mutilated bodies, many passengers were trapped in or beneath the twisted coaches. Some of the worst injured were those who had been standing because they were violently tossed around inside the somersaulting carriages. The lucky ones had managed to escape through broken windows or through sides of carriages which had been ripped open. Many of the passengers on the Basingstoke train had climbed across carriage roofs to the embankment.

The two trains had telescoped into each other. The crash caused the back wheels of the Basingstoke train to fall off, smashing through a window on the Bournemouth express where they severed a man in half. The Bournemouth train's own wheels smashed upward through the floor and the roof fell in. A man standing in the gap between the first and second carriages was crushed to death. Those sitting in the rear of the Basingstoke train recounted how the lights went out, all the seats collapsed and the walls caved in. 'Everything had been perfectly normal,' said one. 'Then we stopped. Suddenly there was an almighty bang, the carriage reared into the air and we were all sent flying over and over.'

Greg Ford, a bank clerk from Poole, was travelling in the front coach of the Bournemouth train. 'A lot of people in the carriage had dozed off,' he recalled. 'I myself was half asleep. Then suddenly there was a big bang. People were thrown all over the place and the luggage came crashing down on us from the racks. I picked myself up and went to help those who were injured. When I got up, I found that I was lying on somebody. I saw there were a couple of people dead on the other side of the carriage.'

John O'Sullivan was a passenger in the same train. 'All hell was let loose,' he said. 'All of the doors were ripped off and there was glass and blood everywhere. It was a horrific scene but strangely there was no real panic. People all around me were badly injured but apart from some initial screams and some pathetic sobbing, there was an eerie silence for a few minutes.'

One poor woman was pinned to her seat by a shaft of metal through her chest.

Mark Barthel had boarded the express at Southampton. With a policeman's truncheon serving as a makeshift splint on his broken arm, he told reporters: 'There was absolute carnage. The man opposite me was trapped by his head and we had to climb over him to get him out and find help. I was sitting in the back of the front carriage and one man in front of me and one behind were both killed. I guess I was just lucky.'

The first problem facing the rescue teams was one of access. The embankment leading up to the road was covered in trees and bushes, making it almost impossible for paramedics to get stretchers to and from the scene and for passengers who had escaped relatively un-scathed to make their way clear of the wreckage. So firefighters used electric saws to rip away large sections of the iron railings at the top and to slice away the shrubbery and cut three pathways down the bank. They then hacked out steps into the paths.

Soon there were fifteen appliances and over 150 firefighters in attendance from stations right across London. They set about freeing the trapped passengers, cutting through the roof of one carriage to release 50 people. In many places, metal and flesh were hideously intertwined. The majority of the injured had fractures or crushed bones and were pinned down by lumps of metal. One victim was found beneath a heavy coupling bogey. Before the casualties could be cut free with acetylene torches and saws, some needed medical treatment. Doctors and nurses set up lines of intravenous drips to passengers trapped beneath the wreckage and administered pain-killing drugs. Firefighters used hydraulic pumps to jack up the fallen carriages in order to create sufficient space for their fellow rescue workers to crawl in and tend to the wounded. It was a delicate operation.

For many, help was immaterial. Vijith Randeniya, a Sub Officer at Lambeth Fire Station, recounted: 'I carried out four people. They were all dead. Their injuries were horrific. I saw other victims in there – their condition was indescribable. When I first got there, the scene was pretty chaotic. Survivors were wandering around dazed and very shaken. As you got closer to the scene of the impact, it became more harrowing. One of the trains had opened up like a tin. I know it sounds like a cliché, but we were all able to get in there and get on with it. Training we might have hoped we would never need to use came into play immediately.'

Over the next four hours, crews fought to free the injured. Some could only be removed after the amputation of limbs. A young woman was found with her hand hanging by a thread. It had to be amputated up to the wrist.

Ambulanceman Bob Dobson was working tirelessly to free a man from the wreckage. 'I was in such a confined space that all I could see were his legs. One was so badly crushed that it probably had to be amputated. All the while the man was conscious and suffering great agony. He was crushed in among other passengers so badly that it was impossible to work out whose limbs were whose. When he was eventually freed, we found four more beneath him.

'In one case there was just a torso from which the head, arms, waist and legs had been severed. We knew there was nothing we could do for a great many so we just concentrated on those still breathing.'

Police Constable Fraser Shaw discovered three people, two of whom were dead. He came across one man as he crawled beneath the wreckage of two coaches which had been crushed together. 'Even the man we found alive had to have both legs amputated,' he said. 'While we were in there, we did not see one complete body.'

The search for survivors was long and dangerous. Steel cables had to be laid over parts of the wreckage to prevent it toppling on to firefighters working below. In the darkest corners where the mass of metal seemed impenetrable, thermal image cameras were used to detect any signs of life. All the while, crews climbed ladders to get on to the roofs of those coaches which were still upright and shared jokes with passengers waiting patiently to be rescued. Jim McMillan,

Assistant Chief Officer of the London Fire Brigade, called the scene 'sheer bloody hell'.

A total of 484 passengers suffered some form of injury in the crash. Many of those who needed hospital treatment were taken to St George's, Tooting – 123 in the course of the morning. Emanuel School continued to help, looking after 120 victims, offering First Aid, tea, sandwiches and the use of telephones to tell relatives and workmates that they were OK. Remarkably, while providing emergency aid, the headmaster managed to keep the school going, taking many lessons himself. A nearby public house also opened its doors to help survivors and rescuers.

What turned out to be the last live casualty was brought out at 12.15 p.m. As television and radio bulletins carried details of the crash, worried families had been besieging railway stations for news of survivors. When passengers retraced their steps and headed home, there was many a tearful reunion at stations along the route.

Alas for all too many, there were no happy returns. Among the dead was Arthur Creech, an off-duty British Rail driver who had been asked to report for work in London on his rest day because of staff shortages. He was travelling up to town on the Bournemouth express.

The search for survivors went on into the night with rescue workers sifting through the wreckage under arc lights. It was a gruesome task, even for those used to picking up the pieces after a disaster. At one point, a paramedic reached down to wipe his hands on what appeared to be a piece of cloth. It turned out to be a severed foot and ankle. Rescuers had spent the afternoon filling a dozen plastic bags with unidentified human remains. As dusk fell, one firefighter changing shift revealed that he had just found a human head.

Slowly but surely, the line was cleared. Some carriages were able to be lifted back on to the tracks and towed away but the Bournemouth buffet car was way beyond repair and was taken apart to be scrapped. The last carriage of the Basingstoke train had to be lifted by two giant cranes and removed by road trailer. Scattered beside the track and among the carriages were all manner of poignant belongings – Christmas presents, shopping bags from a Guildford department store, smart briefcases and a filofax, its pages covered in blood.

Back at Bournemouth Station that evening, the rows of uncollected cars told their own story. Over the next few days, passengers on the 6.30 would note which familiar faces were suddenly no longer there – people who they didn't know by name but who were simply part of the early morning commuter club. Now they were missing . . . presumed dead.

The gang of four survived. Many others were less fortunate. One victim was eventually identified by his wedding ring. He had been in the front coach of the Bournemouth train. He always liked to sit there because it was nearest to the ticket barrier at Waterloo and saved him wasting valuable time queuing to get out.

The official report into the Clapham Junction rail crash established that it had been caused by faulty wiring work on the signals. For most of those passengers who had escaped serious injury, life gradually returned to normal. Many owed their survival not only to the sterling work of the emergency services but also to the pupils and staff of Emanuel School. Young Terry Stoppani said that his mum was terrified when she heard about the crash on the radio. 'If she'd known I was there, she wouldn't have let me go down near the carriages. And in all the dashing to and fro, I completely forgot that it was my birthday.'

* * *

A small boy in Whitstable, Kent, enjoyed nothing more than running around the kitchen with a saucepan on his head. Unfortunately, one day he chose a saucepan size too small and when he came to take it off, he found that it was stuck fast. His mother pulled and tugged furiously until she was weak with exhaustion. There was only one thing for it – she would have to call the Fire Brigade.

The intrepid firefighters took one look at the situation and prescribed washing-up liquid. The boy, whose initial excitement at seeing all these men in uniform had begun to give way to a certain apprehension, had to sit quietly while the sides of his head were coated in the green liquid. A twist here, a twist there, and eventually – after the best part of an hour – the recalcitrant saucepan was coaxed off the boy's head. Thereafter, saucepans were kept well out of his reach.

* * *

Red for Danger

Just twelve weeks after the Clapham Junction disaster, the nation was stunned by another major rail crash in Greater London, this time at

Purley, just nine miles south of Clapham. The casualties were not as heavy but this was only because the Purley crash happened on a quiet Saturday lunchtime rather than the busy morning rush hour. Had it taken place at a different time, Purley would have become every bit as synonymous with rail disaster as Clapham Junction.

Purley is an affluent suburb, situated a few miles north of the Surrey border. Indeed, most of the residents prefer to think of themselves as living in Surrey rather than the capital. It is populated with respectable, professional couples, some retired, who live in large houses with neat borders and splendidly manicured lawns. The railway line, leading from London Victoria to Gatwick Airport and Brighton, cuts through the heart of Purley. Backing on to it, just north of Purley Station, are the smart houses of Glenn Avenue and Whytecliffe Road.

Among the residents of Whytecliffe Road was 75-year-old retired police sergeant James Taylor. Like most of his neighbours, he was a keen gardener and spent a lot of his time in his greenhouse where he grew chrysanthemums. Shortly after 1.30 p.m. on Saturday 4 March 1989, he went out to his greenhouse to water his beloved flowers. He made sure each one had a good drink, pottered a little and then returned to the conservatory at the back of the house.

Suddenly, he heard an almighty crash. He turned round to see four railway carriages toppling down the 40 foot tree-lined embankment at the end of his garden. The front coach smashed into his greenhouse, where he had been standing just a few minutes earlier, reducing it to nothing. Mr Taylor was left open mouthed, reflecting that, in some respects, it was his lucky day.

There had been no hint of the drama to come when the 12.17 Littlehampton–Victoria express had pulled out of the genteel south-coast resort. Soon it was racing through Sussex and into Surrey. Heading in the same direction, but on the slow line, was the 12.50 stopping train from Horsham to Victoria. Some passengers were on their way to the theatre, others were going for an afternoon's shopping in the West End.

The Horsham train was running three minutes late when it stopped at Purley Station. As it pulled out of the station, it was switched from the slow to the fast line, a manoeuvre controlled from an automatic signal box near Crawley. At 1.39 p.m., the train was travelling at around 25 mph as the driver took it through the cross-over. It was about three coach-lengths on to the fast line when the driver felt a 'severe violent crash' from the rear of the train. The Littlehampton express, which should have stopped at the red signal at Purley Station, had instead roared through the station at 60 mph. When the driver of the express, Robert Morgan, saw the slow train move across to his track, he slammed on the brakes but he was travelling too fast to avoid clipping it. The impact forced six carriages of the express down the embankment. The front coach rolled through 180 degrees and went on to crush James Taylor's greenhouse. It was only prevented from wreaking further havoc by the fact that it came up against some immovable trees. The carriage finally came to rest just fifteen yards from his house, by the gate of his allotment.

After being rooted to the spot for a few moments, Mr Taylor quickly recovered from the unexpected invasion of his privacy and ran to fetch two ladders. He propped these up at either end of the upside-down carriage and began to open the doors. 'The guard was injured and lying in his guard room,' recalled Mr Taylor. 'He had blood all over him and he had lost his glasses. His chest appeared to be injured and he was complaining about pains in his ribs.'

Despite his injuries, the guard, Tony Squires, managed to scramble up the muddy embankment to warn other trains before going back down to help those who were more seriously hurt than himself. He later recalled being in the brake van when he saw the emergency brake light come on. 'The next minute we were bouncing along the track. Then we went over the bank and it was like autumn leaves tumbling, all falling about.'

Thankfully, the four-carriage Horsham train was not derailed. After feeling the impact, its driver immediately shut off the power and applied the brakes before climbing down on to the track to ascertain precisely what had happened. The driver of another train which was waiting at the signal outside the station when the crash occurred climbed down on the track to alert signalmen and then helped passengers to walk to Purley Station, ensuring that they stayed clear of the electric rail.

The alarm was raised by a neighbour who had been looking out of the kitchen window of her house when she saw the coaches plunging down the embankment into the garden next door. Mrs Rosemary Jetten of Glenn Avenue also witnessed the falling carriages. She said: 'I heard a loud bang and looked out of my back window. I saw a cloud of smoke and trees flying through the air and could see the train coming off the bank into my garden.'

Soon 30 fire appliances, 22 ambulances and four police helicopters were converging on Purley, ready to free and tend to the casualties. In the meantime, initial help was provided by local residents and passengers waiting at Purley Station who had watched aghast as the two trains collided.

One of the first on the scene was an off-duty police officer, James Taylor's son Andrew. 'It was absolute devastation,' he said. 'I saw the carriage upside-down in my father's garden and ran to have a look. There were about half a dozen injured people inside. One old lady had been very badly hurt and another girl was trapped in the luggage rack. All the neighbours came running up with blankets and ladders. The people inside the carriages who weren't too badly hurt were climbing out of windows and doors. I carried at least two injured people to safety myself. There was no screaming – everyone was very calm. Some people were just asking: "Can you come and help me please?" Others were saying: "I'm trapped, I'm trapped." '

Fourteen-year-old Kevin Sullivan had just missed the Horsham train. Seconds later, instead of cursing his luck, he was counting his blessings. He ran along the trackside to help and saw the driver of the express lying on the ground. 'He was conscious and just muttering to himself. He looked pretty bad and the carriage was a complete write-off.' A neighbour later found the driver staggering about in her garden and made sure that he received medical attention.

Passengers were lurching out of the carriages dripping in blood. Those in the centre of the Littlehampton train jumped out and slithered down the embankment. Survivors helped each other out while local residents brought chairs and blankets and made cups of tea. The area was scattered with people's coats, cast aside by the force of the crash. Other passengers were thrown through windows. One regained consciousness to find himself in a 4 foot gap under one of the carriages. A woman was pacing along the top of the embankment calling for her children. Beneath the debris, an elderly lady lay on her back. She was dead.

Alan Wilcox was travelling in the second-class half of the front carriage of the express to meet his wife and two children who were on their way down from Wales. He described the sensation after impact as 'like being in a cement mixer. We were bouncing off walls, the ceiling and the floor. I heard the brakes go on rapidly and sharply and also repeated bangs like a detonator. Then we just seemed to stop rolling. We seemed to slide along the track as if the brakes were locked. Then we hit something. I flew forward and hit the wall. Next we were off the track and down the embankment. When we stopped, I was wedged in a corner of the carriage, dazed, and bleeding from my head.'

A number of passengers ended up covered in branches from where the carriages of the express had slewed into the line of trees. Twenty-two-year-old Fiona Donnelly from Hove was thrown clear of her carriage and landed in a tree. She spoke of the moments after the collision. 'I just grabbed my seat and closed my eyes. I seemed to be thrown all over the place – it was like a rollercoaster ride that had gone wrong. The front carriage seemed to jump up and down. When the train stopped rolling down the embankment, I found that I was covered in glass. It was up my nose and in my head and my hands.'

Civil servant Peter Fawcett usually drove to work in London from his home in Wivelsfield Green, East Sussex. But he wanted to see whether the train was preferable to a two-and-a-half-hour drive and so that Saturday he boarded the Littlehampton express. It was his first rail journey in over twenty years. It left him with back injuries sustained after he had been catapulted through the air and pinned under the carriage door.

Derek Pearson was in the second carriage of the Littlehampton train with his wife Janet and two teenage daughters. 'We had just gone through Purley Station when we heard three bangs as if we were coming off the rails or had hit the platform. A couple of seconds later, we were falling. One of the guards came flying through the air from one end of the carriage to the other and landed on top of me. The carriage was tipping down the embankment. I was trapped where I landed and showered with glass. I thought I was finished . . .'

Amazingly, only five people were killed in the Purley crash although 87 passengers were injured. Two died at the scene of the crash, the remaining three in hospital. The dead included two pensioners from Hove. Fifteen people were trapped in the derailed express for around half an hour. While the Mayday Hospital, Croydon, was put on red alert, emergency crews used the houses along Glenn Avenue and Whytecliffe Road as through routes for ferrying the injured to waiting ambulances. The steep gradient of the embankment made access to the coaches particularly awkward and some rescue workers had to be pulled up by ropes. The overhanging trees also hindered the rescue process although helpful residents, notably James Taylor, had taken the step of sawing away branches which were blocking access to the carriages. There is no doubt that without the marvellous assistance of the people of Purley, fire and ambulance crews would have had a much tougher job and many passengers would have stayed trapped for considerably longer than they were.

The youngest casualty was four-year-old James Watson who insisted on reading *Thomas the Tank Engine* books in hospital!

Inside the carriages, fire crews worked tirelessly to free those trapped under the wreckage. Cutting equipment sliced through the metal, just inches away from human limbs, the patients constantly reassured with comforting words, supplemented in the more serious cases by pain-killers.

Those travelling in the Horsham train began to tell their side of the story. John Lawrence and his daughter Tanya were passengers in the crowded rear smoking carriage of the slow train. They had journeyed up from Redhill, planning to see the stage show *Starlight Express* as a leaving present for Tanya who was flying out to Lanzarote the following Thursday to begin a career in public relations. Tanya Lawrence said: 'The ironic thing was we were just talking about accidents and then there were bodies flying and glass everywhere. There was a couple sitting on the opposite side of the carriage. The woman just flew across and ended up unconscious on the floor. The husband finished up in my father's lap. He was covered in glass – there was glass sticking out of his eyes.'

Reza Estakhrian had boarded the Horsham train at Coulsdon to do some shopping in London. 'I felt our train judder and then I saw some of the derailed compartments of the express lying in gardens at least twenty feet beneath me. Some were on top of garden sheds and others were still in the trees. People down the embankment were crying and moaning and I heard someone who seemed to be the driver shouting: "Where's the guard? Where's the guard?"'

The emergency services spent the rest of the day clearing wreckage and debris. The carriages on the embankment were still in a precarious position and there was considerable concern that they might roll further down the embankment on to the houses below. As a precaution, families in thirteen nearby houses were sent to stay with friends or were put up in hotels at British Rail's expense. The carriages were uncoupled and a 300-ton crane was brought in the following day to lift them clear of the embankment. To accommodate the crane, a garage had to be demolished. In Glenn Road, householders looked out to see a newly lifted carriage standing upright on the tarmac where cars were normally parked.

The cause of the crash was found to be driver error. Robert Morgan, the driver of the express, subsequently pleaded guilty to two charges of manslaughter and was sentenced to eighteen months' imprisonment with twelve months suspended. The Appeal Court later reduced the custodial term to four months.

Deputy Assistant Chief Officer Brian Ash, the officer in charge of the Brigade operation, had also been at Clapham Junction. He was in no doubt that Purley could have been every bit as disastrous as its notorious predecessor. Speaking at the scene of the crash, he said: 'It was lucky that this didn't happen during the rush hour when the trains would have been packed. The degree of damage to the trains was the same as at Clapham.'

*   *   *

A 37-year-old man from Birtley, Tyne and Wear, drank so much celebrating a £786,000 pools win in October 1993 that he hardly felt a thing as he spent 30 minutes with his leg impaled on iron railings. The alcohol did, however, have the advantage of numbing the pain while firefighters fought to cut him free.

*   *   *

48 Hours after Purley . . .

The dust had barely settled at Purley when there was a third major train crash in Britain in the space of little over three months.

This latest dent to public confidence in the rail network occurred two days after Purley – 6 March 1989 – when two trains operating the same service but in different directions collided at a junction near Bellgrove Station in Glasgow. One of the drivers and a passenger were killed and 54 people injured as the front of an eastbound Milngavie–Springburn train mounted a westbound Springburn–Milngavie unit.

The head-on crash happened at 12.47 p.m., 300 yards east of Bellgrove Station in a deep cutting near a tunnel on the Glasgow North electric line. The 12.20 p.m. Milngavie–Springburn train had just left the station when it apparently ran on to the wrong line, crossing the points and moving directly into the path of the oncoming 12.39 Springburn–Milngavie train. Seconds before the collision, a signalman, who had seen an irregular movement on his display panel, attempted to warn the driver of the eastbound train by activating two detonators on the track, but it was too late to prevent the crash.

The trains were travelling at around 30 mph. The service from Milngavie careered over the top of the other train. Carriages toppled over and passengers were hurled about the compartments. Some who were comparatively unscathed scrambled clear of the wreckage across neighbouring lines and up the embankments. Many more stayed behind in order to tend to their fellow travellers-in-distress. Among the injured was a six-month-old baby.

Anthony McVeigh was standing at Bellgrove signal box when he heard the detonators explode. 'I saw the two trains. One seemed to be slowing down and there was an almighty crash. I ran along to see what I could do to help. When I got there, people in the carriages at the back were battering at the doors and windows with their hands. They were desperate to get out. I helped drag one old woman out. She was covered in blood. One of the guards was in a terrible mess too. His face was covered in blood but he did not seem to realise he had been hurt.'

The worst of the damage was to the front of the westbound train. Its driver was killed as was a passenger travelling in the second carriage. It was two hours before the latter was cut free.

Logistically, the emergency services had to overcome similar problems to those experienced at Clapham Junction. Here too they had to descend steep embankments to gain access to the coaches, making the removal of casualties on stretchers to waiting ambulances all the more time consuming. Rail crashes rarely seem to happen at convenient spots.

On the plus side, the Glasgow accident happened at a much quieter time of the day when the trains were not packed to capacity.

Strathclyde fire crews set about freeing the trapped passengers. 'It was pretty chaotic,' said one of the firefighters. 'There were people staggering out of doors with blood pouring down their faces. They seemed to think they were all right, but they could hardly stand. Inside was just a pile of metal. Everything was topsy-turvy. You'd make your way along the carriage, thinking it was empty, and then you'd hear a faint moan and you knew that somebody was stuck under that lot.'

The rescue teams began gently lifting off the rubble and debris. They had to be careful that, in moving one shaft of metal, they didn't cause another to fall on to the victim. As always, they maintained a constant dialogue with casualties, assuring them that freedom was only a matter of minutes away.

Some needed a lot of reassurance. The driver of the Milngavie–Springburn train was trapped for some two hours. Before he could be freed, he had to have part of his left leg amputated by surgeons. The last out was 80-year-old John McCulloch, a former British Rail engineering worker who had been sitting in the front carriage of the westbound train. He was trapped for nigh on four hours. 'I saw the accident coming,' he said later in hospital. 'I was just ten feet from the front of the first carriage. A bar came down right across my feet, but I felt no real pain. I was more worried because my right foot was trapped.'

As the emergency crews headed back to base, they must have hoped that the old saying about things coming in threes was true. For after this third big rail accident in the space of a few months, nobody wanted to see another.

* * *

In 1994, a Sunderland man had to be rescued by fire crews after using a manhole cover to smash a shop window then stepping back and falling down the hole!

* * *

One Foggy Morning

Jonathan Brett-Andrews had always been interested in trains. The 36-year-old from Caterham in Surrey was a genuine railway enthusiast and was able to combine his hobby with his work as a British Rail guard. His ambition was to be a driver and from time to time he would travel in the driver's cab, taking everything in, picking up first-hand experience. On the morning of Saturday 15 October 1994, his passion was to cost him his life.

That day, he was rostered as guard on the 8 a.m. train from Uckfield in Sussex to Oxted, Surrey. The Uckfield–Oxted line is one of those quiet little branch lines that time and Dr Beeching seemed to have forgotten. Linking affluent Home Counties villages, the ten-station shuttle line is at its busiest on rush-hour weekdays when it takes commuters to and from London. Otherwise, it mainly serves the villages and, because of its limited use, the service is principally hourly. The majority of the line is dual track but there is a four-mile stretch of single track, between Ashurst and Hever, approximately halfway along the line. In the middle of the section is Cowden Station. This stretch was reduced from double to single track in 1989, leading to complaints from local commuter groups who were worried about the possibility of a collision.

The early-morning train from Uckfield on a Saturday was rarely crowded, so Jonathan Brett-Andrews was not unduly overworked. This gave him the chance to ride in the cab with the driver even though his bosses had twice before warned him not to do so. The view from the cab was usually nice, the line cutting through some of the most pleasant countryside in the south of England. Not that there was much of a view that Saturday – long stretches of the line were shrouded in fog.

Autumn is generally a problem for our railways, forever plagued with leaves on the line. To the general public, it always seems that one errant oak leaf can bring the entire network grinding to a halt. Network South Central were taking no chances that Saturday. Both the 8 a.m. Uckfield to Oxted train and the 8.04 a.m. Oxted to Uckfield service were given six carriages instead of the usual three in order to provide extra traction against the menace of fallen leaves on the line.

The two trains were scheduled to pass each other on the dual track at Ashurst Station, the next stop south of Cowden. That morning, both trains were running late. According to Network South Central, the train from Uckfield should have waited at Ashurst for the other to pass. It didn't.

Thus, the two trains found themselves heading towards one another on a single track in thick fog. For an agonising fifteen minutes, the signalman in charge of the single-track section could tell that the two trains were on collision course but was powerless to prevent it. For while the trains were equipped with portable telephones in their cabs, these could only be used for outgoing calls. Neither driver could be warned that he was about to crash. All the signalman could do was ring the Railtrack control room in Croydon to tell them to call out the emergency services because there was about to be a crash.

The inevitable happened at 8.50, on a bend 300 yards south of

Cowden Station. The train from Uckfield was slowing down to approach the station, the other was picking up speed as it left. The impact speed was about 80 mph.

The force of the head-on impact caused both front carriages to be derailed. The southbound train destroyed the front carriage of the train from Uckfield, ripping off the driver's cab and the roof and crushing the superstructure against its first passenger carriage. The leading carriage of the train from Oxted shot up into the air and flew off the track, finishing up dangling over a 30 foot high embankment.

A passenger on the train from Uckfield told how the train appeared to slither into the collision after attempting to brake. He added: 'There was an almighty bang and we were all thrown to the floor. I got out and went to see what had happened. The front carriage was completely destroyed. I could hear people screaming with pain.'

Passenger Barbara Lawton from Solihull added: 'I went flying through the air and landed on the opposite side of the carriage. It all went very quiet. I waited a few minutes before getting out of the train because I didn't think it was a serious accident at that time, but then when I saw the state of some of the people's injuries, I realised it was. I stayed around, helping and comforting other passengers for about half an hour.'

The alarm was raised by Michael Steadman, a retired philosophy teacher travelling to London on the Uckfield–Oxted train. He scrambled from the wreckage and ran 400 yards down the line to a farmhouse. Banging on the door, he implored the occupiers: 'For God's sake stop the trains because there's been a crash!'

The farmer summoned the emergency services and soon more than 70 firefighters and paramedics were searching for survivors and bodies in the mangled wreckage. Both drivers were killed, as was Jonathan Brett-Andrews who had the misfortune to be in the driver's cab at the moment of impact. Had he been further back in the train, he would surely have survived. Two other people were killed – a middle-aged couple who were passengers on the train from Uckfield.

The rescue teams worked through the day to free the trapped passengers. Paramedics administered pain-killing drugs while firefighters cut away the metal with hydraulic equipment. Eleven injured passengers were taken to the Kent and Sussex Hospital, Tunbridge Wells, but all were later released.

One firefighter said: 'Some of the wreckage was the worst I've ever seen. It was horribly twisted. The two drivers who took the full force wouldn't have stood an earthly. We just had to pick up the pieces and get those who were trapped out as quickly as safety permittted.'

It was a delicate rescue, particularly to free those trapped in the carriage hanging over the embankment, and passengers had to be helped to the ground down a series of ladders. The operation continued into the night under floodlights and a pair of 200-ton cranes were brought in by road to remove those coaches which were balanced precariously or were damaged beyond repair. Such was the state of the cab of the Oxted–Uckfield train that it was not until the Monday that crews were able to release the body of the driver.

The inquest was told that the driver of the northbound train from Uckfield, an experienced employee, ignored four separate warning signals and overrode an automatic brake prior to the crash. There was speculation that the presence of the guard may have distracted him or even that the guard himself may have taken the controls for a short while, although there was no evidence to support or disprove this theory. The coroner concluded: 'Whoever was driving, why did he not stop at the signals? I fear that question will never be answered satisfactorily.'

8 Chemical Incidents

Operation Cloudburst

The residents of Ellesmere Port in Cheshire had lived for years in trepidation of the giant chemical factories which line the southern bank of the River Mersey. And the dreadful events at Chernobyl in 1986 had further served to heighten the fear of poisonous clouds being released into the atmosphere as the result of an explosion.

Among the plants at Ellesmere Port is Associated Octel Number One which operates 24 hours a day, making lead additives for petrol. On the night of 1 February 1994, a huge fire at the plant threatened to send a cloud of toxic gas drifting towards thousands of homes.

The incident began shortly after 8.30 p.m. when a quantity of highly flammable ethyl chloride liquid escaped from a reactor. An Octel worker, one of 150 on the site that Tuesday night, heard a leak alarm and immediately called the Fire Brigade. The first 999 call was received at 8.41 p.m. and four Cheshire fire crews arrived at the plant at 9.02 p.m.

By now, the leaking ethyl chloride, which decomposes into hydrochloric acid and phosgene, had vaporised, forcing the fire crews to don chemical protection suits before they could attempt to disperse the cloud of toxic gas. With winds gusting up to 57 mph, there was a grave danger that the colourless gases would be blown towards residential areas. Therefore, Cheshire's well rehearsed serious incident procedure, Operation Cloudburst, was put into effect.

The plant was shut down at once and police broadcast warnings on the radio, urging people to stay indoors and to lock all doors and windows. The chilling warning was reiterated to householders in the nearby villages of Helsby, Frodsham, Ince, Elton and Hapsford by officers aboard a police helicopter using a Skyshout loudhailer system. It was the message so many had been dreading.

Parents immediately began to worry about children who had gone round to friends' houses; wives agonised over husbands who were still making their way home from work; and men fretted over wives and girlfriends who had gone to evening classes or out for a drink. Would they all hear the warnings? Soon the telephone lines of North Cheshire were red hot with people anxiously relaying the message to loved ones.

Families living near the plant were evacuated to a community centre and just after 9.30 p.m., fire chiefs decided to evacuate other factories in the area – ICI, Shell, Kemira and Cabot Carbon. Fortunately, the easterly wind was sweeping the gases away from the centre of Ellesmere Port itself but across instead to the Manchester Ship Canal and the Mersey. Accordingly, the crew of a 6000-ton ship, which was docked nearby, were also moved out. Shipping in general was advised to steer clear of Ellesmere Port and motorists on the M53 were turned back between junctions 9 and 10. All emergency services within a 60-mile radius were put on full alert.

At the county's emergency headquarters in Chester, four staff began liaising with social services, river and wildlife experts, receiving 30-minute updates from CHEMET, the chemical meteorological office.

By 10 p.m., crews from seventeen appliances seemed to have brought the leak under control. It appeared that the worst was over. Then eight minutes later, disaster struck. Flames appeared beneath the reactor containing 30 tons of ethyl chloride liquid and the poisonous gases exploded into a wall of fire. The sudden explosion threw the Associated Octel Number One works back into turmoil.

As the ethyl chloride ignited, it sent flames soaring 150 feet into the air, illuminating the night sky for miles around. Eight more pumps were ordered to the scene, from Merseyside and Clwyd, bringing the total number of firefighters present to around 150. In addition, 50 ambulancemen waited to tend any injuries and rush casualties to hospital.

At the outbreak of the fire, crews rapidly deployed high-powered cannons, creating a wall of foam and water around the plant to prevent the blaze spreading. The big danger was that the ethyl chloride itself would explode, putting the firefighters in real peril. Three times over the next two hours, they were withdrawn because of the risk of explosion – and three times they returned to pump some 200,000 litres of foam on to the fire.

Octel had taken the precaution of coating the container housing the ethyl chloride with a substance which kept it safe from fire for a minimum of two hours and possibly for as long as three. This meant that while the firefighters could feel reasonably secure at first, chiefs would have to keep a constant eye on the clock. It made for a nerve-racking period as the crews fought to bring the blaze under control.

Shortly before 11 p.m., the wind began to shift direction and as a result Merseyside's own emergency plan was activated. By 11.25, the flames had taken hold of the lagging underneath the vessel. Thick black toxic gases were hanging in the air. It looked as if the fire crews were fighting a losing battle. They were fast running out of time.

More and more foam was pumped in. All the while, fire chiefs were anxiously monitoring the clock, working out how much longer it was safe to leave the crews in there. It was a momentous decision to have to make. For if the teams were withdrawn, the fire would be allowed to burn freely. And that would enable the ethyl chloride to be released into the fire, causing a potentially horrendous explosion.

The clock ticked on. Then at 11.50 p.m., nearly two hours into the fire, just as senior officers were beginning to contemplate mass withdrawal, the blaze was finally brought under control.

Fire Chief Dennis Davis breathed a sigh of relief. He said afterwards: 'Because the company had gone to the trouble of protecting the vessel, we knew we had two or three hours to play with. That was quite crucial during the phase up to about 1 a.m. It was an unprecedented fire which broke with a high degree of severity. It was also very unpredictable and we knew that sooner or later we would have had to take a decision about withdrawing the crews for their own safety. We were getting towards that decision to withdraw to a safe distance and leave it to itself. That would have left us in a situation where we left it to burn. Once those couple of hours were up, the product could well have gone.'

Although under control, the fire continued to burn throughout the night until 8.30 the next morning. The state of emergency lasted sixteen hours 52 minutes.

A total of seventeen firefighters needed medical attention. Two were taken to hospital after the chemical came into contact with their skin. The Octel worker who raised the alarm was also treated in the Countess of Chester Hospital after breathing in fumes. Octel showered the firefighters with fulsome praise, a company spokesman commenting: 'We were very impressed with the courage and commitment shown.'

Fire Chief Davis was adamant that, because of the wind direction, residents of Ellesmere Port were not at risk that night. But Ralph

Ryder of the Ellesmere Port Clean Air Society remained concerned about the presence of chemical factories. He said: 'It was only by the grace of God that the wind wasn't blowing in the other direction because, if it had been, who knows what the effect might have been on the people living in Ellesmere Port.'

* * *

On 1 March 1996, Wiltshire crews had to deal with one of the most unsociable incidents in the firefighters' manual when 30 tons of dung caught fire at a farm near Salisbury. It took two crews almost three hours to extinguish the heap of trouble. Not surprisingly, they were all keen to wear breathing apparatus sets.

* * *

An Alarming Discovery

The May Day Bank Holiday Monday usually marks the start of the serious holiday season in North Norfolk. Given favourable weather, a few hardy souls will venture there over Easter but it is the first week in May when the caravans and trailers really begin to descend on the area in earnest.

William Sinclair liked to walk his dogs along the shingle beach near Weybourne early in the morning before it became too crowded. But his gentle dawn stroll on 6 May 1991 resulted in a find which was to see over 1000 people, trippers and locals alike, evacuated from their homes in a full-scale chemical scare.

The morning wasn't exactly the best one for a walk. It was cold, grey, damp and generally miserable, the only advantage being that it guaranteed him the freedom of the beach. There was not a deck chair or 'Kiss Me Quick' hat in sight. At 7 a.m., Mr Sinclair was contemplating the joys of solitude when he spotted two huge containers lying some 200 yards apart on the shore. Suspecting that they had been washed up on the tide, he went over to investigate, but as he drew nearer he was driven back by the awful smell emanating from them. He promptly rang the coastguards and suggested that they shut Weybourne beach.

Other residents had detected a strange smell in the air that morning. One described it as 'a metallic smell, a bit like fertiliser'.

The emergency services were called in to take a closer look. The two tanks turned out to be 24-ton lorry trailers, each containing 24,000 litres of ethyl acrylate, a chemical commonly used in acrylic-based paints and resins. It is classed as a dangerous fire risk. Mixed with air, the gas emitted can cause explosions. Absorbed through the skin, it can cause respiratory problems. It appeared that the tanks had been among four swept overboard the previous Friday from a Swedish-registered cargo vessel, *Nordic Pride*, during bad weather. At the height of a Force 8 gale on their journey from Zeebrugge to Immingham, the trailers had seemingly slipped the chains lashing them to the deck of the ship. Now they had been carried ashore to haunt the people of North Norfolk.

Already the tanks were releasing a cloud of poisonous fumes into the air. The leak would have to be stemmed and then the trailers moved as quickly and as safely as possible. As firefighters in chemical protection gear assessed the situation, the winds began blowing the toxic gas inland towards the villages of Kelling and Salthouse. Clearly the public were now at risk.

The order to evacuate Kelling was made just before 10 a.m. and tourists visiting the nearby Muckleburgh military museum were advised to leave the area. Caravanners at a cliff-top site were also told of the potential danger of toxic fumes.

Although firefighters succeeded in slowing the leak, the threat persisted throughout the day. The evacuation area was extended to two square miles around Weybourne village and all householders living within a further eight miles were told by the police to keep all windows and doors shut until the danger had passed. Over 150 people were evacuated to a primary school at Sheringham for the night, where the emergency services provided camp-beds and blankets. People returning from a Bank Holiday break found their homes within the evacuation zone and had to spend the night in the school.

During the day, 45 people were taken to hospitals in Cromer and Norwich, complaining of nausea and breathing difficulties as well as sore throats and runny eyes. All of the victims were later released.

It had been hoped that the families would be able to return to their homes the following day but instead the evacuation area was extended and nearly 1000 people spent the night away from home while experts tried to halt the flow of the toxic chemicals. By now, the smell of the leak was polluting the North Sea breeze over an area of 50 square miles. Inland, it was like a ghost town. Villages, which were expecting to be alive with the sound of ringing tills, lay abandoned, the only sound coming from dogs that had been left to bark in deserted country lanes.

High-level discussions continued between the Fire Brigade and North Norfolk Council's environmental officers. The biggest obstacle to overcome was the inaccessibility of the steep shingle beach. The plan was to decant the chemical from the trailers into containers but first a temporary roadway would have to be built to allow tankers to reach the site. So civil engineering contractors with bulldozers and excavators set about cutting two 50-yard paths through a 30 foot high shingle flood protection bank before men from the Royal Corps of Transport moved in to build a temporary roadway for tankers to gain access to the trailers. The tankers then pumped off the ethyl acrylate and the empty trailers were removed. At last, North Norfolk could return to a sense of normality.

The chemical spillage had meant a miserable Bank Holiday for many people in North Norfolk but none more so than the Keeling family from Mansfield. After being forced to leave their tent and join the evacuees in Sheringham, Gary and Jane Keeling and their two children headed back disconsolately to Mansfield, only to discover that police had sealed off the area around their home following another chemical alert, this time caused by a fire at a plastics factory!

*　　*　　*

Exercising in the playground at a school in Wakefield, a small boy succeeded in getting his knee trapped between the wall of the building and a drainpipe. When teachers and fellow pupils were unable to free him, they called out West Yorkshire Fire Brigade who promptly set about dismantling the pipe from the roof. Within half an hour of their arrival, the boy was released with a sore knee and a reminder to keep away from drainpipes.

*　　*　　*

Rocked by Dawn Blast

Seventy-two-year-old Molly Handley had lived in her house near the massive Silkolene petrochemical plant in Belper, Derbyshire, for 30 years. A multinational company was not exactly her ideal choice as neighbours. Not only was the plant something of a blot on the landscape, but for local residents it presented a constant fear of explosion. So Molly was by no means alone in being worried about living in its shadow.

In 1990, her 48-year-old daughter Sandra was living with her. Since their house was the closest to the plant, they had often thought about what would happen if there was a major fire at Silkolene but hoped they would never be in a position to find out. On 9 August 1990, they were when an almighty explosion ripped through the oil refinery.

It was just after five o'clock in the morning when Sandra was startled from her slumbers by what she described as 'a terrific whooshing sound'. She went over to the window and, to her horror, saw flames shooting up into the sky. Instinct told her to get out of the house as quickly as possible. She ran downstairs to rouse her mother, picked up their dog and two cats, and the two women fled for their lives. 'Having got mum, my first reaction was to get out,' said Sandra. 'We had no idea whether or not the whole thing was going to blow, so we just ran.'

It was a similar story in adjoining streets as the loud blast rattled windows throughout the town and could be heard several miles away. 'It sounded as though a plane had come down,' said one eye-witness. 'I looked out of my window and there was a ball of flames rising fifty to a hundred feet in the air, and a huge roaring noise. A massive pall of smoke was going up over Belper.'

Another stated: 'I was woken up by a loud crackling noise and at first I thought some of the trees along the railway line were on fire. I was very worried when I realised it was Silkolene because I thought it might explode.'

The blast had torn through a 12,000-gallon storage tank. Fire and police were immediately put on major disaster alert and roads and the railway leading into the town were sealed off. Dozens of local residents were evacuated to a local school although some, like the Handleys, had already left home by the time the police had arrived to escort them to safety. The Spencer family's departure was less frantic. When police officers told them they had to leave, they calmly packed teabags and cups into a bag and headed for the school. Their only regret was having to leave their two dogs and two cats behind.

Firefighters arrived to tackle the blaze within minutes of the alarm being sounded. Soon there were 70 present from all over Derbyshire. Their first task was to confine the fire as best as they could. It had quickly spread to five other tanks and there was a danger that it might engulf the whole plant. The crews' tactics had been tried and tested in similar circumstances. High-pressure water jets were positioned so as to form a high curtain of spray around the tanks, thereby preventing the flames from spreading to adjoining containers. Meanwhile the flames themselves were smothered with gallons of foam. As a result of Derbyshire Fire Service's swift and efficient response, a potential catastrophe was averted.

By 7 a.m., fire chiefs announced that the danger had passed. Shortly afterwards, people started to drift back to their homes, to try and pick up the threads of the day. Six fire crews stayed on to dampen down the blaze and used a thermal image camera to detect any hot spots or concealed seats of fire.

Although there were no casualties, the explosion increased locals' demands that the plant be closed.

'There's a school next door to the plant,' said one angry resident. 'It was only by pure chance that the fire happened during the school holidays.'

* * *

West Sussex firefighters were sent to free a six-year-old girl with her hand trapped in the slot of a video recorder. She had been rummaging around looking for her favourite tape, Disney's *The Lion King*, and thought that it must already have been in the machine. She reached in to check but stretched too far and got her hand jammed. Her mother rang the Fire Brigade who solved the problem by greasing the girl's palm . . . but not with silver.

* * *

Double Refinery Blaze

Essex firefighters had never known a day like it. Two unconnected, but potentially deadly, oil refinery fires broke out within two miles and two hours of each other. And for good measure, on the same day there was a major glassworks fire in another part of the county. To say resources were stretched for a while would be an understatement.

Tuesday 26 February 1991 had started quietly enough for fire stations in the Basildon area but shortly after 10 a.m., the pit beneath a crude oil storage tank at the giant Mobil refinery at Coryton suddenly erupted in flames. It was believed to have started as a result of a spillage from the huge tank which was undergoing routine maintenance at the time. The oil poured from the container and escaped into the pit underneath which ignited. The pit held 350,000 gallons of naptha, a petroleum product.

When the oil leaked, three Mobil firefighters immediately put a precautionary foam blanket across the tank but they were forced to retreat to the evacuation point by the burning naptha which quickly reached temperatures of 2000 degrees Centigrade. Flames as high as 40 feet leapt into the air, producing plumes of thick black smoke as hundreds of workers fled the site.

One witness said: 'There was only a mild bang followed by intense heat. We just got the hell out of there. The whole place was chaos. People were running everywhere – screaming and shouting.'

An engine and a foam pump from Basildon raced out to Coryton, to be joined by appliances from Corringham, Grays and Tilbury. Later, the number of pumps present was increased to ten.

The blaze could be seen from miles away across the Thames in Kent. Crews set up the familiar curtain of spray to prevent the fire from spreading and by 11.30 a.m., they had succeeded in bringing it under control.

Then, as they continued to fight that fire, a second blaze broke out at the nearby Shell refinery just before noon. An unusually large flare in a flare stack, caused by a processing upset, had rained on to the ground and ignited at the base of the stack. Shell firefighters tackled the blaze, supported by seven Brigade appliances. This second fire was dealt with by 12.20 but not before five people had been treated for smoke inhalation and minor burns.

Wearily, the crews headed back to their respective stations, only to learn of a major glassworks fire at Harlow. All in all, it was quite a day.

* * *

On 20 November 1983, a 34-year-old man slipped while climbing a crane at Bristol City Docks and dangled 130 feet above the pavement for over an hour with his ankles snagged in the boom. He was eventually rescued by firefighters and taken to hospital with a broken leg.

* * *

Clouds Over Yorkshire

During the late summer of 1992, Yorkshire was rocked by two major fires at chemical plants. Although they took place at a time interval of two months and 30 miles apart, the two incidents were to be inextricably linked in the minds and stomachs of over 100 firefighters.

The first fire occurred at the Allied Colloid plant at Low Moor, Bradford, on 21 July. The company makes acrylic polymers for the printing, textile and paper industries as well as products for use in paint and weedkiller.

The fire broke out in the oxidising department of a raw materials warehouse. Kegs of a volatile chemical, AZDN, ruptured and spilled on to bags of sodium persulphate. The contact between the two chemicals led to ignition. The fire quickly spread to a second warehouse, sending lethal fireballs bursting out into the open. Surrounding streets were evacuated and householders and drivers within a three-mile radius were told to close all windows and ventilators. In addition, two main roads were closed.

West Yorkshire fire crews were faced with a ferocious inferno. The only redeeming feature was that nobody was trapped inside either warehouse – indeed none of the plant's 300 workers were hurt. No matter how much water they poured on to the buildings with high-powered jets, they needed more. Supplies were running short as they fought to confine the blaze to the two warehouses and so extra pumps were called in. Soon there were 31 appliances at the scene and over 150 firefighters. A pillar of black smoke from the fire could be seen twenty miles away.

As crews in breathing apparatus ventured into the burning buildings, fire chiefs enlisted the assistance of a police helicopter hovering overhead to guide them towards the trouble spots. The combination of flames, smoke and chemicals made it a particularly hazardous operation and there was mounting concern for the welfare of some of the firefighters. Accordingly, cardiac monitors and a saline solution for eye irritations were taken into the buildings. Six ambulances stood by because of the large quantities of toxic materials close to the seat of the fire.

'It was a horrible fire,' said one firefighter. 'Breathing was difficult through the smoke and we had to be on our guard with the chemicals. Some of the lads felt this awful itching sensation around their eyes. We were glad to get out.'

After three hours, the crews had succeeded in bringing the blaze under control. Thirty-five members of the emergency services were treated for various injuries and five firefighters were detained in hospital overnight, suffering from smoke inhalation and minor chemical burns.

Although the fire was extinguished with no loss of human life, the incident was a disaster in environmental terms. For the cocktail of 400 chemicals swept out of the plant by the four million gallons of water used to fight the fire got into rivers and killed several thousand fish as far down the River Calder as Castleford 30 miles away.

It was in Castleford, two months later to the day on 21 September, that the second big chemical fire took place. Tragically, on this occasion, five people were killed and seventeen badly injured.

Situated some ten miles south-east of Leeds, Castleford is generally known for its Rugby League club and for being among the unemployment blackspots of Britain. The Hickson and Welch plant is one of Castleford's biggest employers, a workforce of 1000 occupying a 175-acre site near the town centre. The plant makes the explosive chemical nitrotoluene which is used in the manufacture of a wide range of products from paint to fertiliser. Derivatives of nitrotoluene help to make dyes, pigments and washing powder whiteners. Among other things, TNT can be extracted from it.

The relationship between the plant and the community had been good, any fears about the presence of a large chemical site being outweighed by the employment provided for the townspeople in an area where jobs are so hard to come by. The most serious incident at the plant had been way back in 1930 when a blast resulted in six deaths.

The nitrotoluene was stored in an 80 foot high distillation tank. At 1.30 p.m. on that September day in 1992, the tank was being cleaned when there was a massive explosion. The tank ruptured, killing one employee instantly. The explosion created a fireball which, with devastating effect, shot 150 yards across a road and into a four-storey office block housing 140 employees. On its journey of destruction, the fireball wiped out a one-storey, prefabricated wooden building, went through an iron fence, in the process melting the railings, and burnt out three cars.

Castleford Rugby League ground is just 100 yards from Hickson and Welch. Head groundsman Steve Kirk saw and heard the explosion. 'I was on a tractor in the middle of the pitch with ear protectors on, but I still heard a huge rumbling sound. Then a big orange cloud floated over the plant away from me and it turned black. I ran indoors and made sure everyone else got inside.'

Another witness, Joyce Colgan, saw flames shoot hundreds of feet into the air. She said: 'There was this sound like an engine getting louder and louder. I thought it was an aeroplane going to crash. I looked round and saw this great ball of fire. It was terrible – I thought the whole place was going to go up. And there was an awful smell in the air. It made you feel sick and it was difficult to breathe. I was scared, really frightened.'

The moment the explosion happened, a warning system, established for the security and reassurance of the townspeople, swung into action. A chain of telephone calls urged employers and schools nearby to keep adults and children inside. Acting on this relay of information, three schools close to the plant immediately shut all doors and windows and waited for news.

The blast had blown debris into neighbouring fields a quarter of a mile away and the plant was now covered in a huge pall of smoke with flames cutting through it.

West Yorkshire Fire Service crews were quickly on the ground in numbers. They had to deal with fires on two fronts – one around the tank, the other in the company offices. The latter assumed particular importance because casualties were involved. Fortunately, because it was lunchtime there were only 30 or 40 people working in the office block – the other 100 were elsewhere on the site, safely out of reach of the fireball. Conversely, it created a problem for the firefighters. They were able to conduct a head count of workers on the site but some had left the plant for lunch. Those unaccounted for could either be safe and well somewhere in Castleford or trapped inside the blazing office block.

Crews in breathing apparatus fought their way through the smoke and flames to reach the workers in the office block. Four members of staff had been killed by the fireball, one as he tried to flee to safety from the office. Many of the victims were badly burnt. One man with 20 per cent burns could not be identified for another five hours because of the severe effect of the scorching and the chemical soot. The heat was so intense that it melted workers' hard hats and safety spectacles.

Bravely, the teams pulled out an eighteen-year-old clerical worker who was suffering from serious burns. Such was her condition that she was taken to hospital by helicopter but, in the course of the airlift, she suffered a heart attack. She was placed on a life-support machine but died a few days later.

Firefighters continued to douse the flames in an effort to isolate the two fires, using water from the Aire and Calder Canal and the River Aire. By now, twenty appliances were in attendance from across the region.

The good news was that it was established that the foul-smelling smoke was not toxic and, although the plant was still burning at 4 p.m., local children were allowed to leave school for home. The blaze was steadily brought under control but was still being dampened down into the night.

But if firefighters thought the demise of the blaze marked an end to their ordeal, they were sadly mistaken. The following day, 143 firefighters and staff were struck down by a mystery 24-hour bug, the symptoms of which were diarrhoea and vomiting. It appeared that the water drawn by firefighters from the river and the canal in order to confine the two fires was still polluted from the Bradford chemical blaze two months earlier. After being hosed on to the burning buildings at Hickson and Welch, the water had evaporated in an area where sandwiches were being laid on for the fire crews. The result was an extremely uncomfortable ending to a gallant day's work.

The official inquiry into the accident heard that the tank containing nitrotoluene was being steam-cleaned for the first time in 30 years. The thermometer being used failed to gauge the temperature of the chemical residue until it topped 90 degrees and exploded. Hickson and Welch were subsequently fined £250,000. The tragic irony is that the sludge in the tank need never have been cleaned out as it did not affect the chemical's distillation. It was a lesson learned – but too late for five people and their families.

9 Historic Buildings

The Great Fire of Windsor

Friday 20 November 1992 will go down in history as the day Windsor Castle went up in flames and the Queen spent her 45th wedding anniversary rescuing priceless treasures from her famous Berkshire home. As 50 foot flames leapt into the air and thick smoke billowed across the town and down the Thames valley, pictures of the fire were flashed around the world. There was enormous public sympathy for Her Majesty at her time of loss. And but for the efforts of 225 firefighters, that loss could have been even more painful to bear. For at one point there was a very real danger that the entire castle could have been destroyed in what became known as the Great Fire of Windsor.

Like most historic buildings, the ravages of time and tourists mean that Windsor Castle (parts of which date back to the eleventh century) and its contents are in almost constant need of repair and restoration. That week, picture restorers were at work in the Queen's private chapel in the north-east corner of the castle. With its magnificent oak-panelled walls painted white and gold, its nineteenth-century organ and beautiful stained glass and carved wood altar, the chapel was the perfect setting for royal christenings. But some of the paintings required a little attention so that they could be returned to their former glory.

The various switches in the chapel were not labelled and so the restorers had no idea which switch operated which light. Therefore, whenever they entered the room to begin work, they were in the habit of turning on all the switches. Unbeknown to the workmen, one of the switches also illuminated the wall-mounted spotlights which were hidden from view by the 30-foot-long curtains screening the altar. It appears that somehow the curtains were brought too close to one of the spotlights and at 11.37 a.m. they caught fire.

Spotting the flames, the three workmen hurried out of the chapel.

Not realising there was an emergency fire phone nearby, they ran instead to the Queen's vestibule where one of them made an emergency call using the internal 222 number directed to the castle switchboard. The alarm was raised both with Berkshire Fire Brigade's Windsor Station and the castle's own salvage corps and fire unit. Windsor Fire Station immediately contacted Reading for assistance.

The castle's own crew were first on the scene but even in the short time it took them to arrive, the fire had taken a hold in the ceiling and roof. At 11.45, the first fire appliances arrived and a well rehearsed operation was put into action. The emergency crews had practised this many times before, using specially prepared architects' blueprints of the castle. Carrying water jets, they approached the seat of the fire – the private chapel – through St George's Hall, but were forced back by the intensity of the flames.

The fire quickly burst through from the chapel to the adjoining St George's Hall, one of the jewels in Windsor's crown with its gilded and embossed panel ceiling painted to look like wood and decorated with hundreds of heraldic shields bearing the coats of arms of the Knights of the Garter. The hall had been accumstomed to staging vast state banquets, latterly for Polish president Lech Walesa and American president Ronald Reagan. But in addition to being a splendid piece of architecture, St George's Hall was also a veritable fire hazard. The enormous timber roof, dating partly from the fourteenth century, and the wood-panelled walls fed the flames which were fanned by the draught in the lofty chamber. The fire spread rapidly down the entire length of the hall and also along a 6 foot high void between the ceiling and the roof.

David Harper, Deputy Chief of Berkshire Fire Brigade, confessed: 'The thing that thwarted us most was the number of hidden voids. St George's Hall was 185 feet long and running above the ceiling was this six foot void. I looked above me and saw a hole in the ceiling suddenly open up. And through the hole I could see the fire raging.'

Clearly, reinforcements were needed to prevent a major catastrophe and fire crews were called in from London, Surrey, Buckinghamshire and Oxfordshire.

The Duke of York had been in the castle precincts when the first alarm sounded. As the gravity of the situation unfolded, he called the Queen at Buckingham Palace on a mobile phone to relay news of the fire. She told him that nobody should risk their lives in trying to save the building or its contents.

Nevertheless, the Duke was determined to help salvage as much as possible from areas threatened by the blaze. He joined soldiers of the Household Cavalry and Gurkha Regiments, policemen, members of the Women's Royal Voluntary Service and 300 castle staff and tradesmen to form human chains to remove valuable objects from the castle rooms. The collections of centuries passed through their hands – priceless paintings by Canaletto, Holbein, Rubens and Rembrandt as well as carpets, curtains, candelabras and tapestries. They brought out ornate tables, cabinets and desks, suits of armour and even a 150 foot long dining table which had to be removed in sections. Soldiers carried away the longest seamless carpet in the world from the Waterloo Chamber, the room directly to the north of St George's Hall. Three hundred clocks were saved as was the Queen's personal collection of miniatures. The Royal Library was emptied of thousands of valuable books, manuscripts and Old Master drawings. But on fire officers' instructions, heavy chests and tables were left behind.

The treasures were assembled on to huge plastic sheets on the north terrace and in the quadrangle, the great central courtyard of the castle. To assist the evacuation, the police had summoned dozens of removal vans from across the Home Counties and these took the works of art, furniture and carpets away to safety in other parts of the castle.

By 12.20 the fire had taken such a hold that the glow in the sky could be seen up to a mile away. The ancient combustible beams, wood panelling and draughty stairwells provided an ideal environment for the fire to spread. And the lack of fire doors meant that it was difficult to contain. The complicated nature of the building hindered the speed with which firefighters, particularly those from stations who were not familiar with its layout, could reach the vital areas. Crews needed directions from the staff but even so there were still plenty of undetected nooks and crannies for the fire to establish a hold before the hoses were able to have any effect.

The speed with which the fire had shot through the void above the ceiling in St George's Hall had stunned fire officers at the scene. The whole of the north-east wing of the castle was now ablaze from the first floor up, including the royal kitchens, the octagonal Brunswick Tower and the Queen's state rooms – the state dining room in the Prince of Wales's Tower, the crimson drawing room and part of the green drawing room. There was now a very real threat of the entire castle burning down.

Conditions for firefighters were becoming more dangerous by the minute. The structure of the castle was very weak in certain areas, leading to the possibility of collapse. Something had to be done quickly to restrict the fire before one of Britain's most celebrated landmarks was razed to the ground. For although there were now 39 appliances in attendance, pouring on over a million gallons of water, the fire showed little sign of abating.

The salvation plan was two-fold. Firstly, fire chiefs decided to cut away part of the roof of St George's Hall so that the fire could vent itself and save the rest of the castle. It was a delicate operation. Exercising great care, teams of firefighters crawled across the roof and used chainsaws to cut large holes, allowing the fire and smoke to escape into the sky. Secondly, building contractors, who were on site at the time, were asked to set up 'firebreaks' of non-flammable materials at two crucial points in order to prevent the fire spreading any further. Fire chiefs ordered that the firebreaks be set up at the clock tower at the west end of St George's Hall and at the southern wall of the green drawing room where the Chester Tower joins the grand corridor. The idea was to hold the fire there. Meanwhile, the Brunswick Tower would be sacrificed and left to burn as a natural flue.

The fire stops were set up around 1.30 p.m., enabling the fire to be brought under some form of control. Smoke and flames continued to billow high into the air as firefighters on two giant hydraulic platforms directed water on to the fire. Elsewhere, crews placed ladders against the castle walls and aimed hoses through windows where the glass had been blown out by the intense heat.

At 3 p.m., the Queen arrived from Buckingham Palace to witness the devastation for herself. She spent an hour at the castle, helping to remove treasures and private papers from her apartments. Meanwhile, the Duke of York described his earlier evacuation to the world's press. 'I just grabbed what I could carry out – pictures, clocks and tables, all sorts of ornaments.' He added that he was immensely relieved that the fire had happened during daylight hours. 'Had it been night, we would have lost a great deal more.' He went on to praise the work of the castle staff. 'There was no panic, fuss or mourning. It is a pretty nasty mess inside but everything we could possibly take out has been taken out.'

By 3.30 the firebreaks had done their job. Fire chiefs reported that the blaze was now surrounded. Their task had been helped by a southerly wind which directed the flames away from most of the state apartments. As darkness descended, floors within the Brunswick

Tower collapsed, adding fuel to the flames. Soon the tower was engulfed in flames which lit up the night sky. Fortunately most of its contents had been removed before the fire had even started, to enable rewiring to be carried out. Later in the evening, the ancient timber roof of St George's Hall also finally succumbed to the blaze.

On two occasions when roofs collapsed, firefighters were temporarily unaccounted for. It was feared that they might be trapped under falling debris. The crews were brought out for head counts but happily the missing men were quickly found unharmed. Nevertheless, in the course of the operation five firefighters had to be taken to hospital for treatment. Three sustained minor burns while the other two were suffering from hypothermia, caused by the use of cold water on a chilly November night.

Falling timbers and the bitter cold were by no means the firefighters' only enemies. With the fire raging on into the night, exhaustion began to set in. Crews had to put on their breathing apparatus up to six times to make repeated trips into the castle.

Watching the family home go up in flames, the Duke of York remarked to reporters: 'It is a lovely place. It is where I was brought up and it's a terrible sadness to see it in this condition.'

The main fire was put out at 11 p.m. although small pockets of fire continued to burn. Crews toured the castle dousing these smouldering pockets of debris while senior officers watched from observation platforms for any new outbreaks. It was not until 2.30 a.m. on Saturday that the fire was finally extinguished. Even so, 60 firefighters remained on duty with eight appliances since it would be several more days before isolated 'hot spots' were dampened down.

As daylight returned, the full extent of the fire became known. On the Saturday morning, the Queen entered the charred ruins of St George's Hall. Its pomp and splendour had been reduced to a cavernous blackened tomb. The roof and floors had fallen in, leaving the hall open to the sky and producing a tangled pile of debris and ashes up to 6 feet deep in places. The lavish grand reception room, adjoining St George's Hall, was also ravaged by fire. Eighty per cent of this exquisite room, decorated in the style of Louis XV, was severely damaged. Most of the richly gilded rococo plaster ceiling collapsed in the fire. Yet a precious mid nineteenth-century urn, given to Queen Victoria by Tsar Nicholas I of Russia and which had been too heavy to remove from its plinth in the window, had miraculously survived. The crimson drawing room was also destroyed by the fire.

This was one of a series of three sumptuous state salons in the private apartments where the Queen entertained important guests. Another room in this suite, the green drawing room, was badly damaged by smoke and water. In total, six rooms and three towers were destroyed or seriously damaged.

Despite the sterling efforts of the rescuers, a few important works of art could not be saved from the fire. These included Sir William Beechey's equestrian portrait of 'George III at a Review', which was too large to remove from its frame. This was the only painting destroyed by the fire. An 18 foot sideboard by Morel & Seddon dating from the 1820s was also lost, along with the nineteenth-century organ built by Henry Willis which graced the private chapel. One brave rescuer, Dean Lansdale, a 21-year-old decorator, burned his hands while removing paintings from the private chapel. He was taken to the royal surgery and then to hospital.

The Queen was full of praise for the unstinting efforts of the firefighters from five counties who had repeatedly risked their lives over a period of fifteen hours to save so much of the castle. A month later, in her Christmas message, she referred to the Great Fire of Windsor as contributing to her 'annus horribilis'. She knew that without the efforts of the nation's firefighters it would have been more horribilis still.

* * *

On 3 April 1996, firefighters had to rescue a twelve-year-old boy after he had got stuck up a 30 foot turret in Newark Castle, Nottinghamshire. The boy climbed over a fence to get into the tower, before scaling it from the inside.

Newark Sub Officer David Smith said: 'He'd got to the top OK, but once he'd done that, he realised he didn't want to be up there any more. The trouble was he couldn't get himself down. In the end he was so terrified that he couldn't even let go of his hand-hold and we had to send one of the lads up on a ladder to coax him down.'

* * *

Saved by the Lord

York Minster is one of the jewels of English architecture. The largest Gothic cathedral in Europe, it took two and a half centuries to complete (beginning in 1220) and thus combines the best of three different architectural periods – early English, decorated and perpendicular. The Minster is a mecca for tourists who flock from all over the world to admire its magnificent medieval stained glass, rivalled only by that of Chartres. In particular, visitors like to gaze in awe at the 125 windows, the most famous of all being the world-renowned Rose Window.

Sadly, like so many old buildings, York Minster was not immune to fire. There had been two sizeable fires since the start of the nineteenth century, but by far the most damaging was the one which took place in the early hours of 9 July 1984.

It was a wild nig`.`t, the sort which could have stepped straight out of a horror movie. Violent electrical storms swept across Yorkshire. Around 2.10 a.m., witnesses saw the storm produce flashes of lightning which appeared to play about the thirteenth-century roof of the south transept of the Minster.

The roof caught fire and the blaze spread rapidly yet it remained undetected for a further, vital twenty minutes due to the siting of smoke alarms, forced upon the authorities by the layout of the building. Owing to the steep pitch of the transept roof, six smoke sensors had to be sited five metres below the apex, thereby creating a void which had to be filled with smoke before the alarms would be activated. This blind spot in the Minster's smoke detectors allowed the flames to burn fiercely for twenty minutes before the automatic alarm system was activated. Had the fire been discovered sooner, much of the ensuing damage could have been prevented.

As it was, the Minster's alarm link with North Yorkshire Fire Brigade headquarters at Northallerton was not sounded until 2.30 a.m. At the same time, passers-by and the night security officer also spotted the blaze and quickly telephoned the emergency services.

But by the time firefighters had arrived, it had taken a strong hold. Flames were leaping into the air, some attaining a height of 200 feet. Two more crucial minutes were lost when the Minster guard, on his first nightshift after three weeks in the job, was unable to find the keys for the two security doors to allow firefighters access to the transept roof.

Fire crews descended on the city from far and wide, desperate to save as much of the Minster as possible. The fire was so well established, almost from the outset, that the operation amounted to a damage-limitation exercise. The highly flammable lead roof and the dry old timbers helped intensify the blaze and meant that the south transept roof was soon beyond salvation. However, it was imperative that the fire be prevented from spreading to the central tower or from seriously damaging the stained glass windows.

At the height of the fire, relays of clergy dashed into the Minster and rescued priceless artefacts from the high altar and lady chapel altar, in the process risking their lives in the face of the flames and showers of molten lead. Only when the beams supporting the roof began to collapse were the clergy obliged to abandon their mission on the orders of fire chiefs. Elsewhere in the building, firefighters and volunteers joined forces to remove furniture and furnishings to places of safety.

After almost three hours, the fire was brought under control. The majority of the Minster, including the Rose Window, had been spared. Even so, damage was estimated at over £1 million and the south transept was totally destroyed, its ancient roof beams and plaster vaults being reduced to a smouldering mass on the floor.

With the fire extinguished, the clearing-up process began and firefighters set about pumping out ankle-deep water which had seeped into the Minster's undercroft.

Some commentators suggested that the fire was divine retribution for the previous week's consecration of the controversial Rt Rev. David Jenkins as the Bishop of Durham. Understandably, these assertions were dismissed by the Archbishop of York as 'ridiculous'. Indeed, Dr Robert Runcie, the Archbishop of Canterbury, said that it was a 'miracle' that the fire had only destroyed the south transept.

The Chief Fire Officer of North Yorkshire added: 'The Lord was on our side as we battled with those flames, and every man in my brigade knew they were doing something special by saving York Minster.'

Four months after the blaze, the North Yorkshire Fire Brigade were presented with the Cross of St William of York for acts of outstanding service to the church. Half an hour after the presentation ceremony, the Brigade were called back to the Minster, but it turned out to be a false alarm.

The fire put everyone on their guard. They knew that in the event of another alarm, there was not a moment to waste. And so when the alarm at the Minster was raised again in May 1992, dozens of firefighters from across the county answered the call, only to find that it had been set off by nothing more dangerous than a French bishop holding a smoking incense burner. The Brigade arrived to find hundreds of tourists already evacuated. When they went inside to investigate, they discovered the bishop and his congregation continuing with the service, totally unaware of the alarm. It transpired that Bishop Mael of the French Orthodox Church had been given permission to hold the service in the crypt but nobody had followed the usual practice of turning off the smoke alarms ...

10 The Broadwater Farm Riot

The Broadwater Farm riot of October 1985 marked an unwanted milestone in the history of the Fire Brigade. Until that fateful night in Tottenham, rioters and demonstrators had always perceived the Fire Brigade as a neutral body and therefore had refrained from subjecting crews to attack when they arrived to deal with burning cars and petrol bombs. Even in sixteen years of trouble in Northern Ireland, no firefighter had sustained serious injuries. But Broadwater Farm was different. The rioters' vicious attacks on the police spilled over to anyone in uniform, anybody who was seen representing authority. Consequently, firefighters too found themselves besieged with lumps of concrete and petrol bombs as they went about their duties. This shocking scenario was to give celebrated playwright Jack Rosenthal the impetus to write the screenplay for the very first story of *London's Burning*. The heart of his film was a riot.

The Broadwater Farm Estate in Tottenham, North London, had been seen at one time as a showpiece development. It had won prizes and was seen to represent all that was good about inner-city housing. But its reputation had deteriorated over the years with an increase in racial tension as Asian traders became the victims of both black and white gangs. Tension was also running high between some residents and the police.

The fuse that was to explode into a bloody, murderous riot was lit on Saturday 5 October 1985 when a black woman, Cynthia Jarrett, collapsed and died during a police search of her home which was situated near the council estate. As word spread throughout the estate, a crowd gathered outside Tottenham Police Station on the Sunday lunchtime to protest at Cynthia Jarrett's death. Appeals for calm from the dead woman's family and community leaders temporarily took the heat out of the situation, but the anger swelled up again and by 2 p.m. there were some 300 people voicing their feelings about the police action. Verbal abuse was hurled at the police and some vehicles were damaged. Traffic in Tottenham High Road was stopped and a stone shattered a window at the police station. Then at 3.30 p.m., two police officers were called to The Avenue, a road leading into the estate. Lumps of concrete were thrown at their car, smashing the windscreen.

A meeting was called on the estate for approximately 6 p.m. The police were not invited. Forty-five minutes later, the police received emergency calls from people complaining about groups of youths throwing stones at doors in The Avenue. Investigating officers were attacked with a storm of missiles, including petrol bombs. By 7 p.m., a full-scale pitched battle was developing around The Avenue, Mount Pleasant Road and Willan Road.

Trouble began to flare up all over the estate, involving some 500 youths, black and white. Pieces of concrete and petrol bombs were lobbed from high-rise blocks on to the unsuspecting police below. Cars were overturned and set on fire. Buildings were set alight. Soon twelve fire tenders carrying 80 firefighters were racing to the riot zone. Some of the missiles which were presumably aimed at the police missed their targets and landed beyond the police frontline in among the ranks of fire and ambulance personnel.

Fires were breaking out everywhere. The crews could not cope with them all, something the rioters knew only too well. Nor was it safe for firefighters to go in and tackle the blazes, unless they could be sure of police protection. A joint incident room was set up to direct operations, thus ensuring maximum co-operation between police, fire and ambulance services. After the initial wave of attacks, the police sealed off the area in an attempt to prevent the trouble spreading to adjoining neighbourhoods. Traffic exclusion zones were established to safeguard routes for emergency vehicles moving in and out of the estate.

Firefighters had to dodge missiles and burning vehicles to go about their work. The burning vehicles were a particular problem that night. They blocked off roads within the estate, preventing fire appliances from gaining access to trouble spots, and the clouds of thick black smoke from burning tyres obscured visibility. Also there was the constant threat of exploding petrol tanks. The noise of the explosions, coupled with the shouting of the rioters and the echo-chamber effect created by the high-rise flats, made for an intimidating atmosphere and one in which verbal communication was extremely difficult.

Shortly after 9 p.m., firefighters did manage to gain access to The Avenue to deal with four burning cars. There were also reports of a fire at a house in Adams Road but police advised firefighters to keep out of the area. It was too dangerous – police feared that it was a trap to lure emergency teams to the scene where they would then come under attack.

At 9.40 p.m., shops in Willan Road were set on fire. The blaze in a supermarket had threatened to take a strong hold and there was concern for the safety of the people living above it. Protected by a group of ten police officers from Hornsey, the firefighters tackled the fire and, at around 10.15 p.m., were preparing to take action to secure the safety of the residents when about 150 youths ran through the shopping area. Fifty or so broke away to chase the rearguard of those police officers who had remained until the last moment to ensure that their colleagues had evacuated the area. Among the rearguard was Police Constable Keith Blakelock, a 40-year-old father of three sons.

Assistant Divisional Fire Officer Trevor Stratford, himself a married man with two children, was caught up in the tragic events which followed. He told journalists: 'It had been very quiet for a while and we had floated out a substantial amount of hose to take into the upper walkway to see what we might have to damp down. Then we saw the youths running towards us. The mob was right behind us hurling bricks, breeze blocks, metal objects and, I think, petrol bombs. We were running up a grass embankment outside the shopping precinct area when I half turned and saw a police constable fall about twenty yards behind me. He just stumbled and went down and they were upon him. It was just mob hysteria. I stopped about forty or fifty feet further on and turned. They had fallen on him and I completely lost sight of him.'

After calling for help, A.D.O. Stratford returned seconds later as the crowd backed away in the face of a surge of police in riot gear. 'I grabbed one lapel of the injured officer's coat and a policeman grabbed the other one. We dragged him bodily across the grass and crouched down to avoid the missiles. I was hit by a brick in the small of my back. I opened up his overalls and it looked as though he had a number of stab wounds in his chest. Then I saw his neck wound. He had a knife, what looked like a kitchen knife, embedded in his neck to the handle. It was underneath his right ear. He wasn't breathing and there was no heartbeat. He was one hell of a mess.'

A.D.O. Stratford dragged PC Blakelock another 150 yards and loaded him into a private ambulance. On the way to North Middlesex Hospital, the fire officer continued to administer heart massage but within fifteen minutes of being admitted, PC Blakelock died.

'It had been like watching a pack of hounds tearing a fox to pieces,' added A.D.O. Stratford. 'He never stood a chance. They looked as though they were going to tear him limb from limb. There were no heroics about rescuing him – it was purely spontaneous.'

The brutal, cowardly hacking to death of PC Blakelock did nothing to quell the violence. After a brief lull, youths emerged from their hiding places to hurl more stones and petrol bombs at police lines in Griffin Road. Petrol was poured across the road, ready to be lit. More alarming still was the fact that, from time to time, someone would discharge a firearm from the front line of rioters before quickly retreating into the safety in numbers of the crowd. A total of eight police officers and members of a television camera crew required treatment for gunshot wounds although fortunately none proved fatal.

At five o'clock on the Monday morning, ten hours after the riot had begun in earnest, the police occupied the final pocket of resistance in Adams Road. On high-rise walkways, they found heavy beer canisters and a further supply of petrol bombs, ready to be dropped on to officers 30 feet below. Of the 1000 police officers brought in to contain the disorder, 248 had been injured.

Daylight revealed the full extent of the rioting – charred buildings, broken glass and some 50 burnt-out cars. As they relived the horrors of the night before, firefighters who had come under attack from the baying mob could only hope that Broadwater Farm would not represent the shape of things to come for the Fire Service.

Alas, in some areas firefighters do seem to have become targets for mindless yobs. In July 1992, crews fighting to control a blaze at a Salford carpet warehouse were pelted by youths and children armed with snooker balls.

11 Trapped

The Boy in the Bog

Eleven-year-old Matthew Davies was spending the weekend with a friend in Brecon, Powys, a few miles from his caravan home at Llanfihangel Talyllyn. On the Saturday afternoon, Saturday 5 September 1992, the two youngsters decided to head off on their bicycles to some land at nearby Llanddew. They were mucking about, as boys do, when one of Matthew's legs sank into a peat bog. It was to be the start of a remarkable 72-hour ordeal which Matthew, displaying remarkable fortitude and presence of mind for one so young, somehow survived against all the odds.

Matthew's leg was trapped and he slowly began to sink waist-deep into the swamp. His friend promptly ran off to a nearby farm where he found a shovel. He came back and tried to dig him out but it was an impossible task. He said he would go off to fetch help – and that was the last time Matthew saw anyone until the following Tuesday.

For three days and three nights, Matthew defied hunger, thirst, exhaustion and the cold in an amazing feat of endurance. He was helped by the fact that, at 5 foot 9 inches he was extremely tall and strong for his age. Whereas most other eleven-year olds would have been almost totally submerged in the four feet of squelchy mud, Matthew was able to keep his face well above the surface, thus enabling him to breathe freely.

He desperately tried to free himself but his leg was stuck fast under tree roots and giant boulders. He ripped off his T-shirt with the intention of wrapping it around a bush or a tree and then pulling himself to safety but the plan proved unsuccessful. As darkness fell and it became obvious that his friend was not going to return with help as promised, Matthew had the sense to spread a layer of mud over his body to retain heat through the cold night. It was an inspired decision, and one which undoubtedly saved his life.

All through the Sunday, Matthew languished in the swamp, praying that someone would pass by. But it was a remote spot, well off the beaten track. He began to wonder whether he would ever see a living soul again.

By the Sunday evening, his mother had become worried that he had not returned home from his weekend in Brecon and duly reported him missing. The police quizzed his friend but the second boy, apparently worried that he would get into trouble over the incident, told them that he had no idea where Matthew was. Meanwhile, Matthew was about to spend a second night in his one-boy battle against the elements.

And so it went on through Monday and Tuesday. In the close-knit community, there was widespread concern over Matthew's whereabouts. Apart from the inevitable fear of abduction, there was the feeling that he was scarcely equipped to cope with three nights out in the open, dressed as he was in nothing but a thin T-shirt and tracksuit bottoms. The locals had reckoned without his inner and outer strength.

The search went on but was no nearer finding him. Hardly surprisingly, he was now cold and weak – he could feel the life beginning to drain slowly away from him. The peat level was now almost up to his shoulders. He was not sure whether he could survive a fourth night under the stars trapped in this hell-hole. If only someone would pass by . . .

Then at 5 p.m. on the Tuesday came the vital breakthrough. Terry Higgins, a 49-year-old electrical engineer, had decided to take his dog for a late afternoon walk. By a stroke of long overdue good fortune, the path he chose took him close to the Llanddew bog. By the side of the footpath, he saw an abandoned bicycle. As he paused to investigate its owner, he heard a faint cry for help.

Mr Higgins ran over to where the cry came from and found Matthew, half naked and stuck in the swamp. 'You could just see his head and shoulders,' said Mr Higgins. 'When I got to him, he grabbed me. For a boy of eleven, he was calm and logical. After taking my shoes and socks off, I walked into the bog with my trousers rolled up, but I couldn't pull him out. His leg was trapped in tree roots and rocks under the mud which must have been at least four feet deep. He was covered in dirt and was very slippery. He was also extremely cold. I told him I was going to get help. As I left him, I said: "Don't go away, will you?" He just smiled weakly back at me.'

Mr Higgins was as good as his word and called the emergency services. Firefighters from Brecon quickly assessed the situation. Since

Matthew's leg was trapped, they would have to dig him out rather than simply attach a line to him. At first, they used spades but then they had to scrape away the peat with their bare hands. However, conditions were so treacherous that, in the course of the dig, three firefighters became trapped in the peat bog and had to be pulled to safety by colleagues. Taking care not to injure the boy's legs, the firefighters gradually managed to shift the rock and the roots sufficiently for Matthew to be pulled clear. The operation took an hour and a half.

Paramedics immediately wrapped him in silver foil so that he would regenerate his body heat. His hands and feet were badly swollen. His feet were grey and very cold and at first there was no sign of any circulation. While struggling in the mud, he had sustained severe bruising across his chest and his back was covered in insect bites.

He was admitted to hospital where he was rehydrated with hot tea and milk. Doctors were amazed that, considering his dreadful ordeal, his body temperature was only two or three degrees below normal. Dr David Johnson said: 'It is incredible that he kept his body temperature as high as he did. His own strength kept him going – he is a very strong boy. I am sure that was a major factor in his survival.'

Nevertheless, Matthew had only just been rescued in time. One of the fire crews admitted: 'The lad's spirit was broken by the time he was found – he would never have survived another night. It was exceptionally difficult to dig him out – the conditions in which we had to work were appalling. He is very lucky to be alive.'

That wasn't quite the end of the Matthew Davies story. On 8 September 1993, a year to the day after his rescue, a helicopter spotted him soaked to the skin on the Brecon Beacons close to the peat bog where he had spent that agonising three days. The police intervened and gave him what they described as 'suitable advice'.

* * *

A 39-year-old Worthing man searching for somewhere to sleep for the night in April 1991, fell into a narrow gap between the roofs of two buildings and plunged down a 20 foot shaft. He lay in the 4 foot square shaft, situated between a china shop and a solicitor's, for nearly six hours. It was not until eight o'clock the following morning that a cleaner, reporting for work, heard his cries for help and raised the alarm. Unable to get the man to climb the ladder in the shaft for fear of aggravating his back injury, firefighters instead had to force a set of doors at the bottom of the shaft. He was then strapped on to a stretcher and taken to hospital from where he was later discharged.

* * *

Buried Alive

It was the morning of 17 June 1986 and the gang of construction workers on the building site in the Hockley district of Birmingham were going about their business as usual, the sound of the JCB punctuated only by the odd verse of 'Danny Boy'. The work was roughly on schedule and everyone was happy.

The mechanical digger was excavating a long trench, some 6 feet wide and 8 feet deep. A group of men were working in the trench when suddenly part of it began to collapse. All of the men bar one managed to scramble out in time but Patrick Kelly was stranded, buried up to just above his waist.

The JCB driver switched off the engine and jumped from his cab. The foreman came running over from the site hut.

'What's happened?' he shouted.

'It's Patrick,' replied one of the workmen. 'The trench has collapsed on him.'

Two of the men tried to reach in and pull Mr Kelly out but he was in too deep and there was always the danger that the activity might prompt a further soil collapse, this time completely burying their colleague. While the foreman rushed to telephone West Midlands Fire Service, Mr Kelly's workmates did their best to keep his spirits up.

'Are you all right, Patrick?' enquired one.

'I can feel pains in my legs below the knee.' He was struggling for breath, clearly winded and shocked. 'It also hurts a little when I breathe.'

'Well, don't worry. The Fire Brigade will be here in a minute and they'll soon have you out of there.'

Mr Kelly smiled weakly. 'I hope so.'

Fire crews responded quickly. Their first task, apart from offering verbal reassurance to the victim, was to check the walls of the trench to determine their stability. The walls were not shored and consisted of a top layer of tarmac, beneath which was a layer of concrete. It was decided that the safest way to remove the soil was by hand and so a team of three firefighters began clawing away the loose earth from around Mr Kelly. A human chain of firefighters waited at the top of the trench to take the soil away in buckets. By now, an ambulance crew had arrived and they fitted an oxygen mask on to the injured man and also set up a saline drip. Throughout the operation, the medical team kept a watchful eye on his condition.

The manual digging continued slowly but surely. Inch by inch, more of Mr Kelly's body became visible. But then they chanced upon a huge concrete and brick boulder in front of him. While it was not actually resting on Mr Kelly, there was a danger that further excavation might loosen the soil and allow the rock, which was some 4 feet in diameter, to topple on to him. The men in the trench had to proceed with extreme caution. Eventually a small hole, just big enough for a firefighter to put his hand in, was carved out beneath the boulder and two slings were positioned, one on either side, to support its weight.

As they dug deeper, the men found Mr Kelly's heavy pneumatic drill. It was lying against his legs and accounted for the pain he was still feeling in that part of his body. One of the firefighters managed to cut the compressor pipe with a hacksaw and the drill was carefully lifted away from the trench.

A second set of slings was placed around the boulder. Exercising all their strength, the surface crews succeeded in moving it a few inches, but there was a risk that it might disintegrate and crumble on to the victim, and so that part of the operation was halted.

Conditions in the trench were at best unpleasant. There was precious little room in which to work as Mr Kelly was pressed firmly against the trench wall and the crews sometimes found themselves almost working upside down as they strove to scrape away the surrounding soil. Thanks to the boulder being supported, they were finally able to remove sufficient soil to enable them to reach the trapped man's legs. Once his legs were free, they could think about winching him to safety. It was not a moment too soon for Mr Kelly, who was beginning to complain of additional pains in his chest and back.

Fitting the parachute harness of the rescue line on to Mr Kelly was no easy matter. Apart from the position of his back, which made access difficult, his legs had been pressed tightly together for over two hours. Unless he could bend them slightly, it would be impossible to thread the straps through in order to secure the harness. The fire crews asked him to make a real effort to bend his legs and he responded sufficiently for the harness to be fitted.

Before the Major Rescue Unit vehicle could be moved into position to winch Mr Kelly to safety, officers had to check that the land around the trench was stable. The last thing they – or the trapped man – needed was for the movement from the vehicle to spark a fresh collapse. Once the stability was established, the vehicle was backed up to the trench and the winch gear fastened to the hook. Gradually, to the relief of all concerned, Patrick Kelly was raised from the trench and placed in the care of ambulance crews. He was rushed to hospital where he was admitted with a lung injury, severe shock and bruising.

Perhaps the most remarkable thing about the whole incident was that his workmates had been so worried about him that, for the first time in living memory, they had forgotten all about their morning tea break.

* * *

Three fire appliances were called to help free a man who had got his hand stuck in a postbox while sending a letter in Stockton, Cleveland, on 29 March 1996. The second-class male was later taken to hospital for a check-up.

* * *

Pole Position

Cyril Terry was pleased to accept the offer of a lift home from work. Sitting in the back of a colleague's car as they left their workplace at Grays, Essex, on the evening of 28 May 1984, Cyril was looking forward to a hearty meal and seeing his wife Jeanette at their home in Chadwell Heath. On the way out, the car had to stop at a barrier gate. Then, as the car moved forward, the barrier suddenly swung part of the way across. Its pole smashed through the front windscreen of the car, by-passed the driver, speared through Cyril's chest and went out through the back window.

Everyone rushed to Cyril's aid. People panicked when they saw what had happened. Yet the calmest person of all was 48-year-old

Cyril himself, even though he had a two-inch diameter pole protruding from the front and back of his chest.

Essex firefighters were called out and they too were stunned by Cyril's laid-back approach. It was just as well he was fairly relaxed since it took them two hours to free him from the car.

The problem was simple. With some 10 feet of pole sticking out of him like a giant kebab, Cyril could not be moved from the car by conventional means. He would not fit out of the door. The crews studied the situation from all angles before deciding to slice the car roof off with cutting equipment. Once they had done that, they were able to saw through the pole, reducing it to a length of 2 feet on either side of his body.

Cyril remained conscious throughout and insisted on climbing into the ambulance on his own. He had to make the journey to hospital sitting upright because it was impossible for him to lie down. When Cyril was admitted, doctors were so amazed that they took photographs of his predicament for their medical records. Surgeons then set about cutting out the offending pole. Unbelievably, it had gone through his body without smashing his rib cage or damaging a single vital organ. However, doctors did point out that he had come within half an inch of a fatal injury.

Cyril's wife Jeanette said: 'When I heard what had happened, I was horrified. I set off for the hospital not knowing whether I would find him dead or alive. I was so thrilled when I found that he'd survived, I nearly fainted. A nurse had to hold me up.'

From his hospital bed, Cyril still thought it was a lot of fuss about nothing. Reliving his experience, he said: 'The pole burst through the windscreen and came at me like something out of a horror 3-D movie. It happened in a flash. At the time I couldn't see the need to cut the roof off the car. When the pole was sawn through, I just wanted to walk out of the door, but they wouldn't let me. Everyone's making a lot of fuss over me. I just want to get back to work.'

This was by no means Cyril's first brush with death. On a previous occasion, he was knocked off his bicycle by a lorry and then run over by a cyclist. He promptly picked himself up and refused to let anyone call an ambulance. Instead he accepted a lift to hospital from the lorry driver.

His wife admitted: 'He's a tough customer who never loses his cool.'

*   *   *

A red-faced young woman turned up at Arnold Fire Station in Nottingham with her boyfriend, pleading to be cut free from the handcuffs which were locked around her wrists. Firefighters some-how managed to keep a straight face as they set about releasing her from her acute embarrassment with a pair of bolt-cutters.'

*   *   *

Rescue from a Silo

Terry Stammers had one of the least enviable jobs known to man. He worked at a silage store in Ipswich where his job was to clean the dozen huge silos in which farm produce was fermenting. The occupa-tion was hot, smelly and decidedly uncomfortable. It could also be dangerous, as he found to his cost on the afternoon of Saturday 29 July 1989.

Mr Stammers, a man in his mid-twenties, used to clean the 70 foot high silos by entering from the top on a plastic bucket seat, through which a long metal pole was attached to a chain pulley. He was then winched down at intervals to clean the inside. The pulley was in turn attached to a solid iron bracket which formed part of the roof truss. That day, he was being lowered into the silo as usual when the chair became detached from the chain pulley and he fell some 50 feet to the very bottom of the silo.

Suffolk Fire Brigade Control were informed of the accident at 1.11 p.m. The slip read: 'Man in industrial bin.' Accordingly, three crews piloting a water tender ladder, turntable ladder and emergency rescue tender were despatched to the scene, arriving within five minutes.

Two officers climbed to the top of the silo and looked down inside. They could just make out the motionless body of the casualty lying on his side, still in the plastic bucket seat. It was obvious that someone would have to enter the silo and ascertain what injuries had been sustained and also to find a method of extricating the victim. One of the crew, Temporary Leading Fireman Pegg, volunteered for the unpleasant task. Since nobody knew what the atmosphere would be like at the bottom of the silo, it was decided that he should wear a breathing apparatus set. He was well aware of the fact that, although it was strictly against all Brigade guidelines, he would be on his own in there and that if anything untoward were to happen, any assistance which his colleagues could give him would be extremely limited.

A doctor from the Suffolk Accident Rescue Service also asked to be allowed down into the silo but fire officers thought it unwise. They had already sent one man into an unknown situation and had no intention of compounding the problem by sending in a second rescuer. Conditions were too hazardous. The temperature at the top of the building was over 100 degrees Fahrenheit and officers were told that it would be even hotter at the bottom of the silo, owing to the lack of ventilation.

Temporary Leading Fireman Pegg was lowered into the silo using the same chain pulley as had Mr Stammers. He was also fastened to a line with the aid of a pulley and a turn taken round another roof truss. When he reached the bottom, which had a steeply sloping base, he informed the crews at the top that, although the victim was unconscious, he had a pulse and was still breathing.

His first task was to extricate Mr Stammers from the plastic seat as carefully as possible so as not to aggravate any injuries. The combination of the sloping floor, the confined space and the excessive heat rendered this extremely difficult. As a safety precaution, a second B.A. set was lowered into the silo and suspended some 3 feet from the bottom, within arm's reach, in case a fault occurred on the set being worn.

The fire officer in charge made pumps two for extra manpower and equipment. By now there were seventeen firefighters present. All crew members with unused lowering lines and general purpose lines were immediately ordered to the top of the silo.

While the firefighter was labouring away 70 feet down and succeeding in removing the plastic seat from beneath Mr Stammers, the doctor was constantly monitoring the situation from above. On his advice, an oxygen mask was lowered to be placed on to Mr Stammers to help his breathing. The doctor also suggested that a special back and neck splint be lowered in which the injured man should be placed before being raised from the silo. This was a new piece of equipment, something which none of the fire service personnel present had come across before, but with directions from the doctor, the firefighter set about trying to fit the special splint.

After approximately ten minutes of trying to fix the splint, the whistle sounded on Temporary Leading Fireman Pegg's B.A. set. Officers were left with a choice of bringing him up immediately or allowing him to remove his face mask and don the second set which had previously been lowered. Aware of the risk he was taking, the firefighter decided to remove his mask and put on the second set. In doing so, he sampled the atmosphere without breathing apparatus and came to the conclusion that he could survive in it unaided. This allowed him to work without the restriction of his set. The used set was removed but the second one was left in position as a safety precaution.

The firefighter was struggling to fit the splint. The doctor again requested that he be allowed to go in and assist and this time fire officers relented. After all, the atmosphere at the bottom was respirable and Temporary Leading Fireman Pegg had been working alone for over an hour in deeply unpleasant conditions. He would probably welcome any help. Also, with the victim still unconscious, expert on-the-spot medical opinion could prove invaluable and there was now sufficient manpower and lines available to reduce the risk of an accident to those in the silo. In total, there were four general-purpose lines, three lowering lines plus the original chain pulley.

The doctor was duly lowered into the silo accompanied by a second B.A. set, suspended as before. Twenty minutes later, the two men had managed to place Mr Stammers into the splint and the crews began to raise him steadily to the top of the silo. It was an anxious wait as the stricken man edged closer to the summit. Once at the top, he was placed on a stretcher, still in the special back and neck brace, and rushed to hospital where his condition was reported as serious but stable.

Then it was time for the two rescuers to be brought up, the firefighter insisting that the doctor be winched up first. Finally, Temporary Leading Fireman Pegg emerged, having spent one hour and 45 minutes in the oppressive heat of the stinking silo. His colleagues offered to buy him a congratulatory drink when he finished duty, on one condition . . . that he had a shower first.

*   *   *

In 1995, Hampshire firefighters were called out to release a two-year-old boy from a cat-flap. Having seen the family pet use it on numerous occasions, the toddler decided to follow suit, but became so firmly wedged that his mother had to summon the Fire Brigade.

After attempts at lubrication proved unsuccessful, the crew were obliged to use a hacksaw to cut into the flap. The boy emerged unscathed and promising never to imitate the cat again.

* * *

The School Party

In dry weather, the Ibbeth Peril cave on the banks of the River Dee at Dent in Cumbria is challenging but relatively safe. Consequently the cave, situated in rugged country on the edge of the Pennines, is a popular destination with potholing centres and also with some schools from the north of England who want their pupils to sample the outdoor life without putting their lives at risk.

But in wet weather, it is a different proposition altogether. The River Dee, which flows by the entrance to the cave, can suddenly rise dangerously, flooding the narrow entrance and torrenting into the large chamber beyond. As it continues to rain, so the level inside the cave rises. In periods of extreme wet weather, of which there are many in that part of the world – even in high summer – the Ibbeth Peril cave is impassable. At such times, the most experienced cavers give it a wide berth, recognising the risk of being cut off for hours, even days.

It was on 4 July 1990 that two teachers from the Ashleigh Centre, a local authority home in Blackburn, set off with a group of three boys and two girls, the youngest twelve and the oldest sixteen, to explore the Ibbeth Peril cave as part of an outdoor activities course. Rain was forecast but those in charge were confident that it posed no threat to the exercise. Both of the teachers were experienced cavers and some of the youngsters had also been caving before.

In the early afternoon, the party reached the entrance. Although rain was already beginning to fall, it was fairly light at that stage. To get into the cave proper, they had to crawl through an inhospitable tunnel, some 300 yards long and only 15 inches high. It was an early test of their caving ability. Yet they managed to negotiate it safely and were greatly relieved when the sewer-like entrance opened out into the 45 foot high main chamber.

This was what they had come for. But their feelings of awe at reaching the large chamber made them oblivious to what was happening all around. For the persistent rain outside was making the river swell alarmingly, turning the once benign waters into a mass of tossing, swirling foam. When they did eventually notice the state of the water, it was too late. To all intents and purposes, their exit route was cut off. The teachers wisely decided that rather than risk the perilous manoeuvre back through the tunnel, an area now lashed by raging floodwater, they should climb to a safe perch high in the chamber and pray that they would be rescued in time.

The party were due back in Blackburn at 6.30 p.m. As that deadline passed and there was no word of explanation regarding their lateness, John Arnold, the officer in charge at the centre, followed the standard safety procedure in such cases and notified the emergency services. All parents were also informed.

Police officers carried out a search of the area and found the team's minibus near the cave. At 9 p.m., the voluntary Cave Rescue Organisation, based at Clapham some twelve miles south of Dent, was alerted. The telephone call to CRO controller Jack Pickup warned that a party of schoolchildren and teachers were feared trapped underground in the notorious 'Peril' pot. John Forder, a former professional caving instructor who lived less than two miles from the cave, was asked to check out the scene, and when he saw that the river had cut off the entrance, a full emergency was declared.

Mr Forder said: 'It was raining when I got there and I would certainly not have gone in there myself. The water was up to my chest and I thought, This is crazy. I was on my own and could have been swept off my feet. There was a curtain of water in front of the entrance and it was clear the passage was flooded – a full rescue call-out was on.'

To speed up the operation, each member of the team called several others in a telephone chain-letter and each brought along vital equipment.

The volunteers sped to Ibbeth Peril cave but the water was cascading out of the entrance at such a rate that there was no hope of an immediate rescue. They spent the evening battling to divert the River Dee but it was still a raging torrent. Conditions were too treacherous and any rescue attempt would simply be placing more lives at risk. Just before midnight, Mr Pickup reluctantly decided to call off the rescue bid for the time being. The crews would have to wait for the rain to stop and for the water levels inside the cave to drop.

He explained: 'There were 50,000 gallons of water a minute

pouring down the river and there was no way we could get in. I decided to leave a small party to work through the night so that the rest of us could return fresh in the morning.'

In the meantime, they poured green dye into the water to let those inside the cave know that help was on the way.

Darkness was falling and the temperature inside the cave was dropping fast. It was very cold and very wet. The group huddled together as best as they could to keep warm in a desperate bid to fend off the onset of hypothermia. The girls in particular were suffering. All too quickly, the excitement of caving, a trip which they had been looking forward to for weeks, had turned into a terrifying nightmare from which there seemed no imminent escape.

Outside, the rescue teams kept vigil through the night. The frustration was gnawing away at them, knowing that with every hour the rescue mission was further delayed, the slimmer were the chances of the school party's survival. But there was nothing they could do except monitor the weather forecasts and be prepared to act the moment that conditions improved.

The main body of rescuers were back at eight o'clock the following morning, joined by a 100-strong emergency team, comprising firefighters, police, ambulance crews and local authority staff. Council vehicles arrived with supplies of sandbags from which a dam could be built to divert the river away from the cave entrance. Everyone pitched in to build the massive dam and, as back-up, a huge mobile crane was brought in ready to lower a steel dam into the river in case the sandbags did not hold.

The water levels were still dangerously high but gradually, as the clouds began to break and drier weather set in, they began to fall. By 10.30 a.m., it was deemed safe enough for a four-man rescue team, including two divers, to be sent in. The water was still thundering past and the rescue team were warned to take no unnecessary risks. Having spent all night in such atrocious conditions, the party would either have found a safe ledge or they would be dead. There was no sense in adding to the toll.

Progress was difficult, but their expertise meant that the big chamber at the end was now accessible. Once in the chamber, they shouted above the sound of the roaring water and the cheering youngsters answered their calls. The rescuers then made their way up to the stranded party who were sheltering on a long ledge in a side passage high above the water.

The first to reach them was firefighter Geoffrey Crossley. He said afterwards: 'As we went in, we were all aware that the only thing between us and millions of gallons of water was a temporary dam built from sandbags. To be honest, we didn't know what we were going to find and were delighted that they were OK. They were so pleased to see us. They had managed to keep dry throughout but the girls had become very weak. It was a good job we got to them when we did – a few hours later and we could have been dealing with a tragedy.'

Not that the pupils' ordeal was over yet, for there still remained the little matter of getting out of the cave against the force of the rushing water. Ropes were linked to the entrance and the children were brought out one by one. The smaller ones had to be hauled out by rope because they could not stand against the force of the water. Clinging to the line, they edged towards the entrance, finally emerging after having spent a total of twenty hours underground.

By now, the girls were only semi-conscious. The moment they were out, they were given emergency medical treatment. All seven members of the party were rushed to hospital in Lancaster, suffering from hypothermia and shock, but were later released.

Once again, the emergency services had saved the day – but it had been touch and go.

* * *

After a long evening touring the pubs of Swindon, the young man was considerably the worse for alcohol. He couldn't face going home and just wanted somewhere to rest his head for the night. In his drunken haze, he opted for the most exclusive bed in Swindon – the top of a high gantry crane overlooking a street in the town centre.

It was not until the following morning, 20 August 1995, when he woke up to find himself perched precariously on the crane's jib 150 feet above the street below that he started to panic. He sobered up with amazing speed. Suddenly it all came back to him. It had seemed like such a wheeze at the time and then he must have fallen asleep. Now he was scared rigid.

His plight was spotted by passers-by who swiftly alerted Wiltshire Fire Brigade. Showing commendable courage, Firefighters Shipway and Pakenham scaled the crane and brought the young man down to safety. From then on, he vowed to catch a cab home . . . or stick to low-alcohol lager.

* * *

The Real Blue Watch

Well of Death

The area around the small resort of Ventnor on the Isle of Wight is notorious for subsidence. Land regularly slips down the steep cliffs into the sea, leaving some of the buildings perched in a somewhat precarious position. Even one of the local attractions is known as The Landslip.

Twenty-two-year-old Ramunas Girenas lived in the picture-postcard village of Godshill – all thatched cottages and cream teas – some four miles north of Ventnor. A Lithuanian by birth, he was single and lived with his family in the village. He was a builder's labourer by trade, but in June 1985 he was out of work and therefore had the time to help friends with various jobs about the house.

One of his friends was Mr Gerald Morgan who lived in a house on Grove Road, Ventnor. On the afternoon of Monday 3 June 1985, Mr Girenas was helping Mr Morgan to lay new drains.

In the back garden, two feet behind the house, Mr Girenas discovered a disused well. It had been unopened for something like ten years. Inside it was dank and dark. Mr Girenas was fascinated by the well and was keen to explore it, in order to find out whether there was any water at the bottom. His friend warned him about the dangers of going down but Mr Girenas insisted that he would be safe. Twice he climbed down by ladder and emerged with his findings. He said the shaft of the well, which was some 50 feet deep, was waisted at the middle and bulged out towards the bottom. Mr Morgan hoped that two visits would satisfy his friend's curiosity but Mr Girenas wanted to take one more look. Again, Mr Morgan pointed out the risk and again Mr Girenas chose to press on regardless.

Then disaster struck. At 5.30 p.m., shortly after Mr Girenas had disappeared below ground for the third time, this time wielding a pick and bucket, Mr Morgan heard 'a tremendous thud. The ladder started shaking violently, the ground trembled and the shaft just filled with debris.' He could only look on helplessly, filled with horror as Mr Girenas was buried beneath the landslide. The sides of the well shaft had caved in.

Mr Morgan ran to telephone the emergency services. The first fire crews arrived and were confronted with the soil-filled well. Their immediate dilemma was that they had no idea how far down the victim was buried, let alone whether he was still alive. But it was soon apparent that if they had to dig with their bare hands, the chances of finding him alive would be slim to say the least. So they sent a request to Isle of Wight Fire Control for a mechanical digger.

The excavator was duly sent over, but it had to be operated with extreme caution and could not work at full speed for fear of putting extra pressure on Mr Girenas.

Working in shifts under floodlights, the rescue teams managed to excavate 20 feet down the shaft by midnight. But there was still no sign of the trapped man. The weather forecast was not good either. There was a threat of rain from northern France. Besides making the soil more difficult to remove, fire chiefs were worried that any rain would percolate into the well via underground channels and thus further reduce the chances of finding him alive.

In the course of the early excavations, the edges of the shaft began crumbling ominously, hinting at another collapse. The sides urgently needed shoring up. Emergency calls were made to the mainland for 20-foot-lengths of steel shoring to be sent over. The shoring was rushed by police escort from Ringwood in Hampshire to Portsmouth to catch the 3 a.m. ferry to Fishbourne. The ferry was held up to wait for this essential cargo.

Meanwhile, John Bowker, the Chief Fire Officer of the Isle of Wight, had held a late-night on-site meeting with representatives of Mowlem Engineering, who had offered their services, the Southern Water Authority and the Isle of Wight coroner. They considered the difficulties already encountered in what was clearly going to be a long, complicated rescue and mulled over alternative solutions.

With the well being situated so close to the wall of the house, it was felt that digging could lead to a collapse of the house itself. So the experts decided that the best approach was to dig a new shaft, 2 feet wider, parallel to the original but further from the house. This would be slow and expensive but would best guarantee the safety of the rescue workers.

To stabilise the new shaft, 60 concrete shoring rings were transported to the island from Nottinghamshire, the first arriving on the morning of Tuesday 4 June. Each ring was made up of five sections, making for some bulky loads to be ferried across the Solent.

The sinking of the new shaft was a tricky business and fire chiefs consulted throughout with geological experts. Miners were brought in from Ryde to do the digging. More and more firefighters were drafted in too, some to act as safety men, others as general labourers shifting the tons of rubble. With chiefs predicting that it would take at least another two days to excavate the new 50 foot shaft, fire crews began operating six-hour shifts in groups of 25. Also taking it in turns to stand vigil at the well-head were relatives of Ramunas Girenas. All they could do was wait . . . and hope.

The first set of support rings were put in place on the Tuesday night. To avoid any sideways movement of the rings, a fast-setting cement slurry mixture was pumped behind each one. Being on previously undisturbed ground, the dig immediately came up against solid firestone rock and firefighters and miners together started drilling through it.

The rescue mission wasn't getting any easier but when Mr Morgan relayed details of his conversation with the victim about the shape of the well, hopes were raised that the sides of the shaft might have closed, thereby creating a substantial air pocket in which Mr Girenas could survive.

Timber props were cut and inserted into the excavation in order to secure it but ground conditions continued to give cause for concern. The land was very unstable. Anyone entering the shaft was ordered to wear a full safety harness attached to a rescue line which was manned by three firefighters. Should the ground collapse beneath the miners, the fire crews would be able to take the strain and prevent a further disaster.

Digging went on throughout the third day. The tough rock made it a painfully slow process. It was taking the miners six hours to dig just 2 feet. By 6 p.m. on the Wednesday, ten concrete rings, each 2 feet deep, were supporting the new shaft, but at a depth of 20 feet the crews were less than halfway to the foot, where it seemed increasingly likely that Mr Girenas was trapped. Inside the shaft, conditions were nigh on unbearable. It was hot and dusty but every man was totally committed to the task of trying to bring the casualty out alive. Dust masks were provided for the diggers and lines supplying compressed air from cylinders were passed down into the shaft to give some much-needed fresh air. By now, the whole of the top section of the ladder by which Mr Girenas had descended into the well had been removed.

The rescue had attracted tremendous press interest which in turn prompted offers of help to the Brigade from far and near. Industrialists and potholers volunteered aid, as did a little old lady who said she was prepared to offer the services of her canary to test for gas. Her gesture was politely declined. All the while, the Brigade were

entering unknown territory in terms of providing equipment for the
operation. It wasn't simply a question of manpower – there were
things to consider like catering, the installation of toilet facilities and
the provision of improved lighting so that the miners could see into
the very depths of the shaft. The relatively small Isle of Wight Brigade
were unaccustomed to an incident of such magnitude. But they rose
to the occasion splendidly.

At 8.10 on the Thursday morning came a real breakthrough. Two
narrow cavities, 8 feet and 4 feet deep respectively, were discovered
running down the sides of the ladder. Hopes of a successful rescue
soared and an air line was lowered into the larger of the two cavities.

John Bowker briefed the press who had been gathering in force
since the second day. 'We have discovered an eight foot cavity,' he
announced. 'We shouted into it, but there was no reply. Its existence
gives us hope that Mr Girenas may be in a similarly large air pocket
further down. By the time we have lined the new shaft down to a
depth of forty feet, we may be in a position to find Mr Girenas in a
cavity. We would then have to decide whether to go on slowly
constructing a lined shaft or whether to get a line around him and try
to snatch him to safety.

'The firestone has in some ways been a bonus. Its strength means
that it is capable of supporting great weights of shale and soil without
breaking.'

By 5 p.m. on the Thursday, the fifteenth ring was safely in position,
indicating that the workers had reached a depth of 30 feet. Although
there was still another 20 feet to go, the renewed sense of optimism
drove them on to overcome all thoughts of exhaustion. At this level,
the miners detected evidence of considerable ground disturbance,
suggesting that this was probably the point where the sides had
collapsed on to the unfortunate Mr Girenas. At 8 p.m., the top of the
lower ladder was exposed.

Work continued through a fourth night. Progress was swifter than
at any other time and by 9.30 on the Friday morning, engineers were
able to report that they were just 8 feet from the foot of the disused
well shaft. And there they would find Mr Girenas, dead or alive.
Everyone present – firefighters, miners, engineers, ambulance crews,
doctors, police officers, local residents and of course the victim's
relatives – held their collective breath. Even the Press waited anxiously.

Inch by inch, the workers forged their way down. The morning gave way to afternoon. And then came the news nobody wanted to hear. At 12.55 p.m., diggers uncovered the head and shoulders of Ramunas Girenas. The Chief Fire Officer escorted a doctor down into the shaft where Mr Girenas was formally pronounced dead. His body had been found upright on the ladder, 6 feet from the bottom of the shaft, suggesting perhaps that, on hearing the first rumble of the collapsing well, he had tried to make his escape.

After the tremendous efforts of all concerned, the grim find was a terrible anti-climax. No matter how remote the chances of finding the victim alive had seemed from the outset, there had always been that possibility that he might have survived. Suddenly the exhaustion which the crews had fought against so valiantly for so long, overcame them. Firefighters and mining crews sat slumped in silence against the machinery at the head of the well.

The rescue attempt had lasted a staggering 91 hours and in that time no fewer than 90 tons of rubble had been excavated.

The inquest showed that Mr Girenas died of asphyxia, probably within a minute of the collapse. He was certainly dead before the first firefighters arrived on the scene. The coroner praised the rescue teams but was unable to offer any real indication as to what may have triggered the collapse. It was suggested that an iron bar dropped down the well may have hit the sides and set off the avalanche but there was no conclusive proof. It will forever remain a mystery.

* * *

A motorcyclist pulled into a Wakefield filling station at 11 p.m. one night in 1988 and proceeded to fill his 600cc machine with petrol. He then decided to test his oil level manually. But it was he who proved to be the dipstick for, having inserted his finger into the oil tank, he couldn't get it out again.

He tugged and twisted but to no avail. Deeply embarrassed, he called to the female cashier who was in the station shop to come and help. But she thought it was a ruse to lure her out on to the forecourt so that he could rob the place and she steadfastly refused to go to his aid.

Having studied his predicament for fifteen minutes or so, she sensed that maybe he was genuine after all and rang West Yorkshire Fire Brigade.

Firefighters tried every ploy known to mankind to release the digit but the cause was hopeless. So they dismantled the tank from the rest of the machine and drove him off to hospital with the oil tank still wedged firmly on the end of his finger.

Arriving at the casualty department, they suggested that the hapless victim should be attended to soon ... but resisted the temptation to tell the doctor to pull his finger out.

* * *

Buried Under a Collapsed Tenement

Anne Zennaiter had travelled from her native New York for an eagerly awaited holiday in Britain, staying in Glasgow at the home of her Scottish aunt. It was an opportunity not only to experience the city's cultural heritage but also to visit other parts of Scotland such as the lochs and the Highlands. She might even have been able to return with a photograph of the Loch Ness Monster. That would impress the folks back home.

Her aunt lived in a flat on the second floor of a three-storey tenement block in the Parkhead district of Glasgow. The sandstone tenements dated from around 1910 but had recently been refurbished. Like much of the city, Parkhead, in the East End, was rapidly changing to make way for new housing. Many of the old tenement blocks, eyesores of a bygone age, were being pulled down. Next to the block was a vacant site. A post office and social security office, had recently been bulldozed and now the plot of land was being excavated so that foundations could be dug for new houses.

On the morning of 29 March 1993, Anne Zennaiter was pottering around the flat. She could scarcely hear herself think above the noise being made by the workmen on the adjoining land. Across the road, the children of St Michael's Primary School had just gone in from their morning playtime. Due to lack of space, they often played in the street.

All of a sudden, at 10.45 a.m., there was a bang and a low rumble. The gable end crashed to the ground in a mound of rubble and dust, carrying Anne Zennaiter with it. As the floors, walls and ceilings of the flat gave way, she plunged two floors and found herself buried beneath 6 feet of fallen masonry.

A witness said: 'I heard what I thought was a gas explosion, ran down the street and saw dust rising. The entire gable end had collapsed. I prayed that nobody had been inside at the time because I didn't think they'd have stood a chance of getting out alive.'

Strathclyde fire crews arrived to witness a scene of desolation. The end of the block had collapsed to reveal a cross-section of the building. A dressing table rocked ominously on the edge of what had, minutes earlier, been a complete bedroom. Now the bedroom door led into an abyss. The bed had vanished completely. A pair of pink curtains fluttered in the wind with only half a window frame on which to adhere.

Rescuers had no idea how many people were trapped in the rubble and so additional crews were drafted in from across the city. Soon 40 firefighters were sifting through the rubble and debris, pulling away buckled baths, crumpled cookers and smashed items of furniture which had been reduced to scraps of wood. It was as if the *Antiques Roadshow* had been involved in a pile-up.

Thermal imagers were used to search for human forms. Only one was located and that was Anne Zennaiter, thankfully still alive, but pinned down by heavy masonry. One other man had been caught in the debris but had managed to free himself. Fire officers were concerned about the possibility of a gas explosion and there was also a very real danger that more of the block would collapse without any prior warning. Residents were evacuated from adjacent blocks and pupils from St Michael's were sent home.

The risk of further collapse prevented the crews from using any machinery to dig at the rubble. So they had to resort to the most basic form of excavation – bare hands. Fortunately fire and medical teams were able to talk to the 55-year-old victim throughout her ordeal, a great advantage because not only was she able to relay how she was feeling but also they were able to provide words of encouragement. It was a question of her hanging on in there until they could reach her.

It was a long job and the longer it went on, the more worrying her condition became. While taking care not to exhaust her, crews tried to maintain a dialogue with her but at one point she went very quiet and became very cold. They feared the worst but she managed to survive until at last they managed to pull her free. She had been buried in the rubble for three hours. She was immediately given oxygen and taken to Glasgow Royal Infirmary, suffering from trauma, cuts and bruises.

Strathclyde's Firemaster, John Jameson, had to admit: 'She was lucky to be alive because she was very badly trapped by her legs and arms. We were just glad we could get her out.'

* * *

When five-year-old Alexandra Pinnick got stuck into her tables at school, she needed firefighters to help her out! In March 1996, Alexandra got her knee trapped in a desk for over an hour at her school at Clifton, Nottingham, and had to be rescued by eight firefighters in two engines.

Sub Officer Dave Thompson, assisted by two colleagues, used a saw to cut through the wooden struts holding Alexandra's knee while the other firemen helped reassure the rest of her class.

'Alexandra was great,' said Sub Officer Thompson afterwards. 'She was smiling all the time.'

Her headmistress added: 'I think Alexandra was wondering if she'd have the table stuck to her knee for the rest of her life . . .'

* * *

Pregnant Woman Plucked from Flood Waters

Torrential rain and gale-force winds created havoc throughout the West Country in December 1995. Farmland was flooded, roads were rendered impassable and homes were cut off as rivers burst their banks. One of the worst affected areas was around the River Avon in Wiltshire and it resulted in a harrowing night-time experience for a seven-months pregnant mother and her three children after their car had been trapped in rising flood water.

The woman was approaching Staverton in the early hours of the morning, unaware that the Avon had burst its banks. The next thing she knew, her car was marooned in 3 feet of water. Fortunately, villagers were alerted to her plight and telephoned Wiltshire Fire Brigade. The call was received at 1.21 a.m.

It was an anxious wait. The woman had no way of getting herself and the children out of the car because the water had caused the electric doors and windows to fail. They were trapped inside . . . and the water was rising steadily. If it started to seep into the car, they could all be drowned. It was a terrifying prospect.

As an added concern, it was a bitterly cold night. Therefore it was imperative that the children kept themselves as warm as possible until help arrived and so they huddled together in the back seat.

The knights in shining armour arrived in the form of sixteen firefighters from Trowbridge. Wading through the icy waters, they assured the woman that they would soon have her out and discussed the most effective means of rescue. The only way to open up the car without flooding it was via the sun roof and so they clambered on to the roof and set about dismantling it. Once the sun roof was removed, firefighters lifted the three children up through it before carefully handing them to colleagues who carried them to waiting ambulances.

Freeing the heavily pregnant mother proved a more exacting task. Her condition necessitated extreme care on the part of the firefighters who felt that they could not risk carrying her through the flood water. So a Brigade inflatable dinghy was mobilised and this was moved into position alongside the car. The woman was lifted through the hole in the roof of her car and then lowered into the dinghy before being towed across the water to an ambulance.

The incident was closed at 2.08 a.m. . . . but it had been the longest 40 minutes of that woman's life.

* * *

On 13 June 1982, Northumberland firefighters cut a 74-year-old man from his bed after he had woken up trapped between the bedsprings and the frame. The warden at the home in Cramlington and policemen had all tried in vain to free him but eventually they were forced to call out the Brigade.

* * *

Death on the Sands

The broad expanses of sand which line the north-west coast of Lancashire add up to an area of outstanding natural beauty, a haven for wildlife. But they are also among the most treacherous spots in Britain. Over the centuries, numerous travellers have been fatally swallowed up by a combination of sinking sands and incoming sea while endeavouring to cross Morecambe Bay on foot at low-tide. A modern version of the tragedy was performed on Tuesday 27 May 1980.

In the wake of a number of recent fatal accidents, the marshland around Flook Hall Sands was dotted with signs, warning of the dangers of attempting to walk or ride across the terrain. Nevertheless, that evening a teenager decided to go for a spin on the sands on his motorcycle. He was enjoying the freedom of the wide open spaces until he ventured a little too far. Suddenly, his machine plunged into deep mud and slithered away beneath him. The lad tried to pull himself up but the mud was thick and clinging. His legs would not move and there was nothing on which to gain any leverage. He was in too deep. And the more he struggled, the deeper he sank. What's more, the tide was coming in . . . fast.

The boy's screams for help were heard half a mile away by a passer-by who in turn alerted the emergency services. Two Lancashire Fire Brigade pumps were despatched to the scene.

Carefully, they picked their way across the sands on foot, occasionally having to make detours to clear the network of deep, water-filled ditches. By the time they reached the boy, he was up to his neck in sea water. His legs were encased in mud. A police constable had bravely waded in and was supporting his neck and tilting his head back in order to keep his mouth clear of the water. But the incoming tide was sweeping in waves with alarming regularity, forcing water up and over the boy's face, leaving him gasping for air. Unless they got him out soon, it would be too late. His life was hanging by a thread.

The nearest firm ground to the stranded boy was a bank some 20 feet away. From there, two firefighters were sent into the water to try and fit a breathing apparatus mask to his face in the hope of buying some time while the crews worked out a rescue plan. All the while, the boy was flapping around, struggling to keep his air passages above the rising water level. But despite the sterling efforts of everyone present, from time to time he dipped beneath the waves. He clearly couldn't hold on much longer.

A line was fastened under the boy's armpits and twenty rescue workers attempted to haul him on to dry land. It was a titanic battle against the grip of the mud and met with little success. By now, the boy was in a really bad way. Knowing that time was against them, they put every ounce of effort into one last concerted pull, but still he would not shift. His legs were stuck fast. To overcome the problem, a firefighter dived beneath the water and secured the line around the boy's knees instead. This would concentrate the maximum leverage on the part of the casualty's body where it was most needed.

The ploy worked and, following another herculean pull, the boy was able to be freed from his watery grave. Firefighters quickly carried him over to the bank, but the ordeal had taken its toll. He was unconscious and all attempts at resuscitation by ambulance crews proved in vain. The notorious Lancashire sands had claimed another life.

*   *   *

In November 1995, Wiltshire Fire Brigade answered a distress call from a Swindon man who had got his penis stuck in the neck of an empty milk bottle. After considering a number of options, few of which appealed to the victim, they decided that the safest solution was to smash the bottle. But first they slid a thin piece of protective cloth between the organ and the bottle to reduce the danger from broken glass. At the moment of impact, the man gritted his teeth, closed his eyes and prayed. As he emerged unscathed, he realised he would never be able to look the milkman in the eye again.

*   *   *

A Sorry Spectacle

In the summer of 1995, writer Magnus Linklater and his wife were busy packing for a holiday abroad. Crossing the hallway, she dropped her spectacles which then slipped through a small hole in the solid stone floor of their nineteenth-century Edinburgh house.

They managed to lift a small section of the floor and, by doing so, were able to see the spectacles, positioned tantalisingly far away. Nevertheless, Mr Linklater calculated that at full stretch, he could just about reach them with his fingertips.

So he lay face down on the floor to get in as close as possible and inserted his left arm. He wiggled his fingers about a bit but was unable to make contact with the glasses. He could go no further so he decided to give it up as a lost cause for the time being. But when he tried to pull his arm free, he found that it was stuck fast, his elbow jammed in the gap between the rock-hard stone and an iron beam.

He pulled with all his might, but it wouldn't budge. His wife suggested greasing his arm with olive oil, but it had no effect. This was no way to prepare for a holiday. They tried to put off the awful moment until eventually there was simply no alternative – she would have to call the Fire Brigade.

Minutes later, from his prone position, Mr Linklater was aware of blue lights flashing in the street outside. Three firefighters entered the room, wielding axes. They were followed by the police and two paramedics.

Hugely embarrassed that half of the city's emergency crews seemed to have come out for him, Mr Linklater then had to listen to the rescue teams discussing the best method of extricating his arm. He sensed that the firefighters were keen to use their axes and that it was with some reluctance that they put them away in favour of a less violent solution suggested by the paramedics. For the paramedics also reckoned that olive oil would do the trick and poured a small quantity down the hole beside the trapped arm. A hefty pull and up it came. As they left, the crews advised using a coathanger next time. He did just that – and sure enough it worked. If only he had thought of that earlier . . .

* * *

Naval medic John Fay was trimming the top of the 10 foot thorn hedge outside his home on a Plymouth naval estate on 9 July 1986 when he lost his balance and fell into it. The more he struggled, the deeper into the hedge he went. Alerted by his cries, neighbours ran to his aid but, despite donning gloves, they were unable to extricate him. Thus it was left to the emergency services to solve his thorny problem and within minutes, fire, police and ambulance had sped to the scene, sirens blaring and lights flashing. They soon pulled 33-year-old John clear with nothing more than a few scratches and a reluctance to sit down for a few hours. Reflecting on his ordeal, he commented: 'The rescue teams were great and said it was all in a day's work, but I was really embarrassed about the whole thing.'

* * *

21 Hours in a Lift

Genny Jones was a temporary secretary with American telecommunications firm Bellcore International which lease offices in a five-storey office block in the City of London. At 11 a.m. on the morning of

Tuesday 5 March 1996, clutching an armful of stationery, 28-year-old Mrs Jones got into the lift on the ground floor of the building, bound for the second floor. It should have been a twenty-second journey, but instead became the start of a terrifying 21-hour ordeal trapped in a space little bigger than a telephone box.

Mrs Jones stepped into the lift alone. The doors closed in front of her and the cage started to climb before suddenly shuddering to a halt short of the first floor. She pressed the button impatiently, convinced that it was just a temperamental hiccup.

Still nothing happened. Her inability to goad the lift into life was beginning to frustrate her, but as the minutes ticked by and she remained motionless, her impatience at not being able to get on with her work was replaced by a distinct feeling of unease.

Clearly the lift was not about to spring into action so she pushed the alarm and waited to be rescued. There was no response. Then it dawned on her that nobody would miss her. The only other worker on the second floor was away – indeed the sole storey in the building to be occupied was the ground floor, by the Nationwide Building Society. In a bid to alert them to her plight, she crouched on the floor and screamed. Nobody heard her.

Sensing that her biggest problem would be a lack of air in the confined space, she managed to force the doors apart a little and slipped SOS notes through the tiny gap on to the unoccupied first floor. Perhaps somebody passing would see them. It was a slim chance, but she reasoned that it was better than simply doing nothing.

As the hours passed, Mrs Jones became resigned to a lengthy incarceration. She had no food or drink. She could survive without the former but the shouting for help had made her extremely thirsty. She tried to conserve energy and take her mind off her parched throat by reading a book, *The Curate's Wife*, which she found in her handbag.

That evening, her surveyor husband Tim returned home to their flat in Streatham to find it empty. 'I kept expecting Genny would walk through the door,' he said, 'but as it got later, I got more and more worried. Eventually I phoned the police who I'm sure thought we'd had a tiff.'

By dawn, he was beside himself with worry. He wondered whether something had happened to her at work and decided to go to her office. He arrived at 8.10 a.m., accompanied by a police officer, and entered the building. Mrs Jones, now numb with cold, heard a banging noise and cried out in desperation. Realising that she was trapped in the lift, they immediately called the Fire Brigade.

Firefighters arrived within minutes and quickly succeeded in prising open the lift doors and hauling Mrs Jones up to safety.

'I was elated,' said Mr Jones. 'As the Fire Brigade broke in, I saw these little notes saying "I am thirsty" and "Please help", so I knew she was all right. It was such a relief to see her alive and well, if a little weepy.'

Straight after the rescue, Mr Jones cooked up the perfect treatment for his wife of two years. 'I took her to a greasy spoon cafe for a fry-up breakfast. She was fine after that.'

* * *

A 90-year-old woman lay helpless for 12 hours after falling and impaling herself on an ornamental fireplace. She had stumbled in her Brighton flat at 7.30 p.m. on 13 December 1992 but was not discovered until the following morning, by a visiting district nurse. The nurse summoned ambulancemen who in turn called the Fire Brigade to help free the victim from a sharp spike in the fireplace which had lodged in the top of her thigh. Still conscious, the woman, described by neighbours as highly independent, was taken to Royal Sussex County Hospital for X-rays.

* * *

The Unkindest Cut

The parks of Central London have long been favourite venues for romantic evening assignations. To the casual passer-by, a car with steamed-up windows and over-active suspension is as sure a sign of lovers on board as a pair of knickers hanging from the aerial. Just occasionally, things get a little out of hand, so to speak ... with highly embarrassing consequences.

On one such evening, a couple were enjoying a full-blooded encounter in the back of a sports car. Space was a little cramped but mutual desire was able to overcome any obstacles. As the man rose to the occasion and their passion reached fever pitch, he let out an anguished cry.

'Was that good?' asked his girlfriend, assuming, not unreasonably, that his excitement was the result of her exquisite performance.

His face told a different story. It was contorted with pain.

'What's the matter?' she demanded urgently.

'It's my back,' he groaned. 'I think I've slipped a disc.'

Realising that play was abandoned for the day, the woman suggested, somewhat curtly, that they begin unravelling their various limbs. But the man was unable to move.

'What do you mean, you can't move?' she demanded from a position not at all becoming of a missionary. 'How am I supposed to get out?'

The atmosphere inside the car was becoming as cold as the air outside.

Desperate to attract attention, she utilised the one part of her anatomy which still retained some form of mobility and managed to twist her leg into a position within reach of the hooter button. She then jammed her foot against it. The sound alerted a member of the public who, seeing that the woman was in some difficulty, volunteered to call the emergency services.

Soon the car was surrounded by firefighters, ambulance crews and a sizeable gathering of interested spectators. The senior fire officer peered inside to take a look. It was not a pretty sight. The man, wearing his trousers around his ankles, was in considerable discomfort and just wanted to be put out of his misery. But no amount of gentle manouevring could separate the couple, who were wedged behind the front seats, nor was there room to lift them en bloc through either of the doors. The only way to get them out was to slice off the back of the car.

While the hydraulic cutting machinery was sent for, local residents passed mugs of hot tea through the car window to soothe the frayed nerves of the unfortunate couple. Two firefighters began scything through the back of the car, the flying sparks illuminating the embarrassment on the faces of the erstwhile lovers. Once the back was off, crews were able to climb in and prise the bodies apart.

The man was carried off in agony, leaving ambulancemen to reassure the girlfriend that he would soon make a full recovery.

'Sod him,' she answered. 'What's worrying me is how I shall explain to my husband what's happened to his car.'

* * *

Two Wiltshire fire appliances were sent to rescue a man who had become trapped by the legs at Biddestone Saw Mills. An engine from Corsham and a rescue tender from Chippenham raced to the mill on the afternoon of 2 November 1995 to find that an employee had got his legs wedged between a line of logs which were waiting to be cut up. Fire crews used special hydraulic spreaders to make a gap between the logs into which a low-pressure air-bag was then fitted. Once in position, the air-bag was inflated, thereby forcing aside the offending logs. The casualty was not thought to be seriously injured but was taken to hospital as a precaution.

* * *

A Miraculous Escape

Born in China, Cunhai Gao had been in Britain for two years, working as a researcher at Cambridge University's Department of Plant Sciences. To all intents and purposes, it seemed an innocuous occupation yet it turned out to be one which very nearly cost Mr Gao his life.

On the morning of 19 April 1995, the 32-year-old geologist had breakfast as usual with his wife, Kiaoling Zhu, and five-year-old son Phil at their home at Arbury, Cambridge, before setting off for a farm at Willingham, some eight miles north of Cambridge. There, he was in the process of collecting underground soil samples as part of his study of the effects of climatic changes which had taken place 120,000 years ago.

His work was being conducted in a trench 20 feet deep and 6 feet wide. He had been taking samples from the bottom of the trench for fifteen minutes that morning when he suddenly heard the driver of a JCB digger nearby yell out a warning. Before Mr Gao even had time to look up, one side of the trench collapsed on him. The hard safety hat he was wearing was knocked off his head and he was buried under several feet of earth.

The JCB driver ran to raise the alarm. Two fire service special units, the fire crew from Cottenham Station, an ambulance, an emergency service doctor and police officers descended on the quiet Fenland village. Assessing the situation, fire chiefs decided that it was far too dangerous to use the JCB to remove the soil from the trench in case it injured Mr Gao. So they began the painstaking job of scraping away the earth with small trowels and their bare hands. If the truth be told, none expected to find Mr Gao alive beneath the avalanche.

For more than an hour, they dug. With each passing minute, they became increasingly convinced that they would be dealing with a fatality. Then they finally reached the hunched-up figure of Mr Gao and, to their amazement and delight, he was still alive. They quickly clawed away the soil surrounding his face and were eventually able to free his entire body. He was then gently lifted into an ambulance and rushed to Addenbrooke's Hospital, Cambridge, suffering from nothing more than hypothermia and a broken arm. After two nights in hospital, he was allowed to return home to his family.

Mr Gao survived for so long because his hard hat had fallen forward in the collapse and had formed an air pocket around his face, enabling him to breathe. It was a miraculous escape.

Cambridgeshire firefighter Geoff Quince admitted: 'We thought we were digging out a body till he started talking to us. He's an extremely lucky man. He was helped because he was doubled up and his hard hat had slipped off his head to create that air pocket around his face.'

Even so, the crews only just pulled him out in time. For Mr Gao revealed that he felt his life slipping away just before he was finally rescued.

Reliving the ordeal, he said: 'I heard the workman shout "Watch out" and then all this earth crashed on top of me. I doubled up with my head forward and my hard hat came off. Everything was pitch black and I was surprised when I found I was able to breathe.

'I prayed that the people on the surface would call the Fire Brigade but after a while, I was convinced I was going to die. I thought there was no escape from the earth all around me. All I could think was how unfair it was. I had had breakfast with my family, I had said goodbye to them and now I was going to die.

'I could hear people on the surface, but I didn't know if they could dig me out in time as it was getting harder and harder to breathe. Then I felt as if I was going to sleep, and it was a really nice feeling. I thought, if this is dying, let it happen. I just wanted to see my wife and son one last time.'

As Mr Gao used up his last supplies of air, he was finally given hope. 'Suddenly I felt the pressure on my back lessen as they lifted the earth away and I saw a hint of daylight in front of my eyes. When I saw the blue sky again, I thought my life was starting all over again. This is my second life now.

'I cannot describe how overjoyed I was as they dug me free. I still can't really believe how I survived – I'm so lucky to be alive. I owe my life to the rescuers and my hard hat. I would probably be dead now if I hadn't been wearing it.'

The emergency crews echoed his sentiments. 'It was a very nasty incident and we got to him just in time.'

* * *

Firefighters had to grease the head of a prisoner to free him after he got his head stuck in a police station cell door at Keighley, West Yorkshire, on 6 January 1994.

* * *

And Finally . . .

West Midlands firefighters' most bizarre call of 1994 was to free a man who had got his penis stuck in the hole in the middle of a large, hardened steel ball bearing.

Egged on by his fiancée, the man had pushed his organ so far into the ball-bearing hole that he was unable to release it. The couple tried everything. They tried to pull it off, they tried lubricating the affected area with a number of substances, including soap, low-fat margarine and washing-up liquid, but it wouldn't shift.

For the next 24 hours, the man hid his embarrassment in his trousers although he looked pleased to see everyone. Going to the toilet proved particularly uncomfortable.

The pain was getting steadily worse. They had exhausted every withdrawal method and so reluctantly decided that he would have to go to hospital for surgical removal. Doctors at the hospital in Walsall took one look at the problem and decided that it was definitely a job for the Fire Brigade.

An officer with the West Midlands Fire Service recalls: 'The man was in great discomfort when we arrived and it was easy to see why. The ball bearing had gone beyond the glans of the penis and there was this huge swelling on the end. But because the bearing was made of hardened steel, none of our cutting equipment would work on it.

'As the hours ticked by, the man was becoming dangerously ill. A surgeon was in attendance and from time to time he had to use a syringe to take blood away from the swelling. It was not a pretty sight.

'We tried every piece of equipment we knew and then we hit upon the idea of having a specialist slitting saw brought in. Obviously, we had to be extremely careful using a razor-sharp saw so close to such a sensitive part of his body and there was no way that we could risk cutting right through to the skin. So we patiently sawed five-sixths of the way through and then cracked the weakened ball bearing open with a hammer and chisel.

'At last, the ball bearing separated. It had taken us twelve hours. I don't know whose relief was greater – ours or the victim's. The surgeon told us that if we hadn't managed to get it off within the next hour, he would have been forced to amputate.

'Over the years, we've had all manner of strange incidents. We've had people with various things up their back passages, including bottles, and we've had to free men with their penises trapped in vacuum cleaners! I must say I've never looked at a vacuum cleaner and thought, "You're going to get it tonight, pal" . . . but I suppose it takes all sorts.'